S0-BMY-492

301.0924
S35a

01412

DATE DUE			

WITHDRAWN
L. R. COLLEGE LIBRARY

JOHN WANAMAKER

KENNIKAT PRESS SCHOLARLY REPRINTS
Dr. Ralph Adams Brown, Senior Editor

Series in
AMERICAN HISTORY AND CULTURE
IN THE NINETEENTH CENTURY
Under the General Editorial Supervision of
Dr. Martin L. Fausold
Professor of History, State University of New York

(Photo. by C. M. Gilbert.)

WANAMAKER AS POSTMASTER GENERAL.

(Photo. by C. M. Gilbert)

WANAMAKER AS POSTMASTER-GENERAL

JOHN WANAMAKER

BY

HERBERT ADAMS GIBBONS

ILLUSTRATED

IN TWO VOLUMES
VOLUME ONE

KENNIKAT PRESS
Port Washington, N. Y./London

CARL A. RUDISILL LIBRARY
LENOIR RHYNE COLLEGE

381.0924
JB5j
81412
Jan. 1973

JOHN WANAMAKER

Copyright, 1926, by Rodman Wanamaker
Reissued in 1971 by Kennikat Press by .
arrangement with Harper & Row, Publishers, Inc.
Library of Congress Catalog Card No: 70-137911
ISBN 0-8046-1479-2

Manufactured by Taylor Publishing Company   Dallas, Texas

KENNIKAT SERIES ON AMERICAN HISTORY AND
CULTURE IN THE NINETEENTH CENTURY

TO
THE SON
WHO IS CARRYING ON
AND TO
ALL WHO ARE HELPING HIM

CONTENTS

CONTENTS

ILLUSTRATIONS

HOLOGRAPHS

HOLOGRAPHS

FOREWORD

JOHN WANAMAKER earned money for seventy-five years. In 1847 the boy of nine turned bricks at two cents a hundred. In 1922 the man of eighty-four jumped out of bed eager for the day's work. He did not die of old age. When the last severe cold compelled him to stop going to his office a few weeks before his death he was mentally alert and physically vigorous, and he was holding in his own hands the many threads of his vast business, religious, and public interests. He did not think that his work was finished. He was not ready to retire. That he was going to die never entered his head.

So no autobiography was written and no complete record of his life put down. For sentiment's sake or to emphasize the consistent growth of a business principle John Wanamaker often looked back over the wonderful years that had been lived, and in his writings and speeches are vivid glimpses of early days and struggles, of hopes and ambitions denied and realized. He was not a man of the type, however, who would write his own story or interest himself in having others write it. He felt that growth was the principle of life, and that when one stopped growing one died. The knowledge that he might rest on his laurels, therefore, did not tempt him. Life was too interesting. What was facing him at the moment always received the best that was in him, and what was ahead lured him, beckoned him on. In his eighties there was the same eagerness to find out what new things life had in store for him that there had been in his teens.

Miraculous health, tireless energy, childlike faith, consummate ability—these are the explanations most people give of Wanamaker's success in life.

But John Wanamaker did not always enjoy good health. He was rejected for active service when as a youngster he volunteered for the Civil War, and through the years he had his share of ailments.

He did not always feel like driving himself; no man does. He yearned for rest and fun and change. His soul is bared in what he wrote on the front porch of his summer home at Cape May Point on July 4, 1903:

There cometh a mist and a weeping rain, and the sea is not the same. We unhook the hammocks and push back the rocking chairs to save us from the storm that forms scurrying cloud walls between us and the many ships and the fourteen miles off breakwater. The sea with its myriad fingers comes up and pats the shore and rushes away as if it had forgotten something. I am glad to be left behind in the quiet and rest, satisfied to be here alone writing with my knee for the desk, willing to pay almost any price for the privilege of doing nothing and for two days to be a boy again. Maybe the world thinks I cannot! I wish it could see—at least once. If it did—and liked such boyishness—I should be tempted to say to the world—I love to work, but I love, too, to lay it all down—all the way down and let the nature of me have its own holiday. So do I soar away to quite another world, sometimes to Mars, sometimes to the Pleiades. I have inverted trolleys that run direct at my bidding to the Southern Cross, to Jupiter, to Saturn. Only it requires time to enjoy these journeys of nature. Time is the only fare that I have to pay. And almost always I must go alone, for nearly all the friends I have are as busy as myself. The pity of it all forever to drudge and never to budge from mostly fudge! The pity of it all.

There were times when his faith was sorely shaken by the loss of those he loved, by the malice and envy of the foes born of his success, by the discovery of his own limitations. And with the innate eagerness to be ever learning from experience, which is the prime quality of greatness, he knew the fallibility of his judgment and longed for the talents that he lacked.

Through more than six decades of achievement what he said and did alike reveal a consciousness, that was never absent, of not having done anything as well as it might have been done. But this dissatisfaction—the stimulating impulse of his life—had in it neither gloom nor unnervement. Every combination of events, every contact with people, interested him. He was building, perplexedly, laboriously, but the materials were fascinating, and the effort itself was a delight.

It would be impossible for the biographer to mention the names of all who have helped him. They have not wanted him to do so. Friends of John Wanamaker's, associates in his many religious and political activities, and above all the old and trusted members of his business family in Philadelphia and New York, have given unstintingly of their time and thought in order that the biographer might have all the material that would throw light upon his subject. Acknowledgment is due also to great merchants in Paris, London, New York, Philadelphia, and Chicago, who have gladly helped in making this record authoritative; to the faculty of the Harvard University Graduate School of Business; to officials of the Department of Commerce; and to the staffs of the Library of Congress, the New York Public Library, and the Princeton University Library.

On the second anniversary of John Wanamaker's death the biographer sat in the merchant's private office in the corner of an upper floor of the great building in Philadelphia. Where thousands were selling to thousands, he was alone in the midst of the papers of which there seemed no end. John Wanamaker was not only a voluminous writer, but he had the habit of saving everything that he wrote, or that anyone wrote to him, in regard to his varied and multi-

tudinous enterprises. During the day an old friend came
into the office to put a flower on the desk.

"You are reading all these?" he asked, with a wave of
the hand around the room.

"Yes," answered the biographer.

"Well," said the old friend, "if you are to know how to
tell the whole story, I suppose that is necessary. But there
is one thing still more necessary, and that is to find in these
papers and to show in every page of your book the spirit
of the man's life. It wasn't religion or business or politics,
although it was all that—and if you don't find it and if you
don't put it into your book you will not be writing about
John Wanamaker."

Without waiting for question or comment, he placed both
hands on the desk, looked the biographer in the eye, and
declared:

"From the 'forties of the nineteenth century right on
through to the end it was radiant adventure, always, always,
always."

Of course I had found it. But I had not before known
how to name it, that spirit. What the old friend said is
true. If this book is not a story of radiant adventure, it is
not a faithful picture.

                                    HERBERT ADAMS GIBBONS.

Princeton, June 1, 1926.

JOHN WANAMAKER

A FAMOUS *painter was engaged upon his own portrait and asked an intimate friend, standing by, for his opinion of the likeness. The reply was, "It would be better if you could keep to your own portrait, but you seem to be trying to improve upon your face."*

There is a great deal in the manner of bringing truth forward in such a way that it is not overpainted and made ineffective. After all, the public is the jury that has the casting vote.

Written on
January 12, 1920.

JOHN WANAMAKER

JOHN WANAMAKER

CHAPTER I

THE BACKGROUND

AMONG immigrants from continental Europe, as late as the beginning of the eighteenth century, family names were just coming into use. In many instances surnames were still taken directly from the locality, a trade, or the father's given name. On ship manifests, oaths of allegiance, and church registers, therefore, the same name did not necessarily imply kinship. Where the Wanamaker name appears, all we can assume is that those who bore it had probably been engaged in making baskets for grapes and butts for wine, an essential craft in the vineyard industry.

The earliest records of Pennsylvania and New Jersey settlers give the name in a variety of spellings. It was not unusual in those days for a man to write his name differently, sometimes in the same document. Registers of the Dutch Reformed and Baptist churches have the Wanamaker name in a dozen variations. All these Wanamakers can be traced back to the Palatinate. Compelled to leave their homes because of religious persecution between 1709 and 1750, they emigrated to America by way of Holland, as did the Pilgrims. One family seems to have stayed in Holland for a decade or more. In the Pennsylvania archives the lists of immigrants who came to Philadelphia from Rotterdam give the first of the name as Johan Wan-

nermacher, in 1710, and the last, Samuel Wanenmacher, in
1749. Georg Wannmacher arrived in 1731; and Jacob
Wannamaker and Conrad Wannemacher in 1738. Georg
seems also to have had a son, Conrad Wannemaker.

From which of these John Wanamaker is descended we
cannot say with certainty. The family history begins with
Henry Wanamaker, John's great-grandfather, who was
living on the New Jersey side of the Delaware River, above
Trenton, when the United States was formed by the union
of thirteen British colonies. The Pennsylvania Dutch belt
extended across the Delaware River into Hunterdon County,
New Jersey. To one who is familiar with the Palatinate it
is easy to understand why this is so. From Trenton to
Easton the valley of the Delaware, with hills coming down
to the water's edge and a rolling country behind, broken by
the valleys of smaller rivers and streams, reminded the
immigrants of their Rhineland. It was the kind of country
they were familiar with, and they knew how to deal with it.
Henry Wanamaker's home was on the river bank, and
immediately behind the house his land went directly up
into the hills. Before the house the river swirled around
and fell over big flat rocks, still graphically known as Tum-
ble Falls.

In the townships of Hunterdon County settled by the
Palatines, large farms and increasing families were impossible. The land lends itself only to small farming, and
even that depends upon keeping the hills in timber. In over
a century the sturdy stone houses have not increased in
number. The little villages like Sand Brook, not far from
the Wanamaker home, preserve their eighteenth-century
atmosphere. But the old names are mostly in the grave-
yards. The Palatine stock in this region became Anglicized
in two generations. The children were compelled to scatter.
The little community of a few dozen families, however, has

given to American history the outstanding names of Wana-maker and Rockefeller.[1]

In his unpublished "Life of Isaiah Williamson" John Wanamaker said: "He was a well-born man. Let the young fellow of good ancestry never forget that he starts with what the lack of to many another is a life-long handi-cap. It is a great thing for any man to be well-born." That John Wanamaker was thinking of his own stock when he wrote these words cannot be doubted. He often spoke with pride of the early achievements of the "Pennsylvania Dutch," their part in the Revolutionary War, their industry, their religious faith, and their eagerness for education. This numerous element in colonial Pennsylvania, he believed, "stood pre-eminent in three things: faith in God; faith in home; faith in education."

The records of the Adjutant-General's office in Trenton show that Henry Wanamaker was an ensign in Captain Crynes Bartolf's company in the regiment raised by Colonel Theunis Dey in North Jersey when the scene of fighting shifted to the region between New York and Trenton. Before the end of 1776 virtually all the young men of Bergen, Essex, and Hunterdon Counties were under arms, and it was this fact that made the British forces realize that they were not only pursuing rebels, but were in an enemy country where treason reigned in every farmhouse.

The deed books of Hunterdon County record the titles to Henry Wanamaker's land, and show that he was a man of substance, who helped his children and his sons-in-law to get a start in life. The original of Henry Wanamaker's will, made on June 12, 1824, and witnessed by Moses Caine

[1] In the cemetery at Larison's Corner, not far from Henry Wanamaker's home, is a monument with the following inscription: "In memory of Johann Peter Rockefeller who came from Germany about the year 1723. Died 1763. He gave this land for a burial place. This monument is erected in 1906 by John Davison Rockefeller a direct descendant."

and Smith Rittenhouse, is in the Hunterdon County Court House. He speaks of himself as "being weak in body, but of sound mind and memory, for which blessing I most devoutly thank my God." [1] With the will is the original of the inventory "of goods and chattels" made by Cornelius Hoppock and Wilson Fisher on March 21, 1831, and the executors' accounting of October 3, 1833. According to the will he had six children, for all of whom he had already provided to a certain extent during his lifetime. One of his daughters had predeceased him, and another daughter, Mary, and his third child, John, had long before gone forth to seek their fortune.

In 1810 Henry Wanamaker gave to John, who was then twenty-three and just married, enough land for a home and farm. He had already done this for the older brother, Nicholas. But if he had hoped that John would settle down in Kingwood Township, he was disappointed. For John's wife, Anna Hann, had the adventurous spirit of her Scotch mother, Hattie Robinson. She shared her husband's pioneering instinct. John and Anna sold their farm, and joined other young people of the vicinity, Opdykes, Rittenhouses, and Colemans, in going out to Ohio, where Judge Symmes of Trenton was developing a tract of land along the Miami, a part of Ohio where rivers run through valleys beautiful with hills.

Shortly after their arrival Samuel, the first son, was born. On October 25, 1811, came Nelson Wanamaker. The fact of these babies may have led the young parents to remain in Dayton, and postpone taking up a farm. Or it

---

[1] This document is signed "Henry Wanamaker." All the many references to the Wanamaker family in the Hunterdon County records give the spelling of the name as it is used to-day, and it is so given in the Revolutionary War registers in Trenton. Virtually all the other continental European names in Hunterdon County had become Anglicized before the end of the first quarter of the nineteenth century, and foreign given names are comparatively rare.

may have been their gregarious nature that led them to elect to live on in the rapidly growing community. Of Anna Hann we know little. But John Wanamaker, senior, showed throughout his life the strong liking to be with people, and to live in the midst of a constantly moving scene, that was so marked a trait of his illustrious grandchild. He became a builder—a well-chosen trade in a place where there were never enough houses. He must have prospered, for the Dayton records show that he bought two lots in 1818 in what is now the heart of a flourishing city. Three more children were added to the family between 1814 and 1819, Wilson, George, and Mary Ann. Then happened the all too common tragedy of pioneer life in America a hundred years ago. The mother died.

Sorrow over the loss of his wife and the problem of caring for five young children far from relatives, influenced John Wanamaker to abandon the Ohio venture and move back East. He settled on the outskirts of Philadelphia near his older sister and her family. His years in Ohio had given him the knowledge and had yielded the savings to start a brickyard. When his children were fairly well grown he married again and began to raise another family.

Nelson Wanamaker grew up in the brickyard and learned the trade in his 'teens. His brothers and sister struck out for themselves. That he was the son who stayed by his father may have been because he went courting in the neighborhood. Not far from where the Wanamakers lived, at Gray's Ferry, was an inn on the bank of the Schuylkill which was the terminus of Nelson's evening walks for several years. Then he carried off the daughter of the house, Elizabeth Kochersperger, to preside over a home of his own, near that of his father, for whom he continued to work. Elizabeth was named for her mother, whose father was a farmer near Darby on the other side of the river. The

Kocherspergers and the Deshongs (an Anglicized form of Des Champs) were Huguenots. Driven from Alsace and France by the revocation of the Edict of Nantes, they had been among the French families who came to Philadelphia in the first decade of Penn's colony.

The oldest child of the union of Nelson Wanamaker and Elizabeth Kochersperger, who was destined to influence profoundly the history of his times, was born on July 11, 1838. No lack of family background, but circumstances over which his parents had little, if any, control, made his childhood one of comparative poverty. He enjoyed the heritage of seventeenth and early eighteenth century Colonial stock. His grandparents were of Palatine, Scotch, Alsatian, and French lineage. But all the families had been settled in the New World long enough to be English-speaking from Colonial days. His Scotch blood and the generations of forbears in America gave him strong individuality, originality, belief in himself, and the passion that never left him, to work things out alone. The continental European strains added the tendency to thrift, the love of industry, and the instincts of cleanliness and color.

John Wanamaker's Birthplace, Painted by Miss Mabel H. Woodrow from Mr. Wanamaker's Personal Description

CHAPTER II

CHILDHOOD

WHEN he was Postmaster-General, in one of his reports to President Harrison, Wanamaker referred to himself as "a country boy," adding that while this fact gave him sympathy with the needs of rural districts, it did not prejudice him against the claims of cities. It seems an amazing statement to the biographer in 1925, who has located the spot where his subject was born. It is on Manton Street above 24th Street, at the beginning of the southern section of Philadelphia, with miles of houses beyond it. Walking leisurely from Wanamaker's birthplace, ten minutes takes one to Bethany Church and twenty-five minutes to the Wanamaker Store. In half an hour on foot one can visit both these scenes of his life work. The old brickyard of his grandfather is lost in the maze of streets and closely-built three-story houses. One goes over railroad tracks in a quarter of an hour to Gray's Ferry, where his father went courting. And yet in his writings and speeches we get a picture of a boy brought up in an atmosphere of flowers and birds, who trudged barefoot through wooded lanes, shying stones at chipmunks. His memories of lessons had to do with a country schoolhouse. The city was another world to which the boy went timidly to find a job.

But we do not have to attribute to the Wanamaker of later years a vivid imagination or a remarkable ability to put himself back where short distances seemed long to little feet. It is not necessary to smile at an old man's fancy when we see on the wall of his private office the water-color

sketch of his childhood home—a frame house surrounded
by flowers—which the artist painted from his description.
In 1911, when, at his Golden Jubilee, his employees handed
him a deed to the land on which had stood his birthplace, he
said:

"It is a very little house that covers the place, but it was
a very little place in which I was born, and I was a very
little person and didn't need a large house. It was part of
the old farm of some of my mother's kindred—the Deshong
family. Part of it was the United States Arsenal that I
think my people gave to the government, if I have the
history of it right."

And five years later he wrote in an editorial:

> An old red barn by the wayside and that flock of pigeons circling over
> it, and the red-cheeked happy-looking lads in the field cutting the corn
> stalks and stocking them, gave a man passing along a sharp spell of home-
> sickness. . . . He had to live over again days long gone by, in a little
> white house with its green shutters and a small garden of marigolds and
> hollyhocks, to say nothing of a well-trodden path over the lots to the
> schoolhouse and its good companionship.

That John Wanamaker should think of himself as a
country boy is simply an illustration of the startling growth
of American cities during the life of one man. From 1838
to 1922 Philadelphia increased tenfold in population and
area, and the growth was not distributed equally over the
eight decades. During Wanamaker's boyhood changes came
very slowly, and when he was nineteen he could still look
from the windows of the South Street cobbler's shop where
he started Bethany Sunday School, over farms and swamps,
broken by rare groups of houses, to the junction of the
Delaware and Schuylkill Rivers.

It is true, then, that he grew up in the country. Buck
Road, where he was born, and Long Lane, that skirted the
brickyard, were what their names imply—country highways

that disappeared years later when the Philadelphia system of right-angle streets was extended southward. Only Gray's Ferry Road remains on the old emplacement, and that because between it and the Schuylkill lay the Naval Home and the Arsenal, government property through which the city could not cut streets.

The first written record we have of the Wanamakers in Philadelphia is in the visitation book of John A. Neff, who canvassed "families west of Broad and south of South Street" in Christmas week, 1847. Still decipherable, although in lead-pencil, we read:

This first visitation for Landreth Sunday School was made Christmas, 1847, by the Superintendent, accompanied by George Hoffner, Sr. and William J. Hurlock. The route embraced all the families then west of Broad and south of South Street. A snowy, but delightful walk, continued until bed time. J. A. N.

The families follow, with names and ages of the children of the senior Wanamaker's second marriage as John W., 13, and Susan, 10. Nelson Wanamaker had at the time four children, John N., 10½, William, 8, Elizabeth, 5½, Mary, 4. He must have missed the baby, for in a second canvass, in July, 1849, Samuel, 3, is added. Right behind the home of John Wanamaker, senior, was the family of cousins. Henry Long had three children—John, 8, Jacob, 6, and Henry, 2½. Almost all the other families recorded seemed to have had three or more children of Sunday-school age; the names indicate old American stock; and Buck Road and Long Lane were the only highways.

As the result of the first survey Trinity Lutheran Church provided the funds for starting a Sunday school, and the Landreths offered the use of their big house on the seed farm near Buck Road, which was for sale at that time. John A. Neff, who was a clerk in a Market Street hardware store, became the superintendent, and William J. Hurlock and Nelson Wanamaker the teachers. At the opening session John Wanamaker, senior, was present to make an address. But scholars were lacking. The children had forgotten about it. Fifty years later Wanamaker told how graphically he remembered Neff and Hurlock and his own father coming out to round up the scholars. They found him with his little brother William in a field. The boys were not too keen about school on Sundays, the only afternoon they had for play. But they became immediately interested. The year before he died John Wanamaker said that he had put in seventy-five years of Sunday afternoons learning and speaking about the Bible, and that it never ceased to be the happiest event of the week.

At a meeting of the Business Men's War Council in 1918, Wanamaker told of the biggest purchase he ever made and the first debt he ever incurred. It was in the Landreth Sunday school, when he bought from his teacher, Mr. Hurlock, a small red leather Bible, about eight inches long and six inches wide. The Bible cost $2.75, an enormous sum to the small boy. He would not let Hurlock give him the book. He paid for it in installments—how small one can guess from the fact that it took a year and a half to wipe out the debt.

At the end of the Wanamaker brickyard was a little frame schoolhouse, presided over by an old fellow named Simpson, whom Wanamaker remembered as "a better switcher than teacher." Simpson was a great man for spelling-bees and St. Patrick. He taught spelling by the competitive method—with a reward. Boys and girls were ranged on opposite sides. Words were given the girls first and passed over to the boys. The first boy who spelled everything correctly was permitted to kiss all the girls. On March 17 Simpson would come to school with a big codfish, and the

(Photo by O. H. Willard)

ELIZABETH DESHONG WANAMAKER, WIFE OF NELSON WANAMAKER AND MOTHER
OF JOHN WANAMAKER

boys provided potatoes. He never asked where they got them, but sometimes irate truck farmers did. The cod was cooked in the yard in an iron pot and the potatoes were roasted in the ashes underneath.

In 1847, when John was nine, the city purchased the big Landreth House and the ground around it. The rest of the property was sold to a new brickmaking company, which began production on a much larger scale than the brickyards of the neighborhood. Thus a good school for the children came at the same moment as competition and discouragement for the parents. John Wanamaker, senior, was the first president of the local school board.

From his reminiscences it is evident that this was John's first real schooling. For in telling about the Christmas celebration of that year, "the first Christmas I remember," he said that he had not learned to write as yet, "but was given a sheet of paper on which I was to trace for my mother, with ink, the words the schoolmaster had written in lead-pencil." We suppose this is the way he learned to write. John's proud mother preserved all her life his first public speech, which he recited presumably at the Landreth School. Its bathos is quite in keeping with what young children were taught to recite up to the end of the Victorian period:

> I had a mother once like you
>   Who o'er my pillow hung,
> Kissed from my cheek the briny dew
>   And taught my faltering tongue.
> But then there came a fearful day
>   I sought my mother's bed,
> Till harsh hands bore me thence away
>   And told me she was dead.[1]

---

[1] Many a reader will remember in his own school days such selections for recitation as the death scene of Little Nell and T. B. Aldrich's "Ballad of Baby Belle."

Just what John got out of his schooling at this early period it is hard to say. Since he was already famous before those who taught him had died, we have their memories and anecdotes, as well as those of schoolmates, in which it is impossible to distinguish the apocryphal from the real. But there is consensus of opinion that he was fond of and excelled in arithmetic, and that he loved to write, using big and unusual words. He himself has confessed that next to reading the Bible his greatest pleasure was poring over the dictionary, but that his boyhood had not been conducive to the leisure and opportunity for reading that would have made acquiring new words profitable.

In the flats of the narrow Neck between the Delaware and Schuylkill there were many truck farms—temptations to purloining—and a number of ponds. Three of these, "Horsey," "Alligator," and "Baby," were near the Wanamaker home. Shallow and mud-bottomed though they were, the boys bathed there and learned to swim. Fishing was possible with kitchen utensils, and John and his brothers used to hunt for frogs with their hands. They stole off to forbidden meetings in the brickyards of an evening with boys from the truck farms, who brought potatoes, corn, and watermelons to the kiln house for a feast. From all accounts John was not good at sports. He got hurt when he tried to play ball, and he was poor at skating. His love for animals made him dislike shooting and fishing. He seemed to show none of the qualities of leadership that later made people say that he was born to command. One of his schoolmates was able to remember nothing about John as a boy except that he was rather dreamy, did not play around with other fellows much, and was "always taking codliver oil."

Until 1840, two years after Wanamaker was born, Gray's Ferry Road was one of the main highways leading out of

Philadelphia. In that year a flood washed away the bridge, and travel was deflected along the western bank of the Schuylkill into Chestnut and Market Streets. Delay in reconstruction was fatal to the angle between Broad Street and Gray's Ferry Road. It changed for the worse rapidly during the childhood of Wanamaker. Railroad tracks, for moving freight from the Delaware River front, were laid just north of Federal Street, circling south of Gray's Ferry Road, thus destroying the hope of the Buck Road region becoming a favored residential section in the development of the city. It was one of those curious fatalities that happens so often in cities. The future of a neighborhood can never be foreseen. Some people living on the outskirts, as the Wanamakers did, have the luck of finding themselves benefited by the city's growth. Either their district is demanded by business, in which case enhanced property values enable them to move away with a bit of capital, or they find themselves in the midst of a prosperous residential section, with good schools and fine churches. The right of way of railroads sealed the doom of the Wanamaker neighborhood.

The swamps to the south were thus not to be reclaimed for home-making for another generation or longer. They became a refuge for criminals and fugitives from justice. A notorious band of toughs, known as the Schuylkill Rangers, operated perilously close to this little community that had started out so well and that had been so happy in the early 'forties. The railroads brought many tramps, too. Living conditions becoming intolerable, those who could moved out rapidly. Questionable neighbors settled in the vacated houses and began to erect new homes.

Brickmaking, through greater demand and greater competition, changed entirely its old character of a trade carried on in a small way by owners of the yards. Cheap labor was introduced, which caused riots and brawls. Because they had their money invested in the industry and owned their homes and had to think of a roof over their young families, people like the Wanamakers did not know how to get out. To keep things going it was necessary to have the help of the older children after school hours. And there was always a new baby in every family. The boys were little helpers and the girls were little mothers. The city gave them the near-by school, and at last they had their Sunday school. But life was a serious proposition, and it is no wonder that we find the bright spots in John Wanamaker's memories of his childhood in mother love, in flowers, in birds. There was little time for fun for the children of the community, and they saw too much of the evil side of human nature in their contacts with outsiders.

JOHN WANAMAKER, SENIOR

CHAPTER III

INDIANA IN 1850

THE opening of the Landreth School solved the problem that had been bothering the Wanamakers about the education of their children; but the school did not make the neighborhood any better. On the contrary, it grew steadily worse.

Because he was an abolitionist, Grandfather John had incurred the enmity of the smaller men in the brick industry. Ignoring the great principle involved and thinking solely of their own interests, these men translated free negroes into terms of cheap labor. To advocate the abolition of slavery, as the elder John Wanamaker did, was to play into the hands of the big interests that were already threatening the brickmaking trade. The boy who was later to be bitterly assailed for upsetting the existing mercantile *status quo* and for compelling small shopkeepers to change their business methods or go under, learned early in life that opposition and unpopularity always attend men who recognize changing conditions and who do not hesitate to sacrifice the immediate personal interests that stand in the path of progress or the realization of ideals. The attitude of parents was reflected in that of children. The little Wanamakers soon knew what it was to have a "friend of niggers" for a grandfather and father.

Henry Wanamaker's oldest daughter had married an Indiana pioneer, and she wrote to Philadelphia glowing letters of the boundless opportunities on the new frontier. She was living in Kosciusko County, which had been ceded to the United States by Indian tribes only fifteen years before. It was a region of many lakes, watered by Tippecanoe River and Turkey Creek. Leesburg, started in 1834 as a fur post for trade with the Indians, she had long been telling her brother, was going to be the "metropolis of the West." All that later happened to Chicago did the Leesburg settlers dream their town would be "after the railroad came."

Grandfather John decided to go on a scouting expedition. Nowadays one takes the train at night in Philadelphia and wakes up in the morning in Indiana. But on July 17, 1848, after an all-day ride John Wanamaker reached the end of the Pennsylvania Railroad at Chambersburg. He took the stage immediately for Pittsburgh and did not get there until the afternoon of July 19. By way of Warren—the post route—traveling day and night, he was not at Cleveland until the evening of July 21. There he had to wait until the next evening for the boat to Toledo. From Toledo to a place called Junction took all night and the next morning. Twelve hours up the river on the sidewheeler *Illinois* brought him to Fort Wayne at 11 P.M. on July 25 after eight days of steady travel from Philadelphia.

He was still some distance from Leesburg. On July 26 he records in his diary:

This day I have been seeking for a passage to Leesburg but find none. Nine o'clock p. m. it is raining very heavy showers and continued all the night. July 27. Rainy morning. Clear at twelve m. Left Fort Wayne at 1:30 for Leesburg. Went fourteen miles to Mr. Wholf's and put up. July 28. Beautiful morning. Left Wholf's and arrived at Wholf's Lake at noon. Sixteen miles. Arrived at Leesburg at nine o'clock p. m.

The next day John Wanamaker left Leesburg bright and early and drove five hours to "Brother Bailey's homestead." An automobile makes the journey in less than twenty minutes in 1925. How our forefathers must have struggled against mud!

The diary gives graphic details of frontier life, and of how, after one week, he "closed the contract with Isaac Metcalf" for the new Wanamaker home after deciding against the land of "Benac the Indian." The account of how he spent his Sundays is worth quoting to show that his grandson and namesake came honestly by his life-long taste for Sabbath activities.

> Sunday, July 30. I went with Brother Bailey to Meeting to Brother Anglin's where we had an old-fashioned Love Feast and Preaching in the morning and a good time, and after Preaching I went to Brother Barchey's and took dinner and in the afternoon I attended a Prayer Meeting where we had a good time. In the evening we had a very heavy rain.

This fact probably prevented the enjoyment of a third service on the day after the arrival of the prospective pioneer. The next Sunday, August 6, the day before his land purchase, he "went to a schoolhouse to Prayer Meeting and after Prayer Meeting I spoke and we had a Proffitable time."

On the return journey the traveler arrived in Fort Wayne in time to be present at "an illumination of Bonfires and several speeches delivered on the Taylor Victory." From Fort Wayne he returned homeward, and visited, after twenty years, Dayton, the scene of his earliest enterprise and the sorrow of his young manhood. The diary brings us back through Columbus and Uniontown to Cumberland, where he "took the Carrs for Baltimore at eight o'clock a. m."

The kind of stuff of which the Wanamakers are made is revealed by this adventure and its aftermath. Grandfather John was over sixty. It is true that he had seen Indiana at its best in the summertime. But there was still the rain and mud, and of the four weeks all except nine days were spent in getting out and back. But Grandfather John had made up his mind without dilly-dallying. He did not hesitate at his age to buy two hundred and sixty acres of land for nearly four thousand dollars, which would mean using up in a new venture virtually all the money he could get for his interest in the brickyard. He did it for his children, for whom he saw no future in Philadelphia under the conditions which had come over their family life.

We cannot think of him as having been in good health. The little diary of the 1848 trip contains cures for rheumatism, cancer, and other ills. For rheumatism John Wanamaker jotted down: "Take Brimstone and Sewe it in a bag and wear it on your Person and Likewise Take a little inward." Cancer could be coped with as easily. "Take the yolk of an egg and mix as much salt as it will take and make a plaster and apply it 2 a day till Cured." The facilities for procuring things in the country to which he was taking his family can be imagined from the notes he made of things people asked him to bring back when he returned next year. Among them we find the man from whom he bought his land asking for "2 Pair of Specticals divided Glass."

What Grandmother Elizabeth thought of the venture we do not know. She had not seen the flowers of Indiana. She had no relatives there. She had never traveled. But when the roads were again passable the following year, Grandfather John left brickmaking and the Nelson Wanamaker family, and set out from Philadelphia with his wife and two children. This time none of the journey was by rail. He drove through to Indiana in his own conveyance, leaving Philadelphia on May 28 and not arriving at Leesburg until June 22.

The farm he had bought was seven miles from Leesburg, and about a mile and a half from the nearest village, North Galveston, now Clunette. It had been cleared hardly a

dozen years before. But there were no bad influences surrounding the children, no unpopularity with neighbors, and
no worry about steadily decreasing returns from an un-
profitable business. A living could be made in Indiana, and
there was a future for the children. Everyone in the
neighborhood, too, set high store on "Preaching and Prayer
Meetings," in which Grandfather John took full part. They
were his "good times."

It was not to be wondered at then, that the bleak difference
in Indiana between summer and winter did not deter the
father from writing to Nelson to give up making bricks and
bring his family out. This is how John Wanamaker, whose
life was so wholly identified with Philadelphia, had one
glorious year of real pioneer life at the impressionable age
of twelve.

In the summer of 1850 Nelson Wanamaker got what
money he could out of the brickyard, shipped his household
goods to Fort Wayne—beyond which there was no receiving
point for freight—and followed his father westward. It
was a formidable journey for a woman with five small
children, especially as the strictest economy was essential.
What little comforts travel by stage and river boat might
have bought had to be foregone. And from Fort Wayne
to Leesburg the family was divided. Many years later
Elizabeth Wanamaker said that she had not been keen about
the trip and that it had nearly killed her and the baby. The
Wanamakers could get no conveyance from Fort Wayne on
to Leesburg large enough to carry the whole family. Hos-
pitable strangers volunteered to give the oldest two boys a
lift. Traveling for several days, separated from their
parents—and for the first time in their lives facing the
unfamiliar—it was a great adventure for the boys. John
looked after Will. Much to the chagrin of his mother,
when they were reunited John told her that they hadn't

missed her care and that they hadn't been afraid. It had been such fun. John Wanamaker never forgot this early venture into the unknown, coupled as it was with the responsibility for his little brother.

The farm was not far from an Indian reservation. And the Indians were real! They lived in wigwams and huts; they wore blankets; the squaws carried papooses on their backs; they cooked venison steaks and fish on hot stones; they baked corn and potatoes in ashes; they traded in furs; and they were not too primitive to love rum and the white man's games of chance. When driven to it by the need of a little ready cash, they helped the settlers spasmodically to clear and till the farms. Of this direct contact as a child with "the redskins" Wanamaker spoke more than sixty years later when a group of Indian chieftains came to visit him and made him a member of their tribe.[1]

It was a dream summer for the boy who had fished for frogs and suckers in shallow pools in the mud flats of the Philadelphia "Neck." He had come to a country where game and fish were abundant in the woods and lakes and streams. It was a part of Indiana that was not monotonous. There was water everywhere. And there were hills. Health-giving activities, of absorbing interest, held the three generations of Wanamakers. But winter brought hardships they had not counted on. The daily tramp to school was nearly two miles. When the deep snows came the Clunette school

[1] En route to the inauguration of President Wilson, in 1913, thirty-two chiefs stopped in Philadelphia for the day to be entertained at the Wanamaker store. They had luncheon with John Wanamaker, and afterward executed a war dance in his private office. They represented eleven tribes. Mountain Chief, of the Blackfeet, took a string of buffalo teeth from his neck, handed it to Wanamaker, and said: "May you live as long as these teeth are old. I now name you High Crow." Honorary membership in this tribe had never before been conferred on a white man. Mountain Chief explained that the teeth had been given him when he was a very young man by his father, who had signed a peace treaty with the United States in the administration of President Pierce.

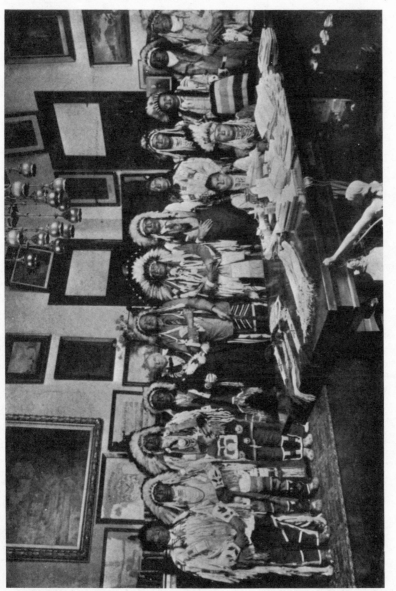

The Visit of the Indian Chiefs to the Private Office, Monday, February 24th, 1913

was closed and John's education was ended. They were virtually marooned on the farm. After the hard winter, the illness and death of Grandfather John came as the culmination of their misfortunes.

Elizabeth and Nelson decided to return to Philadelphia. There was not much to go back to; but they did not care for farming. And they were city folk. Nelson had always been peculiarly dependent upon his father. He was the one son who had stayed with him. Elizabeth had been homesick from the beginning. She missed her family and friends; she loved to be with people that loved her. For the children's sake they had made the move to Indiana. They were still young, and hoped for better luck back home.

The loss of the grandfather who had been a large part in his life was a great blow to the boy of thirteen. Nearly half a century later he said:

"My grandfather was a pioneer. I attended his funeral in Indiana. I will not in my lifetime forget the inscription on his gravestone, reading my own name on it. Standing at the grave, I prayed that I might become as good a man as he was."

CHAPTER IV

FIRST JOBS

THE Nelson Wanamaker family returned to Buck Road. It was not their choice, and they had no intention of staying on indefinitely in the neighborhood which they had disliked enough to make the Indiana venture. But brick-making was the trade that Nelson knew, and he went back to it. Before going to Indiana young John had earned some money before and after school, turning bricks. He never forgot his first earnings, which were also savings—seven copper cents. Those pennies he spoke of frequently, making them a text for a homily on thrift. We found in his desk a small slip of paper on which was written: "The small boy with his first dime feels as rich as a man with his first million."

John could have found a job as carry-away boy in the yard where his father worked; for he had now nearly finished growing and was sturdy enough to wheel a barrow. But neither the work nor the companionship appealed to his parents. Caught they were in the vise of necessity, but that did not mean that the children could not get away from it. Nelson and Elizabeth Wanamaker were not of the foolish type that wishes it could live its life over again, and that fails to see that the wish can be gloriously fulfilled in the next generation. They were consumed with ambition for their children. John was not thrust out into the world to find a job. They prayed over the question with the good friend, John A. Neff, and he suggested that Brown & Robb, young lawyers, needed an office boy. Why not launch John in an atmosphere of books?

In after life John Wanamaker recalled this first job when he was speaking of how he learned to admire and respect the legal profession. Had his parents not begun to need the earnings of the older sons and had his health in adolescence been better, John might have gone on to copyist and clerk and have found in the law his life work. In those days high school, college, and law school were not necessary steps to admittance to the bar. But it was impossible to keep a delicate boy, dependent upon out-of-doors life, cooped up in a dark little anteroom.

When Neff found that Troutman & Hayes, on Market Street below Fifth, publishers of Zell's Encyclopedia and other books of reference, needed an errand boy, John was shifted to business. He had the long walk into the city in the morning and back at night, and was using arms and legs all day. The salary was $1.25 a week. In a sketch of John Wanamaker's life found among his papers, the statement occurs, "John gave his mother all the money that he saved." The word "saved" is crossed out and in the merchant's unmistakable handwriting is written over it, "earned." Small as the wages were, they were needed in the home on Buck Road, where two more babies came to join the other five in the years immediately after the return from Indiana.

Nearly full grown in his fourteenth year, and contributing to the family support, John was still a child. He never forgot the bulldog that sometimes held the road of a morning and made a détour through fields necessary. He never forgot how, in order to keep his boots clean, he had to walk barefoot when it was muddy and put on the boots when he reached the beginning of pavement, wiping one foot after the other on paper brought along for that purpose. The resulting condition of the inside of the boots did not satisfy him, of course, but he was getting an early lesson in the inconvenience—and the pretense—of keeping up appearances.

Hayes, like all early employers of successful men, became inordinately proud of having once bossed John Wanamaker. He told a reporter:

"We had two messenger boys in the office. If we sent one of them on an errand, we were certain that he would go straight to the place and return as quickly as possible. Organ grinders with monkeys, beautiful store windows and all that sort of thing, could not make the boy swerve from a straight path. With the other lad it was different. As soon as the clang of a fire bell sounded, out he would rush to the engine house or the burning building.

"Years passed. I left the city for a time during the Civil War. After my return in 1866, I was passing along the street, when suddenly, at the corner of Sixth and Market, I saw a sign that almost took my breath away. Above the door of a big clothing establishment in large letters I read the name, John Wanamaker. You can imagine my surprise at seeing our old errand boy transformed so quickly into a successful merchant.

"A few days later I was walking down Delaware Avenue. Over on a pier beside a molasses hogshead I saw a man lying in a drunken stupor. I went and rolled him over. Can you guess who I found? Our other errand boy."

This story is quoted, not for its intrinsic value, but to illustrate the despair of the biographer in finding anecdotes of John Wanamaker's boyhood that do not represent him as a good little boy. For a youngster he was undoubtedly thoughtful and serious. The economic urge had him in its grip too early in life. But with all the problems of a livelihood to earn and parents to help, John must still have been

(Photo. by O. H. Willard)

NELSON WANAMAKER

a youngster with a keen sense of humor. What carried him over rough places later could not have been absent in early years. It is impossible to believe that he never listened to an organ grinder or looked in a shop window. But a generation ago biography was still written like tracts. The interest in recording the achievements of a man seemed to be to emphasize the moral that the reward of industry and of being good in childhood was success in manhood. Since the leaders of mankind almost invariably build their careers upon a foundation of a normal, healthy, average boyhood, it is natural for us to wonder if most of the anecdotes of the childhood of great Americans from Washington to Wanamaker are not largely legendary.

The midday meal, when he did not carry it, consisted of "a piece of zweibach and a glass of milk," to use his own words, generally at the Red Curtain, a vender's stand wedged in between stalls in the Market Street sheds. He had been working more than a year before he was able to substitute pie for the dry bread.

This was when he changed to the clothing store of Barclay Lippincott at the southwest corner of Fourth and Market Streets, just before Christmas in 1852. He was still a utility boy, but at the larger salary of $2.50. He swept the store and dusted the top layers of clothing, put out the mannekins, and had everything ready for business at half past seven. This meant getting up long before six and walking to the city in the dark in the winter. About this time the second son, Will, also found a job in town. Nelson Wanamaker now felt that the time had come to move. The economic and social interests of the wage-earners of the new generation were becoming more important than his. He found a little house on Tenth Street, near Wharton Street, which made going to work and coming home easier for the

boys.[1] This was the end of "country life" for John Wanamaker. Until he went to Lindenhurst years later he spent
both summers and winters in the city.

Barclay Lippincott did not realize that his young helper
was growing into a man. Raises grudgingly consented to up
to $5 represented his estimate of the limit of John Wana-
maker's usefulness. The boy was learning a lot about the
clothing business but he was given no opportunity to use
what he was learning. One morning he brought to his
employer the idea that the clothing on the mannekins outside should fit the weather and that Tower Hall in the
block above paid attention to the barometer in its offerings.
With the love for rhyming words that never left him he
said to Mr. Lippincott what has become our first record of
a John Wanamaker business principle. "Not only goods
reasonable, but also goods seasonable," was the way he expressed himself. The presumptuous boy was invited to go
to Tower Hall, seeing that he liked their ways better. He
did, and found to his delight that Colonel Bennett was
willing to give him $6. Not many years later was Barclay
Lippincott to learn that the unknown name of the boy whose
advice he did not want was meaning to Philadelphians a
thousand times more in the clothing business than his own
old and honored name.

There are indications that John had wanted to get a job
at Tower Hall before he went to Barclay Lippincott. The
big granite building (it is still standing) at 518 Market
Street, its size, its unique advertising, its methods of display,
appealed strongly to the boy. It was the best clothing business in the city. Throughout his life John Wanamaker
always wanted to have "the best" and to be identified with

---

[1] We find in a rent receipt book preserved in John Wanamaker's safe that
his father moved still nearer to the center of town in 1855. The Nelson
Wanamaker family lived at 800 Lombard Street from November 12, 1855,
to February 13, 1858.

"the biggest." It had not taken long for him, when he was still the errand boy of the publishing house, to decide that if he was going in the clothing business Tower Hall was the goal. Colonel Bennett, Tower Hall's picturesque owner, considered eccentric on Market Street because he was progressive, had known John's grandfather and was a friend of his father and mother.

To many people this fact would have made Colonel Bennett the logical person with whom to put John. But Nelson and Elizabeth Wanamaker were proud and independent. Hard luck they had had for years, and Nelson Wanamaker may not have been efficient and energetic. He may not have wanted to be. Some men are too devoted as husbands and fathers to have time for business success. But if they stand on their own feet, as Nelson and Elizabeth Wanamaker did, the children are likely to justify the investment of love and personal care.[1] For generations the Wanamakers had been proud of what they were and not of what they had. John Wanamaker went to Colonel Bennett only when he was sure that he was worth something to Tower Hall. He asked for a chance, and this he interpreted in terms of a cloth and brass polish, as he went to work on the massive knobs of the front door. Faithfulness in polishing and not the claim of friendship was his understanding of the path to a position as salesman.

From his sixteenth to his nineteenth year John Wanamaker learned the clothing business in Tower Hall. When he knew the stock by handling it he became a salesman, and was soon put in charge of the men's furnishing department. He persuaded Colonel Bennett to allow him to buy collars

[1] The year before John Wanamaker died he spoke of his father as "a busy father, much absent, hard pressed with laborious work and unending cares, but he never forgets the true son, for whom he would at any time give up his life. The softness, gentleness, and sweetness of the mother are ever a full alabaster box; but the boy remembers that his father's strong, steady arm always seemed to him in his first years as mighty as that of Samson."

and cuffs, shirts, suspenders, handkerchiefs, and socks. This was his first experience in buying and selling, the complementary activities of the merchant; and at the same time he became acquainted with advertising. One of his fellow-salesmen, Mr. Dela, wrote spirited advertising in the form of verses, which Colonel Bennett printed on the first page of the *Public Ledger*. One remarkable feature of the Bennett business was the movement of goods, in lot and single orders, to all parts of the South and West—a business built up entirely by advertising and direct correspondence. In the store there was no phase of the business that escaped John's observation and study.

He soon became aware of the fact that every rung in the ladder a merchant had to climb could be represented by the same word—savings. It was the first rung—and all the other rungs. A healthy business had to be a growing business. No business could grow without a steady increase of capital. In seeking new and larger credits the merchant had to contribute his share of new and larger capital. Long after his father's death Wanamaker told how deeply the lesson of his own family fortunes had impressed itself upon his youthful mind. "When I was in Tower Hall," he said, "the idea came to me that if I was ever to do better than my father, I would have to learn how to save."

He learned, too, that there were times when unforseen circumstances were likely to arise in a business that could ruin the most able merchants, despite what would be regarded in normal times as sound and conservative financing. The great panic of 1857 made a deep impression upon the young salesman, although he confessed half a century later, after he had gone through several panics and was in the last of these himself on the verge of failure, that he had only partly learned its lesson. Among the Philadelphia failures the most startling was that of Caleb Cope, whose great granite store in the block below Tower Hall had been completed only a few years before. It was generally believed that the panic was due to the downward revision of the tariff under the Buchanan administration. It helped to make the new generation of Philadelphians protectionists and lifelong Republicans.

Just when hard times hit every line of business in Philadelphia, John Wanamaker broke down in health. He had scarcely finished growing when he went to Tower Hall. Tall and thin, the long hours behind the counter were cruelly confining, and he had been giving all his outside hours to religious work. The physician he consulted was peremptory. John was told to get out of the atmosphere of a Market Street clothing store, and to go off somewhere for a complete rest.

It was just before this event that he had definitely decided upon his career, despite the strong pull of the church. He recalled how he had come to his decision in these words:

I took an enormous sheet of brown paper and wrote down on it all the different things I thought I should like to be. I remember very clearly to this day. I put down architect because I had always been interested in the making of buildings. I put down journalist and doctor and clergyman—the latter a vocation which my mother was very anxious to have me take up. After several others which I do not recall, I wrote merchant. One by one I went over the list and, after careful deliberation, struck out various words for one reason or another. Finally merchant was left, and I turned my attention seriously to work.

But the door seemed to have closed definitely upon this career. Colonel Bennett was deeply concerned. He offered to finance a long vacation for John, for he knew the burden the boy had been bearing, and that there was no money in the family. But John was able to answer, "I have something saved, sir."

CHAPTER V

NOT BY BREAD ALONE

AFTER John Wanamaker died, James Dobson, a Philadelphia manufacturer who had been a close friend to
him for sixty years, expressed in one laconic sentence the
secret of his friend's buoyancy: "Mr. Wanamaker's religious
temperament kept him afloat." How true this was none
who studies Wanamaker's life can fail to realize. His childlike faith and his consciousness of God's presence and help
pulled him through every crisis. He sincerely believed
the promise: "Seek ye first the Kingdom of God, and all
these things shall be added unto you." His religion could
be more fairly called his life than a part of his life; for it
was always with him. This fact makes of prime importance
the story of his early religious experience.

Grandfather John was a lay preacher in the Methodist
Church, and we have had a glimpse of his delight in prayer-
meetings. We have seen how his father taught in the first
Sunday school which young John attended. His mother did
not disguise her hope of a "call to the ministry" for her
oldest son. Frequently she told him that it would make
her supremely happy to have him become a minister. His
relatives and the friends of the family were all church-going
people, whose chief reading was the Bible and who prayed
for guidance about everything that came along. But they
were not sectarians. Grandfather and father, though of
Baptist stock, were Methodists.[1] His mother cherished the

[1] A memorial window in the M. E. Church of the Covenant, 18th and
Spruce Streets, Philadelphia, bears record of the membership of John Wanamaker, Sr., and Nelson Wanamaker.

REV. JOHN CHAMBERS, D.D.

"DRAWN AND ENGRAVED BY J. SARTAIN"

Dr. Chambers, of the First Independent Church of Philadelphia, was John Wanamaker's first pastor

Reformed faith of her Huguenot ancestors. The Landreth Sunday school was Lutheran. Strong individualism and receptiveness to new ideas made them think less of creeds than of practical Christianity. Indicative of their attitude toward denominations is the fact that when John became interested in a church that had no ecclesiastical affiliations and a preacher who was a law unto himself, they encouraged him to go where the spirit led him.

John Chambers, whose photograph is on the wall of every room of John Wanamaker's private offices—and in a place where it can readily be seen—was the most noted preacher in Philadelphia.[1] He was a sensationalist, a fearless crusader against vice, and is said to have been the first preacher in Philadelphia to use advertising space in newspapers. When he was a licentiate of the Presbytery of Philadelphia, some of his sermons were considered unorthodox. The ultra-Fundamentalists of the day were laying for him when he came up for ordination. He refused to subscribe to all the dogmas of the Westminster Confession, and was rejected by the Presbytery. But he secured ordination from the Congregational Union of New Haven, and returned to Philadelphia to become pastor of the Ninth Presbyterian Church. This bold defiance of the Presbytery led to court action, in which his followers lost the church property. A lot was bought at Broad and Sansom Streets for $400, and there was established the First Independent Church.

Dr. Chambers was thoroughly orthodox. His quarrel with the Presbyterians had been over non-essentials, and were it not for the fact that church splits seem to be inevitable in most Protestant communions, we should be puzzled to discover why a man of John Chambers' strong and mili-

---

[1] In the old home at Lindenhurst, too, there was a memorial window to John Chambers, in which his portrait was graphically and beautifully reproduced. It was destroyed by the fire of 1907.

tant evangelical faith should have been read out of the
Presbyterian Church as a heretic. He was one of the
earliest Philadelphia preachers to make total abstinence a
test of morals, and by becoming a temperance advocate he
showed his great courage. Most of his people loved their
whisky, and some of them who had been liberal in church
support were distillers. Chambers was a splendid physical
specimen, emotional but practical in his appeal, and there
is more truth than fiction in the comment of an unfriendly
critic that he "roared like the bull of Bashan."

The first time John heard him was when he was still an
errand boy with Troutman & Hayes. Dr. Chambers was
appealing for help in building a new church, and he said that
if anyone in the congregation could not give money he might
give goods. The first response was a voice from the gallery,
crying, "I'll give a load of bricks from my father's brickyard." It started a flood of donations more than sufficient
to put up the new building.[1] It created a precedent, too;
for in the twenty-odd years that he continued to hold forth
at Broad and Sansom Streets, John Chambers never appealed
in vain to John Wanamaker.

When the Wanamakers moved in town—even before that,
according to some accounts—John became a faithful attend-

[1] Several years later, when John had become secretary of the Y. M. C. A.,
he helped again with bricks. A new sidewalk was needed, but the trustees
voted against it because there were no funds. Young Wanamaker went
around among his father's friends and competitors, and got a gift of a load
of bricks from several of them. With volunteer help of the young men and
boys of the church the walk was laid on Broad Street and Sansom Street
between Wednesday-night prayer-meeting and Sunday. When Dr. Chambers
came to the church on Sunday morning and started to go into the study, he
realized that his feet were standing on a new pavement. His young
parishioner, concealed behind one of the wooden columns in front of the
church, watched the pastor take off his glasses and rub them to see if he
was not mistaken, and then bend over and look down at the pavement
without any glasses. Then he spied John. The anecdote is preserved in the
private files, without any comment, so there is no reason to doubt its authen-
ticity. There are several anecdotes that show the close and affectionate relations between the great preacher and the youth still in his teens.

CHAMBERS PRESBYTERIAN CHURCH

ant of the First Independent Church. In his first year at Tower Hall, when he was barely eighteen, at a midweek service, a hatter named Walton, with whom his Sunday school and business activities were destined to become closely linked, gave a talk on the practical side of religion, which made John Wanamaker decide to join the church. As he regarded this as the most significant event of his life, we are glad to be able to describe it in his own words:

> As the people went out from the meeting I stayed. I wanted to see the minister. I did not know just where he was, but the people kept passing out, and finally there was no one in the room except the sexton and myself. The minister had gone into another room, and now re-entered the prayer-meeting room.
>
> As he was coming down the aisle toward the door he saw a country boy coming up the aisle toward him.
>
> That chap was myself. I went up to him, and told him that I wanted him to know that I had settled the matter that night, and had given my heart to God. He took my hand and told me how glad he was to know this.
>
> "God bless you, my boy," he said; "you will never regret the step you have taken."

No more zealous convert was ever received into the church by Dr. Chambers. The young clothing salesman accepted his pastor's instruction and Gospel message fully and unreservedly, in spirit and in letter. Dr. Chambers taught that the true Christian should remember that his time and talents no longer belonged to himself, should never miss an opportunity of bringing others to Christ, should keep the Sabbath, should fight rum, and should always be willing to go out of his way to help to their feet men that had fallen. We have in Wanamaker's own writing these cardinal obligations of a Christian, as Dr. Chambers saw them. They might be called the constitution and by-laws of his religious activities:

1. Christ demands full surrender.
2. Every follower of Christ is His messenger of good tidings.
3. Sunday is the Lord's day: it belongs to Him.
4. Alcohol is Satan's most powerful ally.
5. No man is beyond redemption.

The echoes of sermons preached in the First Independent Church were soon heard at Tower Hall. Colonel Bennett was a good Methodist, but not a very devout man, and he noted with some amusement the first efforts of his young salesman to do missionary work. But he was not unsympathetic, and there were other employees at Tower Hall under the spell of Dr. Chambers. Some of them were Sunday comrades, carrying, as he did, their lunch to church, and eating it before the Sunday school opened in a basement room at the corner of Broad and Sansom Streets. They stood by him and helped him when he circulated a little black book with a temperance pledge in it among the Tower Hall force.

In 1856 John became a Sunday-school teacher. No class was assigned to him. That would not have satisfied him. He went out into the street and mustered in his own class. In reminiscences of old Philadelphia one of these boys, Colonel William Lynn, wrote in the *Public Ledger* on June 18, 1923:

Young John Wanamaker had a Sunday-school class in the basement of the old John Chambers Church. He gathered the boys who were loitering around the neighborhood. I went in with the others. He wore a nice black coat and a stiff choker collar. The boys called him "Stiffie." We wore hickory shirts, and there wasn't a collar or a pair of cuffs among us.

In the early part of 1857 came a great revival, and John got the habit of devoting his lunch hour to prayer-meetings in Jaynes's Hall. He had become a member of the Y. M. C. A., and entered into its work with all the zeal that he showed in business and in his Sunday activities at the John Chambers Church. The growth of the noonday meetings at Jaynes's Hall from a small group to the capacity of the largest auditorium in Philadelphia in a few weeks was the first demonstration of John Wanamaker's organizing ability. It seems that he gave several evenings a week also to meetings in engine and hose houses of the volunteer fire companies.

Unflagging devotion to Tower Hall, coupled with these religious activities, proved too great a strain. Carbuncles began to trouble him. There were signs that his lungs were affected. It was then, as we have seen, that medical advice had to be listened to. Like Colonel Bennett, several of the friends he had made through the Y. M. C. A. assured him that he could draw on them. The important thing at that moment was to get back his health. The physician had recommended a complete change and rest.

The boy could not rest. He did not know how to rest, and he never learned. But he did see the wisdom of a change, and he had enough money to fulfill the dream he had in Indiana of seeing what lay beyond. He went out to Chicago, which was easier to reach than Indiana had been seven years earlier. Great progress had been made in railway construction. He had read about the explorations of Father Hennepin, and Longfellow's recently published "Hiawatha" had fired his imagination. So he penetrated (the word is advisedly used) to the Northwest, which was being rapidly opened up. He translated vacation into terms of constant movement and observation, and his pioneering blood was stirred with the vision of the future place of these new regions in the United States. One letter of this period is worth quoting to show how the boy of nineteen had already formed the habit of devoting a large part of his attention and thought to matters of religion. We preserve the capitalization and punctuation:

Since my absence from home I have wandered over three thousand five hundred miles of our country. Seen much to call forth admiration—much to regret. Sailed up the great father of Rivers—the beautiful Mississippi and from the high bluffs around about St. Paul—Minnesota—looked upon the once happy hunting grounds and homes of the Red Men of the Forest. Sad was it to witness their desolation and listen to the story of their sufferings and wrongs—Oh! that their history could be blotted from the page of remembrance for alas! It is a bitter reflection upon the humanity and christianity of the White Man. In viewing the scenery of our beloved America its lofty mountains that rear their heads in grandeur towards the sky—the broad prairies that are covered with golden grain and waving corn stretching out Ocean like before you—the beautiful rivers that raft from shore to shore the products of the surrounding country. The noble lakes upon whose bosom float ships of all nations—the beautiful "Laughing Waters" of the Falls of Minnehaha and last though not least the glories of Niagara sublimely beautiful. I say while feasting upon the magnificient scenery of our native land—where is the American heart that will not swell with joy and burst forth in gratitude for the blessings we enjoy? wonder we but then—Why? we are the pride of the Nations of the world ——I said I saw much to regret—it is with a sad heart I refer to the carelessness and indifference manifested in many places to those principles of vital godliness upon which I sincerely believe rests the foundation of the peace and Prosperity of the land—I feel as we cultivate holiness of heart and spread the glorious tidings of peace—inculcating the truth as it is in Jesus—so do we bind together our beloved Union—inseperable with our prosperity is the religion of the Bible as we grow in the grace of our Lord Jesus Christ—so will our beloved land prosper and advance to that glorious position of Excelsior.

In view of these facts I find an exhortation to the Christian people of the United States—to be faithful and true to their profession—that they shed abroad by their example a power that will grow and expand in the hearts of those around and induce them to join with us in hastening the day and bringing about that Millenium when righteousness will cover the earth even as the waters cover the deep—when every voice shall be tuned in praise and our lovely hills and valleys resound with the melody of Glory to God in the highest.

I am thankful my Bro—that I have the pleasure to say to you that my health has been in a great measure restored and shall, the Lord willing, soon return, I hope with renewed energy to engage in the service of the Lord. In conclusion I ask an interest in your prayers that I may be an *humble* and *faithful* child of God. May God bless and keep you in the way of all truth and may you abound in every good work is the prayer of

Your humble brother in Christ,

JOHN WANAMAKER.

As far as we have been able to discover, the traveler did not write voluminously of this trip, and he seems to have made no record of it after his return. In reminiscences of his youth he rarely referred either to it or to the great crisis through which he was passing. Once he said that when he was West he came face to face with realities and made up his mind that he would have to reckon with his health in deciding upon his life work. He had come to understand how one little defect or weakness could throw a man out of kelter and make him ineffectual. This thought he often afterward expressed, but never more forcefully than when he was running for the gubernatorial nomination in 1898. Referring to a recent trip to Europe he said:

"There was only a screw loose in the great engine of the *Kaiser Wilhelm der Grosse*, the greatest of all the ocean greyhounds, the pride of the North German Lloyd. When she was making her maiden voyage, it was my privilege to be a passenger on board the splendid ship, the triumph of modern shipbuilding, and I saw her flounder her way over the sea. She flew, but it was like a bird with a broken wing."

When funds gave out and his physical condition seemed greatly improved, John returned East, stopping to see his parents at Chambersburg, where they were visiting. Both father and mother were bitterly opposed to any thought of his going back into business.   It seemed like tempting Providence.   And John's mind ever since the great revival had been on the Church.   He wondered if there were not some way in which he could study for the ministry.   But he did not have the necessary foundation of education to go on to college and a theological seminary, and to start in on an intensive course of study would have menaced his health as much as working in a store.

Still uncertain as to the future, but eager to get back to the old circle of friends in Chambers Church and the Y. M. C. A., John Wanamaker returned to Philadelphia at the end of 1857. Within a few weeks he had launched the enterprise that was the beginning of Bethany, and had found a unique position in religious work, which enabled him to earn his living while doing the thing that he wanted most to do.

CHAPTER VI

Y. M. C. A. SECRETARY

BORN of the brain of a great English merchant, the Young Men's Christian Association was an attempt on the part of laymen to meet a religious need caused by the growth of cities, which the church was unwilling or unable to face. Young men were drifting in large numbers from the country to the city. Social and economic conditions were so changed for them in their new city life that the Church, if it was allowed to get any place at all, did not and could not mean for them what it had meant in the places from which they came. In small towns and rural communities the Church was the accepted meeting place for people who knew one another, a community center. When home ties were broken, the newcomers to city life found church attendance without friends cold and unattractive.

George Williams felt that Christian laymen, banded together, could do something to help young men solve the problems and temptation that come from the appalling loneliness of big cities. His conception of the Y. M. C. A. was a co-operative agency with the churches in religious education and devotional exercises. Its distinctive sphere was getting young men together, guiding their activities in the right direction, and giving them opportunities for personal social contacts that would lead to church affiliation.

The Philadelphia Y. M. C. A. was founded under the presidency of George H. Stuart in 1854. Despite the evident need for it, most pastors and churches looked upon the new movement with suspicion, and some were actively hostile.

Pride made them feel that the churches were sufficient. They were unwilling to admit the weakness of Protestantism in meeting the changing conditions of social life. But the John Chambers type of preacher welcomed it as an ally and believed in it as a field in which young men who were in the Church could fulfill their Christian duty towards those outside the fold. In Philadelphia, as everywhere else, the growth from modest beginnings was encouraging. The influence of the movement in the religious life of the city had been manifest in the revival of 1857. More and more prominent churchmen rallied to its support, and young men like John Wanamaker found in it the instrument for directing their zeal for militant Christian service.

But three years of conscientious effort proved to its organizers that wholly volunteer work was haphazard and a makeshift. They decided that the Y. M. C. A. could measure up to its opportunities only by employing a secretary, on a business basis, with a fixed salary and definite budget. During the revival the organization was incorporated, and moved from its single room on Chestnut Street, which had not been much used, to larger quarters on Arch Street below Ninth.

The idea was an innovation, and many felt that it would make the Y. M. C. A. seem more like a competitor of the churches than before. But it appealed to men who had become impressed with the boundless opportunity and their own limitations. Young Wanamaker had returned to Philadelphia without a job. He was not ready to go back into business. He was not ready to enter the ministry. But he was eager to do religious work, and his ability and devotion had been demonstrated. To George H. Stuart this unknown boy appeared to be providentially indicated for the new position. The unplowed field and the opposition to the idea challenged his spirit of adventure.

John Wanamaker thus became the first full-time secretary of the Y. M. C. A. in the United States, with a salary
of one thousand dollars, which was excellent pay for a man
of twenty in 1858. He was the pioneer in a new profession,
which, largely because of his efficiency in the work, had
come to stay. It is now followed by thousands all over the
world.

The conditions facing John Wanamaker were far from
encouraging. The fact of anyone except a clergyman taking
a salary for religious work was new, and therefore startling
and repugnant to many. Even those who accepted the
reasonableness and justice of the innovation demurred at
the size of the stipend. Why, it was more than John could
earn in the clothing business! Then, the salary was only
guaranteed by George H. Stuart. John soon found that it
was part of his job to induce men interested in the Y. M.
C. A. to increase their contributions to meet new needs,
including the secretary's salary, and to find a larger circle
of friends for the support of the Y. M. C. A. Aware of the
criticism, he shrank from asking for money. It seemed like
passing the hat for himself. He had to overcome the opposition of pastors, some of whom were jealous of his organization. Not only did they have to cease being enemies of
the new movement that was to do so much for the evangelical life of Philadelphia, but they had to be won over to
co-operation.

The most distressing fact of all was to find that many of
those whose names were on the list of directors did not
know about Stuart's scheme until after it had gone through.
When he called on them for pledges the new secretary was
treated coolly, sometimes discourteously. One man, after
having at first refused to see him, told Wanamaker that
there was nothing more contemptible than trying to make
money out of religion, and showed him the door before an

answer could be made. Young Wanamaker, despite his sensitiveness, enjoyed opposition when an opportunity was given him to meet it. But it was hard to forgive the man who insulted him and to forget how he had been refused the opportunity of explaining his ideas for the Y. M. C. A. when he went to him with the eagerness and conviction of youth.

At the annual meeting of 1857, George H. Stuart called for the secretary's report, and introduced his young friend, as a man "with a queer name that nobody has ever heard of." Five years before, when the Philadelphia Y. M. C. A. was organized, it began with fifty-seven members. But there were listed seventeen vice-presidents and thirty-three managers. This would seem to have left only seven ordinary members. It was still a small organization, with one room, in 1858, and its activities—aside from those connected with the revival of 1857—had amounted to hardly more than a few evening meetings and having a room with newspapers in it and some old books for young men who might think of spending an evening there. But in the first year of his secretaryship, John Wanamaker reported two thousand new members; tireless visitation of those who dropped in, who were met by chance, or whose names were sent in by pastors in home towns; the distribution of hundreds of Testaments; many names appended to a total-abstinence pledge; noonday prayer-meetings at which young men learned to speak and express themselves in prayer; and the placing of over forty teachers in various Sunday schools. The secretary's salary had been subscribed, and, in addition, more money had come in as contributions and dues than during the previous four years of the organization's existence.

Simple and concise, but full of ideas and suggestions, the report justified in the minds of the board the wisdom of having a paid secretary. The news of Wanamaker's success traveled all over the country, and permanent paid secretaries were engaged in half a dozen cities. But none ever achieved at the beginning the success of John Wanamaker. Many of the secretaries were better educated than the one in Philadelphia; several were far more fluent speakers; probably all of them were as devoted to the work.

Many years later Wanamaker explained his success in this first great work, by saying, "I went out into the byways and hedges, and compelled them to come in." The statement is literally true. There are letters which show the thoroughness and the unflagging zeal of John Wanamaker in finding recruits for the Y. M. C. A. and keeping up the interest of those who entered the old quarters on Chestnut Street. Wanamaker never failed to call—and keep calling until he found his man in—soon after making the memorandum of an address. As the organization grew this task of following up the men in their homes and lodgings became exceedingly strenuous; but John seemed to have the will power and endurance to form personal contacts with young men who came to Philadelphia to seek their fortunes. He kept after them, and detailed them to bring others to the Y. M. C. A. rooms. He was always on hand at fixed hours to welcome both old friends and newcomers. He found jobs for members. When they went to other cities, he wrote letters of introduction for them.

The president and directors were in hearty agreement with the belief of the young secretary that aggressive evangelistic work should be undertaken by the organization to supplement his personal work. They put their hands deeper into their own pockets and got others to help, so that a summer tent meeting, under the care of an evangelist, might be organized to keep alive the spirit of the great revival. This was one of the activities that Wanamaker enjoyed most. To show how strenuous was the evangelistic program conceived by him, we quote a letter in his own handwriting, found in the private files. Writing on May 1, 1859, to George J. Mingins, he said:

Dear Brother,

You have been appointed by the Young Men's Christian Association of Philadelphia to have charge of the Union Tent, and will be required to observe the following letter of instructions:

1st. The name by which you shall be known in your connection with the Tent shall be *Superintendent of the Union Tent*.

2d. You hereby have full authority to protect the property of the Tent during the time it may remain under your care.

3d. The Services in the Tent shall be as follows:
On Sabbath:
Union Prayer Meeting at 7 o'clock A. M.,
Union Prayer Meeting at 4 o'clock P. M.,
Preaching at 4:30 o'clock P. M.,
Preaching at 8 o'clock P. M.
During the other part of the week there shall be:
Union Prayer Meetings about sunrise every morning (Sabbath excepted).
Preaching on Monday, Tuesday, Thursday, and Friday evenings by Ministers of various Evangelical denominations.
On Wednesday night there shall be services conducted by Laymen (consisting of short addresses).
On Wednesday and Saturday afternoons there shall be meetings held for children.
Other meetings—*viz.*, for the anxious—prayer meetings in neighboring houses. Wherever the Tent may be located, shall be at the discretion of the Supt. to be reported to the Committee as early as possible.
There shall be no services held in the Tent other than those of a strictly religious character.

4th. The selection of Ministers shall be made only from such denominations as are represented in the Association, and as a general rule the different denominations shall succeed each other.

5th. The Supt. shall make the necessary daily purchases for the Tent, mark the bills, correct and hand them to the chairman of the Tent Committee.

6th. He shall keep a daily Journal and register therein the number and character of the meetings, names of preachers, attendance and other items of interest that may have an immediate bearing on the enterprise.

7th. When the proper Committee (Committee on Worship) is not present, whose duty it is to take up the collections, the Supt. shall select such persons as he may think proper and have the collection taken up, which shall be deposited with the Treasuer of the Association as soon as practicable.

8th. The salary of the Supt. shall be sixty-six 66/100 dollars ($66.66) per month to commence from the 25th day of April, 1859, and to continue until dismissed.

By order of the Committee of the Young Men's Christian Association on Union Tent.

(Sgd.)   JOHN WANAMAKER,
Chairman.

But John Wanamaker did not ask of others what he was not doing himself. As we shall see, his own Sunday work at Bethany started when he became secretary of the Philadelphia Y. M. C. A. Throughout his life he found time to do for Bethany, in addition to many other religious activities, as much as, if not more than, he required of the evangelist at the Union Tent in 1859. And with all that he did for Bethany, when he was developing his own business, he never lost interest in the Y. M. C. A. Beginning with the convention at New Orleans in 1860, he took an interest in the national work of the organization, and he was one of the prime movers and supporters later in the extension of the movement throughout the world.

It was with money saved from three years of this service that the Wanamaker business was founded. It proved a precious stepping-stone. But Wanamaker did not consider his work for the Philadelphia organization finished when he resigned his paid secretaryship. During the Civil War, Stuart and he diverted their attention largely to army work. Immediately after the war was over, 1210 Chestnut Street was leased, and Wanamaker started to raise money for the purchase of this building.[1] Thirty-five thousand dollars was paid for it in 1868, and the next year, John Wanamaker, presiding at the fifteenth anniversary, said:

"I want to be not only in Chestnut Street, but way down among the foundries in Southwark where the young men have no place to go at night. We want rooms away out in Kensington, where so many are working who at night have no place to go but the saloon that shines and allures them in."

This year he succeeded Stuart as president of the Philadelphia branch, and organized two hundred and seventy-five open-air religious meetings in twenty-five sections of the city. In 1870 he initiated work in the colleges, and rented a house on Lombard Street for a colored branch. In 1871 the Young Women's Christian Association was started with his encouragement, and he was once more a pioneer when he leased a building to provide lodgings and a restaurant for young men who were strangers in the city. In 1872 he picked out and financed the purchase of a large tract of land at 15th and Chestnut Streets and started a new drive for the building that was to be for forty years a landmark in Philadelphia. His own substantial contribution of $5,000 heads the list.[2] On the second page is the following entry in his handwriting:

PRAISE THE LORD

Mr. Alex Brown calls at my office at Oak Hall this morning at 9½ o'clk and says that his father authorizes him to subscribe $25,000 to the Young Men's Christian Association for the Building fund, with but a single condition that the Building and Property be free of debt when completed—that his father does not prescribe any kind of a building, or

[1] In his safe we find a leather-bound subscription book. The first entry is Bethany Sunday School, on February 21, 1866. In the back, in his own handwriting, are estimated figures of the cost of altering the building for Y. M. C. A. purposes.

[2] A second $5,000 was entered in 1873.

Old Y. M. C. A. Building, 15th & Chestnut Streets, Philadelphia

fix the sum it shall cost, but that if a $200,000 or $100,000 house will answer, it will be satisfactory to his father—that he will sign a book at once dating his subscription, so that no tax can be taken from it if paid after his father's death.

JOHN WANAMAKER.

Up to 1887 he remained the active head of the Philadelphia Y. M. C. A., and resigned only after he had arranged for the mortgage to be cleared by annual payments, and had financed the building of several fully equipped branches. Thus did he acquit his obligation to the Y. M. C. A.

In more ways than in enabling him to save the capital he needed to go into business was the secretaryship a great help in Wanamaker's career. When he made his first report in 1859 we remember that President Stuart had referred to him as the young man "with a queer name that nobody had ever heard of." The man and the name were known, before the end of 1860—and favorably known—by Philadelphians of influence who would never have met the salesman in Tower Hall. The Y. M. C. A. movement had attracted many of the most influential bankers and business men of the city. What they saw of the secretary's energy and ability was of inestimable value to the founder of Oak Hall and had a direct bearing upon the fortunes not only of that venture, but also of the bigger venture that followed.

Of the friendship formed with Stuart, and its value to a young man starting in life, Wanamaker has himself spoken:

A precious legacy was left to me by an old Market Street merchant of sixty years ago; and he never knew what he was doing for me. A modest man he was, of good mind, well educated, industrious, successful in his business, and greatly respected by all who knew him.

I used to see him almost daily, and from his unvarying example without a single direct word to me I picked up, almost unconsciously, from him three of the most valuable things of life. First, he never complained;

second, he never spoke ill of anyone; third, he always had a good word to say of everybody.

Dear old man, if he had left me a hundred thousand dollars in his will it wouldn't have been worth as much to me as this.

8 Resolved that ~~we~~ in the name
of ~~[struck]~~ our gracious Father +
His Son our precious Saviour
+ for the glory of the ~~the~~ Triune
God we ~~[struck]~~ confess our
faults in the failures of the
past + hereby pledge ourselves
to take a step forward by
the organization of a Bible
Union of Men to spread the
Word of God – + first of all
bring men to
Christ — to show them the way build ~~them~~ up
in ~~[struck]~~ Christian lives +
do humble work for Christ's Kingdom

A PAGE FROM THE FIRST DRAFT OF THE PLAN FOR BETHANY BIBLE UNION

CHAPTER VII

THE FOUNDING OF BETHANY

THE correspondence and records in his private office
show that Bethany was the greatest interest of John
Wanamaker's life—an earlier undertaking than his family
and his business and an enterprise to which he was consistently faithful to the day of his death. Like every successful man Wanamaker sometimes sacrificed family life
and interests to business. But he never let business interfere
with Bethany. And, although Wanamaker got joy and intense satisfaction out of his home life, he gave his Sundays
to Bethany. There were times when he let business go, as
the four years in Washington as Postmaster-General attest.
But Bethany was never out of heart and mind. Bethany
problems and duties encroached upon business hours. Bethany demanded time each day during vacations. Whether
he was in Europe or in Florida, he never felt away from
Bethany.

The Wanamaker Stores are a greater and more permanent
achievement than Bethany Church and Sunday School, and
John Wanamaker was undoubtedly a greater influence in
the business than in the religious world. But he himself
did not think so. He became a pioneer and leader in religious activities in Philadelphia when he was in his teens;
and he founded Bethany three years before Oak Hall, and
two years before he married. His sweetheart was a girl
whom he had met in church work and who was willing to
allow church activities to invade her home life. His business
associates of the week-day were almost all spending their

Sundays as he spent them, and some of them were life-long coadjutors at Bethany. His peculiar sense of values—we say peculiar because they were so different from what the world would suppose a man of his type to have after success came—betrayed him into checking and resisting the natural inclination to relax, to play, to give a lot of time to home and family. He invested most of his leisure hours in a church organization and among people that he outgrew but never knew that he did.

Once he wrote:

Is Bethany the glory or the tragedy of my life? Do you remember the name of the famous queen who, when told by her medical adviser that she had not long to live, said, "A million pounds for a minute of time"? Daylight, dawn and nightfall chase each other hard, and before we know it, one-seventh of the week is gone. Those Bethany Sundays are precious pearls making up the necklace of years. At times I feel that I starved and cheated myself, however, and that I starved and cheated those dear to me by driving so hard all day Sunday, by never being willing to leave it, to change, to modify. But why should I? I have always been happy in Bethany. It was the earliest habit I formed. It has been a blessing. It was a great tie for Mother Mary B. W. and myself in the early days and has so remained. I might have done other things with greater effect. But if you are happy? Why people think my Bethany work is either virtue or pose, I cannot imagine. I have just always liked it. And there isn't anything else, not business certainly, that I have just always liked and have gotten always satisfaction and blessing, not worrry, out of.

So from the viewpoint of the biographer, if not of the world, the first Sunday of Bethany is as important a milestone to record as the opening day of Oak Hall.

When he came back from his Western trip and entered upon his work with the Y. M. C. A., John Wanamaker had made up his mind not to return to the First Independent Church, but to launch a mission of his own. It was a long-

cherished dream. That he was only nineteen and not robust
and tackling a new job did not act as a deterrent.

The family was moving out Lombard Street to No. 1926,
and he wanted to find a place that needed a Sunday school
near his new home. From the experiences of childhood he
knew that there was plenty of work to be done in the
Schuylkill River district. On February 7, 1858, he went
with the missionary of the Philadelphia Sabbath School Association on a scouting expedition. Toland led him to a
vacant house on Pine Street, near 24th, where he arranged
to have a dozen or more boys waiting to hear about the new
venture. Then Toland disappeared. He had another
appointment. Wanamaker led the way up a dark staircase
to a second-story room. After prayers and a chapter of
Scripture, hurriedly read, he began to explain his plan to
organize a Sunday school. But a crowd had assembled
outside, which grew noisy, and the audience bolted. Down
the stairs, out into the back yard, and over the fence they
went. When Wanamaker appeared at the door he was
hooted and jeered at and advised to leave the neighborhood
immediately if he did not want his "head mashed." Some
of the toughs were carrying clubs and there was real danger.
It was impossible to gather again the scattered group.

During the week Wanamaker canvassed the neighborhood, and before the next Sunday he had secured the use
of two rooms over Andrew Kincaid's cobbler shop at 2135
South Street. This was the extreme limit of the built-up
portion of the city. From the windows of the room in which
Bethany met one could look directly south for about three
miles, beyond the brickyards and marshes, to where the
Delaware and Schuylkill Rivers converge. Kincaid was
sympathetic to the idea of a Sunday school, but he warned
young Wanamaker that the neighborhood would likely

prove too tough for the success of his project and that he must be prepared for trouble.

Saturday, the Wanamakers moved from 800 Lombard Street to the new home, which was not more than a mile from where they had lived in the early years. South is the next street to Lombard, and No. 2135 was hardly two blocks away. The next afternoon, February 14, Bethany Mission Sunday School was organized. It was a purely personal enterprise. After the experience of the previous week John told the two girls who had volunteered to teach, his sister Mary and a friend of hers, that it would be wise for them to wait while he went around and saw how things were. But they insisted on going along with him. It was encouraging to find twenty-seven children. The young superintendent formally opened the school, and the children listened for a while to his exposition of the lesson without too much disorder. Then the door was broken in and rowdies chased the children out. They warned John and the girls not to show their faces again on South Street.

Once more he looked over the ground during the week. Even if Kincaid had been willing to risk a second session, John had not the money to pay for the damage that might be done to the property. So he picked out a broken-down building where South Street ended, beyond 23d Street, and got permission to use the deserted ground-floor store. On February 21 he and his teachers reappeared. John took scantlings and piled bricks under them. These were the benches. It was a snowy afternoon, and there was no way of having a fire. But fifty children and some interested grown-ups walked in. Again the hoodlums arrived. Again the audience was driven out. But John stood his ground, and was pelted with snowballs and rotten eggs. Neighborhood people intervened to protect Mary Wanamaker and Mary Brown.

Richard Croker once said that the only way a youngster could come to the front on the East Side of New York was by taking punishment. If he aspired to leadership he would be jumped on, and as he could not "fight all the bunch at once," he would have to know how "to stand the gaff." Similar conditions prevailed where Bethany was founded. Because John stood the gaff, he won out. The snowballing and egging awakened the sympathy of some who had seen it. They admired the boy's pluck. The volunteer firemen of the district decided that he was going to have a square deal. They let the neighborhood know that they would be on hand the next Sunday and that people need not be afraid to come. Some brought their own children.

This put an end to rowdyism, and Bethany began to grow from week to week. On July 18 the school was moved to a tent on the north side of South Street, west of 21st, with ceremonies attended by over three hundred children. The tent was made of old sails picked up on the docks and sewed together by mothers of the children. Evangelistic services on week-day nights were started by the young superintendent, and a number of friends volunteered to teach in the Sunday school.

The work grew so rapidly that within six months a building by popular subscription was feasible. The lot on which the tent stood was purchased, and on October 18 the corner stone of Bethany Chapel was laid. A scheme of shares at five cents was devised by the superintendent, and he had stock certificates printed. The child who gave five cents got just as big and imposing a paper as the subscriber to a hundred or a thousand shares. Eighteen kiddies put in their nickels to start the ball a-rolling. It was an audacious undertaking when we consider that all the expenses of the enterprise up to October 18 had amounted to less than $70. Significant among the items are: "Advertising, June 24 to

October 6—$17.81. Posters and handbills—$6.25." In this earliest venture of his, Wanamaker put more than twenty-five per cent of the receipts into making it known. He was his own bookkeeper—as he was when he began Oak Hall.

Bethany Chapel was John Wanamaker's first building enterprise. When the cornerstone was laid, the mission school's balance was $2.45 and there was ninety cents in the building fund. Three months later the chapel was dedicated. It cost $3,700, and all obligations were covered by pledges that could be collected. Mortgage capacity had been absorbed in the purchase of the lot. Wanamaker supervised every detail in the construction, kept the accounts, and raised the money to meet bills for material and labor as they came in. It was a bold but thoroughly sound financial operation. When he read the report of the building committee at the dedication exercises on January 27, 1859, the twenty-year-old superintendent stated that what had been accomplished was only a beginning. To illustrate the possibilities of this neighborhood which the missionary of the Sabbath School Association had given up in despair, Wanamaker called the roll. Seventeen teachers and 275 scholars answered.

Among them was the girl who had seen him pelted with snowballs and eggs less than a year before, and who had not known that she was being called upon to make the first of many professions of faith in John Wanamaker when she agreed with him that he was not crazy to think of starting a Sunday school in the South Street district. The intimacy that had begun in the old church at Broad and Sansom Streets, and that had deepened during two years of Sunday work for Bethany, resulted in John Wanamaker pointing out to Mary Brown that there were two obligations in the summary of the Ten Commandments. It was not hard for the girl of nineteen to agree with her Sunday school super-intendent's logical and forceful exposition of this text.

We shall tell later the story of the development of Bethany into the largest Sunday school in America and into one of the leading churches of the Presbyterian denomina-tion. Always a pioneer, its superintendent remained as long as he lived in the position he had created and to which he had appointed himself. When Oak Hall was founded, Bethany was over three years old and was already attracting attention in the city. Out of these three years at Bethany he got confidence in himself, much business experience and sense of responsibility for a youngster, and, best of all, a wife who was with him and Bethany for over sixty years.

EARLY PHOTOGRAPH OF JOHN WANAMAKER
(Year not known)

CHAPTER VIII

THE CHOICE OF A CAREER

THE conclusion at which John Wanamaker and Mary Brown arrived did not find ready acceptance with the hard-headed Scotch-Irish grocer who was Mary's father. Thomas Brown liked young Wanamaker. Everybody did. He was in full sympathy with the boy's ideals and principles. But any father would hesitate before giving his daughter to a youthful visionary whose ability and energy were being concentrated in an original way upon unproductive religious activities. The salary was enough to live on—at first—but Y. M. C. A. work was a new way of earning money. Would it last? What would John do if it did not? What destiny had in store for John Wanamaker none knew. He was not yet the successful merchant whose spectacular performances were to startle Philadelphia. Then, too, war clouds were already looming up on the horizon. The presidential campaign was being conducted with a bitterness and fury that presaged secession. Most people believed that if this happened Philadelphia would be ruined. How the boy—he was still that—prevailed upon the grocer we do not know. But John and Mary had their way, as young folks genuinely in love always do. They were married in the summer of 1860, when the world seemed to be going to smash.

Families and friends admitted the striking success of the Y. M. C. A. and Bethany under John's leadership. But he had no job, as the world understands a job, and coupled with this was his own uncertainty in the choice of a career.

Those who were interested in the young man were anxious about his marked individualism. Unconcealed impatience with tradition and precedent is a healthy sign of youth. When the expression of it reveals the intention to go ahead, defying conventions, it becomes alarming. John bubbled over with ideas. That did not matter. But when he sought to carry them out he came into conflict with older people, who assumed that age and experience should count for more than a young man's fancy, especially when it seemed that John did not feel sure of what he wanted to do.

No movement ever became more rapidly standardized than that of the Y. M. C. A. The Philadelphia example of having a regular secretary and a budget was followed everywhere. When the convention met at New Orleans, less than two years after the Philadelphia innovation, the national organization was already looking towards conformity in methods and program. Probably this was necessary in a movement that had been launched by busy laymen, most of whom, when they saw that it was becoming a going concern, were only too glad to shift responsibility and limit their part to contributions. This did not suit Wanamaker. It chafed him to work in harness and under orders.

It was suggested that he might become a pastor and take a country charge, where he could build up his health, if religion was to be his life interest. In after years John Wanamaker explained his decision not to go into the ministry on the ground that he felt he could do more good as a merchant. He said that he believed that his influence in Christian work as a layman would be more effective than as a clergyman. Given his temperament, it was a sound conclusion. His experience in the Y. M. C. A. had taught him that he could neither be happy nor find full play for his ideas in an enterprise that he was not running himself. The youth whose ideal of a pastor was John Chambers could not easily conform to the doctrine and constitution of any church. He did not see himself content with a church session passing upon his methods and a Presbytery controlling his interpretation of Scripture and presentation of the Gospel. He never said it, but he must have regarded holy orders as a straitjacket.

With all his love for John Chambers and the First Independent Church, had he not gone out and started his own show? Instinctively his adventurous spirit and the innate craving to work out his own ideas carried him along, in religion as well as business, to the creation and running of his own enterprises. A cog in the machine he could not be. It is the destiny of dynamic personalities to build and run their own machines, letting others become the cogs.

In his career four things stand out. Their combination in one man make him unique among American pioneers. None developed during his life. They were all present when he started, and manifested themselves immediately. He found his work on his doorstep. He had the genius of engaging in widely different activities simultaneously, giving the best that was in him to all without detriment to any one of them. He did not lose interest in the enterprises created in his youth, but continued to father them as long as he lived. His creative instinct, because it never slept or died, enabled him to regard every enterprise that he directed as a joyous asset and not an irksome liability.

The first fact we have already noted. Pioneer though he was, his business life began and ended on Market Street in the city where he was born and died. Although his religious interests and influence, like those of his business, gradually encircled the world, it was through the Philadelphia Y. M. C. A. and through Bethany Sunday School that the contact was made and maintained.

The second fact, which never ceased to puzzle all who

knew him, was first noticed by Colonel Bennett. At Tower Hall the boy was diligent in business to a fault, a wide-awake student of his job and a tireless salesman, and yet he seemed to have plenty of time to devote himself to persistent and enthusiastic personal religious work. The beginning of Bethany, as we have seen, coincided with the new departure in the Y. M. C. A. It was because they thought that he could not compass it that those who loved him best were worried about the frail boy's combination of a new business undertaking with the heavy commitments at Bethany and the continued participation in Y. M. C. A. work which, during the Civil War, meant the Christian Commission. At Bethany, Superintendent Wanamaker never could deliver the usual homily on the text, "This one thing I do," without his tongue in his cheek.

On the third and fourth facts we need not elaborate. The third is the content of our book, and the fourth is the *leitmotiv* that runs through the story and makes it a song. We are not writing about moving goods over a counter or expounding Sunday-school lessons.

All these things in the life of the man she had chosen a normal twenty-year-old girl could not have analyzed. But as they were already present in promise, like another Mary, she may have pondered them in her heart. The prophetic vision is never keener than when one is on the threshold of life, else it would not be given to so many to choose the right mate. With the keen sense of the peculiarities of the man she was marrying, Mary Brown encouraged him to follow the pioneering instinct that led him to explore several fields at once. If she were willing to stake everything on the working out of his ideas, what else mattered? With a wife like Mary Brown, John Wanamaker could be a law to himself, unfettered, ready to take chances, and with only his sense of right and wrong and his innate business judgment to guide him.

When he had made up his mind to choose an independent mercantile career, however, Wanamaker was not without some experience. Aside from the three years at Bethany and in the Y. M. C. A., there had been an independent business venture.[1] He had for several years been interested with his younger brother William in a dried-meat shop on Market Street, west of City Hall Square. His other duties had kept him from helping to run the shop. But he passed on the buying, hired the help, did the bookkeeping, and one evening a week he paid wages and bills and sent out accounts. There was not much money in this for the brothers, but it enabled them to send provisions to the parents and to help at home a little more than they could otherwise have done.

Not that Nelson Wanamaker was dependent on his children except for their part in the upkeep of the home. The father was a director of the Spruce and Pine Streets Street Railway, and when he moved to Chambersburg after only two months in the 1926 Lombard Street house we know that he had $1,000 to invest in a new brickmaking venture there. But he died just about the time John married, leaving virtually no estate. The mother returned to Philadelphia. The care of her, as he wrote at the time, was a "blessed privilege." Thanks to his almost immediate financial success, it did not become a burden. We must not forget, however, that he faced this problem, with all the others, at the very moment of going into business for himself.

Enough has been said as to why John Wanamaker did not enter the ministry or remain with the Y. M. C. A.

[1] In a letter to a clergyman in St. Louis dated May 26, 1921, we find a reference to a still earlier undertaking. "I commenced business when I was a boy," wrote Mr. Wanamaker. "My first venture was to join with another boy in preparing and bottling cologne, which we sold and got a little money out of, but nothing to speak of."

But the choice was not regarded by him as meaning that he was going to take away from Bethany the time and thought he had been devoting to that work for three years. Nor, as we shall see, did it mean that he was oblivious of the call of duty in his country's greatest hour of need.

His choice of a business career did not diminish his interest in the coming of the Kingdom of God and the fortunes of his country. In his pocket, alongside the account book and figures jotted down on the backs of envelopes, he carried a New Testament with a tiny folded flag marking the passage to be read that day. Once he had embarked upon the adventure of Oak Hall, he found himself under the pressure of business problems that were never to leave him. But they could not claim all his time or even encroach upon other interests that came ahead of business.

ORIGINAL BUILDING OCCUPIED BY OAK HALL
(From a drawing)

CHAPTER IX

THE FIRST YEAR AT OAK HALL

THE Tower Hall experience had impressed upon the youth in his teens the fertility of retail selling as a field of experimenting in new ideas. The trails to be blazed in merchandising challenged him. When he was thinking of a business career Colonel Bennett, whom he trusted and who knew John's ability, came into the young man's head as a possible partner. He proposed buying a small interest in Tower Hall. Bennett would have been glad to have his old salesman back, but he wanted no partner. He thought so highly of Wanamaker that it was certainly not the absurdly small amount of capital that influenced Bennett. He had plenty of money, and to spare. But he must have feared being swept off his feet. He knew his former employee's pervasiveness and insistency.

The refusal was the best thing that could have happened. John's adventurous spirit demanded hardships, hazards, constant uncertainty, the lack of faith of friends, and the bitter and determined opposition of competitors. And it was always to be that way with him.

He turned to his brother-in-law, Nathan Brown, and proposed that they pool their resources of less than four thousand dollars to go into the men's clothing business. Nathan agreed. But family and friends tried to dissuade them. The time was unpropitious; the capital was insufficient; and what did the youngsters know about running a clothing business, anyway? George H. Stuart, most intimate of counselors, was greatly troubled. He did not discount

his young friend's ability and energy, and he knew that
people who waited until they had enough capital never got
anywhere in business. But the United States was inevitably
drifting into the Civil War. None but an adventurer would
have dreamed of starting a new business at such a time.
"War is certain," he declared, "and soon grass will be
growing on Market Street."

When young people seek advice, they are not after wisdom
or the advantage of the experience of their elders. What
they want is confirmation of their own judgment, and failing to get it does not deter them from going ahead with
their plans. In March, 1861, John and Nathan began to
figure on store fixtures and initial stock. Before the young
partners had a roof over their heads they were compelled to
pay $375 for fixtures and over $700 for the first stock of
cloth. On April 3, when they signed the lease, there was
an additional outlay for rent in advance. The capital was
hazardously small to start a clothing business. If they laid
in ready-make clothing, which was beginning to come into
popularity, many sizes would be required in different qualities and styles. If they started as custom tailors they would
risk carrying a larger pay roll than could be met by orders.
The partners were to have no salaries at first, but, seeing
that they had put their all into the venture, they had to have
a drawing account for living expenses, which amounted to
almost the same thing.

They were lucky in securing a good location, right in the
heart of the retail section, which was slowly moving westward. It was the corner shop in the six-story building (so
large for the time it was built that it was called McNeille's
Folly) at the southeast corner of Sixth and Market Streets,
only a few doors west of Tower Hall. J. R. Houghton, one
of Bennett's cutters, threw in his lot with them at a salary

of $1,300 for the first year, more than either of his employers had ever earned.[1]

The first part of Stuart's prophecy was fulfilled. Oak Hall opened its doors for business on Monday morning, April 8. Before the end of the week Fort Sumter had been fired upon and had surrendered, and the following Monday President Lincoln called for seventy-five thousand volunteers for three months. None expected a long war; people never do at the beginning of a great struggle. It was thought that a determined show of force would end the dispute. The South would be taught a lesson by the occupation of Richmond.

There was no change in the routine of life. The crisis had been too long brewing, and the consternation was only of the moment. Philadelphians went on living normally in abnormal times, and there was not the disorganization of business that had been anticipated. Not until after Bull Run, on July 21, was it realized that the war would be long. Nor did the question of the duty of military service come up until midsummer. Wanamaker's first child was born ten days before Oak Hall was opened. None believed that married men would be needed in the army.

The risks which every one delighted in pointing out to the two "rash young men" were the probability of a temporary suspension of the power or desire to buy and the difficulty of securing credit for any new business. Philadelphia, with its prosperity so largely due to trade with the South, seemed bound to be gravely affected, even if the war did not last long.

[1] In *Everybody's Journal* for November, 1885, we read: "Mr. John R. Houghton, the gentleman that cut the first cloth for Oak Hall clothing, helped to fight its first battles, witnessed its early struggles, is still living to rejoice in its success. Though nearly twenty-five years have passed, he is still with us in an important position, and, judging from his surroundings, handsome property, and elegant turnout, he made no mistake in casting in his lot with ours."

On the morning of the opening day, before the sign was up, came the first customer. James Dunlap's name is worth recording. A mother of several children once said to the eldest, "I do not love you more, but I have loved you longer." It was the kind of boast that James Dunlap was able to make about Wanamaker's for the rest of his life. The junior partner unrolled bolts of cloth. A pair of trousers was ordered. It was not a suit or an overcoat, to be sure, but it was an order! The senior partner took the measurements, and Houghton's scissors got busy immediately. As Dunlap walked out, accompanied to the door by the firm, he wished them good luck. At that moment the exit was blocked by the ladder of the painter, putting up

WANAMAKER & BROWN

"How long is it going to stay there?" ventured Dunlap. He did not live to see it come down, nor has anyone else; for it is still there.

Several others looked at the goods, but there were no more sales that day. Through the window the anxious experimenters watched people pass without so much as a glance at the new store. When the sign was in place it conveyed no meaning. Nathan wanted to "give them time," but he had to agree with John that waiting for what might happen was a risk Wanamaker & Brown could not run. They had to have business right away. Instead of seeking to explain the lack of customers by adverse conditions, Wanamaker declared that the fault lay in the meagerness and unattractive character of the stock.

"We must have goods that will sell right away, and plenty of them, and then we must let people know that we have them," he said.

The next morning the staff of Oak Hall was reduced to the junior partner and the errand boy. The senior partner was off to New York to buy goods, taking Houghton with him. Before leaving he asked Brown to hire a tailor to help Houghton.

New York seemed to the two Philadelphians more upset than Philadelphia over the impending war. As they went from place to place it was difficult to keep the conversation on business. They learned a lot about qualities and styles of summer woolens, but also that Wanamaker & Brown were expected to pay cash. Cash they did not have. To save expenses they shared a room at a modest hotel on Tuesday night. The next morning the weary and disheartening round of wholesalers was continued. Finally back at A. T. Stewart & Co., where they had been turned down the day before, William Libbey allowed them to take several hundred dollars' worth of woolens. The terms, thirty days, were almost as bad as spot cash, but it was the best they could do. Bright and early Thursday morning—the day the first shot of the Civil War was fired—the goods from New York were on display.

Orders still failed to come in. A fortunate opportunity presented itself of buying up several lots of ready-made clothing left on the manufacturers' hands through canceled orders. Because they could not otherwise have been sold, wholesalers were willing to let the new firm have them on credit. The first advertisement appeared in the *Public Ledger* on April 27 to announce this bargain stock. It read as follows:

OAK HALL CLOTHING BAZAAR

Southeast corner Sixth & Market Streets

Wanamaker & Brown desire to say to their many friends and the public generally, that they open to-day with an entire new and complete stock of ready-made clothing; and having purchased their goods under the pressure of the times at very low rates, will sell them accordingly.

WHOLE SUITS FOR THREE DOLLARS

Attracted by the low price, scores of purchasers were readily found for the three-dollar suits. Of profit there was virtually none, but the money that kept coming in was a godsend to meet bills due at the beginning of May. The advertisement had cost $24. With suits at $3 the volume of sales had to be pretty big to make that pay. This was not the way they looked at advertising outlay, however—John Wanamaker and Nathan Brown needed to get their names known. If they could simply carry on from month to month, investing their ready cash in advertising, the turnover would take less time and grow in volume.

The problem of finding money for advertising was solved by going out after business, with the promise of immediate filling of orders and delivery as the sales talk. It was learned that the Philadelphia Custom House needed uniforms. Wanamaker & Brown got the business. John Wanamaker delivered the suits in a wheelbarrow, and was paid cash. On the way back he left his barrow outside the *Inquirer* office and went in to invest most of the money in more advertising. Having ascertained that the rate was the same, he broke up his announcement into half a dozen two-line insertions. It brought in enough trade to meet bills due on May 6 and to pay the first month's salaries.

The Oak Hall account book tells the story of the strictest economy except in increasing stocks and advertising. The partners did all the work except cutting and sewing. They brought in the goods, broke up the packing boxes for firewood, looked after the stove, swept the store, kept the books, and delivered the orders. The errand boy seems to have been dispensed with. Even luncheon money went into advertising. It is true that the new firm, not having laid in stocks already, was lucky in getting goods that wholesalers could dispose of only in the local market at a substantial reduction, and which John and Nathan were in a position to retail without competing with existing stocks. It is true that if the wholesalers had not been in straits they would have refused to grant Wanamaker & Brown easy terms. But the greatest handicap in favor of the Oak Hall partners was the very inexperience and youth that everyone thought would work against them. For the new conditions demanded above all things unbounded faith and tireless energy.

In the first weeks at Oak Hall the business policy of John Wanamaker was decided upon. He was going to buy all the goods he could and keep telling the public about what he had to sell.

Had the youthful partners foreseen the necessity of this policy, they might have hesitated before they opened Oak Hall with a capital of less than four thousand dollars and with credit yet to be established. It was hard sledding when they realized that competition on the main thoroughfare of Philadelphia demanded distinctive goods, and that advertising would have to feature variety and quality as well as price. Moving job lots quickly over the counter was a way to make money, perhaps, but it was drab business —and ephemeral. Just to buy and sell was not Wanamaker's conception of a mercantile career. Making Oak Hall a clearing house for bargains was a danger to be avoided.

At this crisis, which arose at the very beginning of the business, the national tragedy aided Wanamaker & Brown instead of breaking them, as all had predicted. The Philadelphia volunteers were calling for uniforms in a rush. Wanamaker figured on the back of an envelope, having in mind not profits, but the opportunity to maintain and enlarge his business equipment and strengthen his credit. He secured the contract to clothe the officers of two regiments.

This was followed by a contract for overcoats. Space on the floor above was rented, tailors were taken on, and an organization for manufacturing clothing was built up within a few months.

Wanamaker & Brown did not become army contractors on any large scale. From the fact that the sales for the first eight months amounted to only $24,000 for all Oak Hall's activities, it is probable that Wanamaker & Brown clothed only officers. They did not attempt to create facilities for volume production. The army contract business required large capital and established manufacturing connections; and with the methods of getting the business Wanamaker did not want to become acquainted. As long as an emergency existed and all the clothing firms were trying to do their share, Oak Hall rendered great service in tiding over the crisis.

John Wanamaker was always proud of having done his bit in clothing the first volunteers before Bull Run. Aside from the money he made out of it, it taught him the value of a certain amount of contract work to help with the overhead of launching and expanding the retail business. He kept on supplying the Custom House guards, and he was successful in getting contracts from Girard College for clothing the cadets and from the city for firemen's and policemen's uniforms. But this field of merchandising interested him no more than seining interests the fisherman. His enjoyment in life, from earliest boyhood, was in contacts with his fellow beings. Retailing was following his natural bent.

The first years meant "heavy plowing early and late," as Wanamaker put it. But the plowing was experimental— new fields, new implements, new seeds, new methods under the stimulus of every conceivable kind of obstacle and opposition.

At Tower Hall he had begun to sense some of the business principles that were to give him wealth and fame. But he had no conception of the war between ideas and cash in hand. He did not know that those who could give credit were generally hostile to experiments of any kind, and particularly in their own line of business. So strong an individualist was the boy and so enthusiastic about his own ideas that the discovery of these facts could hardly have been safely made with an older and more experienced man as partner. It was good for Colonel Bennett, as well as for himself, that he had not been given a partnership in Tower Hall.

Nathan Brown was the ideal partner for John Wanamaker. They had both learned in childhood habits of thrift and industry. It was no hardship for them to work long hours, to master details, and to practice rigid economy in personal expenditures. They had never known what it was to be interested in anything except their jobs and church work. They were agreed that profits were to be put into the business. Nathan was not gifted with imagination, and he never saw far ahead. But he did have faith in John and he was always willing to let John go ahead and do things. If Nathan had misgivings, he generally kept them to himself. He formed the habit of walking away and letting John do the listening when friends came in to argue and remonstrate, or when Houghton made observations.

Greater than Nathan's faith in John was that of Nathan's sister. His stake was a small sum of money. Hers was everything. She had been willing to marry a youngster who did not know what he was going to do or how he was going to do it. She could not even count upon his health. The ugly menace of war, with separation and possibly death, lay ahead. But Mary Brown married the man she loved, gave him a son, consented to the risk of every cent he had in the Oak Hall venture, and never by word or deed demanded that her husband play safe. On the contrary, she encouraged him to take risk after risk. When failure would have hit her hardest, she expressed no doubts as to the soundness of her husband's ideas. She joined with him in his Bethany work on Sundays; she managed at home so that most of the money that came in could go back into the business; and she urged him to give time and thought to public activities. From the day she became Wanamaker's partner, Mary Brown adapted herself to his active and restless temperament, embarking with him in a gay spirit on uncharted seas. When advised to insist that her husband cast anchor in the first port, Mary answered that she enjoyed voyaging.

CHAPTER X

THE CIVIL WAR

DURING the presidential campaign of 1916 when Roosevelt spoke for Hughes at Cooper Union, the chairman of the memorable meeting that brought the Bull-Moosers back into the Republican party said:

"I stand by Lincoln's side as I did in Philadelphia on Washington's birthday, forty-five years ago, and he bids to me to speak to you the very words of his lips, spoken in Independence Hall at the flag raising on the old State House. Let us remember what he said: 'The Declaration of Independence gave liberty not alone to the people of this country, but hope for the world for all future times. It gave promise that in due time the weights would be lifted from the shoulders of all men, and that all should have an equal chance. If this country cannot be saved without giving up that principle, I would rather be assassinated on this spot than surrender it. I have said nothing but what I am willing to live by, and, in the pleasure of Almighty God, to die by.'"

One felt that John Wanamaker did not have to refer to notes to repeat after half a century words heard by the boy of twenty three. One felt that he was not using his imagination in applying the prophecy of Lincoln to the world mission before the United States as the European war was entering its third year. The patriotism of the generation that lived its teens and twenties from 1855 to 1865 seems curiously subjective to us who were born many years after the Civil War. We know the United States only as our

73

common country. We think of the Stars and Stripes as a flag unquestioningly revered by all. We have no conception of the horror of fratricidal strife, of the widespread ruin of internal war, of the abiding influence on men's minds of living through a period when liberty and unity were ideals demanding the sacrifice of life itself.

The political atmosphere of Wanamaker's boyhood and on through the years when he was beginning his life work was surcharged with bitterness and uncertainty. Preservation of the Union and emancipation of the slaves were issues that affected profoundly every phase of American life. Philadelphia more than any other great city had felt the impending menace of Civil War. Ideals and patriotism were in conflict with interests. The Southern States, rich and luxury-loving, took the greater part of what Philadelphia produced and imported. Cheap freight rates by sea and land had long made Philadelphia the logical shopping center of the South; and on this trade depended the prosperity of Philadelphia merchants and manufacturers. Philadelphia dreaded the influx of freed slaves. It was the first great city of the North to which they would naturally flock. The important Quaker element was paradoxically both abolitionist and pacifist. Some of Lincoln's advisers were not sure that the President-elect could come to Philadelphia without causing trouble.

But there was no lack of heartiness in the welcome that greeted him when he stepped out on the balcony of the Continental Hotel on the evening of February 21, 1861, to address the crowd that packed Chestnut Street. Young John Wanamaker stood on the sidewalk, jammed up against the building which was to be his first Chestnut Street store eight years later. And the next morning, "hardly more than a country lad," as he was fond of saying, he was present at the flag raising at Independence Hall, and heard the

words that he was to repeat in Cooper Union after a lapse
of more than fifty years.

He had been a Lincoln man since the Douglas debate.
He had cast his first vote for Lincoln. Throughout his
whole life he believed that 1861 was the most critical year
in American history, and that on Washington's birthday of
that year he had heard a greater man than Washington
speak. The intensity of his conviction of the sacredness of
the cause for which Lincoln prophetically expressed his
willingness to be assassinated was due to the teaching and
example of Wanamaker's grandfather and father, as well as
to his own youthful enthusiasm. When we place this conviction alongside of the young man's bold and active temperament we can well understand the bitter disappointment
that followed rejection for military service.

When the Civil War broke out, simultaneously with the
opening of Oak Hall, Thomas B. Wanamaker had just
arrived. He was less than two weeks old when Lincoln
issued the first call for volunteers. It was not expected that
married men, especially those whose families were dependent upon them, should enlist. Wanamaker had a mother,
wife, and son to look after, as well as a business even younger
than the child. But after Bull Run there was no holding
him back. He had been talking up the army at Bethany.
One of the first companies to leave Philadelphia had been
from his Sunday school. Now it was his turn, and he was
eager to go.

But the skinny volunteer with what seemed to be a chronic
cough did not pass the preliminary inspection. He was
unceremoniously yanked out of the line and told that if he
didn't take care of himself death would come without going
to seek Confederate bullets.

It was a humiliated and despondent young man that went
home to his bride of a year and told her that he guessed he

was "no good." The occasion was unique in his life. We have record of no other time during the eighty-five years that his faith was shaken in himself and his destiny. The tension of the times and the feeling of youth that physical prowess counts above all things were responsible for it. He had been preaching the duty of arms. Now it was denied him.

The girl of twenty-one rose to the crisis. She concealed her alarm over the ominous verdict of the physicians and gave proof of wise moderation by not sympathizing too much with her man about something that could not be changed. On the other hand, she hid, too, her joy at his not being taken. She pointed out that another way would open up for him to serve his country. Right in the business venture he was launching with her brother, might he not serve more effectively than by shouldering a musket? He had already helped out in clothing the first volunteers. And had not George H. Stuart and other friends of the Y. M. C. A. been talking of army activities? If he felt that he must get into the fray, his wife added, and every man was needed, perhaps the physical disability would pass away or the examination later would not be so strict.

The year before his death, when Philadelphia was celebrating the sixtieth anniversary of John Wanamaker's career as a merchant, a friend said to him, "How you must look back with joy and pride to April, 1861!"

"Why should I be joyful and proud of recalling my greatest humiliation?" he answered.

"How so?" asked the astonished friend.

"Everybody takes for granted that the disappointments, the unfulfilled ambitions, the sorrows of youth are forgotten or wholly crowded out by the events of a long and busy life," replied Wanamaker. "But I doubt if any man worth his salt who was old enough to have fought in the Civil

War, and who for whatever reason did not, ever lived down
—to himself—the fact that he was not among those who
cried, 'We are coming, Father Abraham, three hundred
thousand strong.' "

The revelation is illuminating. In the Spanish-American
War Wanamaker offered to lead the regiment he raised
in his stores. During the World War he often said that
the men who bled and died should have all the glory.
What Oak Hall grew into, his own civilian service through
the Civil War,[1] and his patriotism and public record that
made him a national figure in a sense in which no man could
become merely as a merchant, did not satisfy him. He
never forgot that he was twenty-three in 1861 and that he
was denied the obvious form of aiding his country that
appealed and that alone could satisfy a man of his age.
Does not this explain his marked love of bands and flags
and military display? His abiding devotion to the memory
of Lincoln and Grant? The store he set by his honorary
membership in the Grand Army of the Republic? And his
almost fanatical political partisanship? How he felt in his
latter years is expressed in a telegram to a G. A. R. gathering in 1916:

My greetings to the men of the Grand Army of the Republic who meet
to observe the anniversary of the Gettysburg speech. Lincoln's love for
humanity was so Christlike that it included even those who were his
enemies. Not a word of bitterness is found in the oration which has
become a world classic. If Lincoln's heart went out to any one set of men
more than to another it was to the boys in blue who never faltered in
their undying love and devotion to him and their country. With the
Master he is waiting with outstretched arms to greet you and the men in
gray when with all the other dear comrades of the past you assemble for
the last grand review before the great white throne of God.

[1] In recognition of these services Wanamaker was invited to become a
member of the George A. Meade Post, No. 1, Grand Army of the Republic,
and was addressed by veterans as "comrade."

Wanamaker's first war service was to recruit a company among his Bethany boys in response to Lincoln's call. When he was denied the privilege of going with the second levy to the front, he and his wife together volunteered for canteen service among the troops passing through Philadelphia.

The need of organized welfare work of national scope, however, was soon apparent. The newly formed Sanitary Commission found that handling the wounded and convalescents in the hospitals, and keeping track of prisoners, was all that it could manage. A group of members of the Philadelphia Y. M. C. A. decided that a parallel opportunity for welfare work among soldiers in the field and in transit existed.

On October 28, 1861, Philadelphia took the initiative in calling a Y. M. C. A. convention to meet in New York on November 14. The call was signed by John Wanamaker as corresponding secretary of the tentative national organization. When all the branches of the Y. M. C. A. came together and formed the Christian Commission he was secretary of the convention, and supported the view of those who believed that the scope of its work should extend beyond spiritual matters, on the ground that there was "a good deal of religion in a warm shirt and a good beefsteak."

Wanamaker accepted the secretaryship of the Christian Commission, and very quickly had his first lesson in official red tape. He learned, too, the incredible fact that jealousy seems always to arise between organizations working for the same objects. He afterward said that this was his initiation into what he called "the great tragedy of mankind—the inability of collective human agencies to do Christ's work in Christ's spirit." Army officers and chaplains put every conceivable hindrance in the way of the Christian Commission, and it was not until September, 1864, when the war was nearly over, that it obtained full privileges in the camps.

But Wanamaker and his associates had kept on insisting that it was "the duty of the Y. M. C. A. to take active measures to promote the spiritual and temporal welfare of soldiers and sailors and marines, in co-operation with the chaplains and others."

The first group that went to the armies was composed of fourteen members of the Philadelphia Y. M. C. A. Their experiences and setbacks did not deter others from following. During four years nearly five thousand volunteers were sent out and over six million dollars in money and supplies was expended. President Lincoln was heart and soul with the work from the beginning. It was supported also by Secretary of War Cameron, who was a Pennsylvanian and who knew personally Stuart, Wanamaker, and the others of the original group. In July, 1863, just after the battle of Gettysburg, John Wanamaker made his first visit to Saratoga Springs to a meeting of the Christian Commission, and there he became acquainted with men who were afterward to be friends and associates in his religious and business life.

In retrospect, we think of Gettysburg, at the beginning of the third year, as the turning-point of the war. This was not realized, however, at the time. As in the recent World War, the last laps were the hardest, and many feared that the process of attrition would result in peace without victory. The first months of 1864 were the period of greatest anxiety. It was then that the rivalry between the Sanitary Commission and the Christian Commission died out. The North was straining every nerve. There were work and glory enough for all. Wanamaker's insatiable activity, which could never find sufficient outlet for his ideas and desires and good will, led him into the thick of the movement to hold a Sanitary Fair in Logan Square in the summer of 1864.

Working up the Sanitary Fair was excellent preparation for the Centennial movement a decade later. It was the kind of thing that never failed to capture Wanamaker's interest. He gladly took on all the work that was given him—and asked for more—in preparing the buildings and making the arrangements. Wooden walls were raised two stories high and sixty feet apart straight across the middle of the square and roofed over, with holes to let the trees through. This main building was a Gothic arch, with the trees serving mostly for pillars. It was surrounded by a single floor rectangle, connected by corridors with the central building. Philadelphians loaned pictures for the gallery, to which admission was charged. Every sort of display and amusement of the period, that it was thought would yield money for the care of soldiers, was solicited.

The Fair was opened on June 7, 1864, by the Governors of Pennsylvania, New Jersey, and Delaware. Its importance was great enough to secure a visit from the President. Despite the pressure upon him at Washington and the cares of his campaign for re-election, he came to Philadelphia on June 17. Escorted by the City Troop, President and Mrs. Lincoln spent part of the day going through the Fair. In 1861 the "country boy" had worshiped from afar. Three years later he was among those presented to the President of the United States.

JOHN WANAMAKER'S FIRST PHOTOGRAPH AUTOGRAPHED FOR HIS SISTER,
MRS. ELIZABETH W. FRY

CHAPTER XI

OAK HALL BUSINESS POLICIES

NONE who has made a success of life escapes being deluged with inquiries as to how he did it. And none escapes telling something of his story. Great men are generally modest, and if they keep on working to the end, as Wanamaker did, there is never time for connected autobiographical retrospect. But we do have fragments and anecdotes. The question arises with the biographer as to how safely he can regard a man's statements as source material. Who remembers in exact detail the story of his own life? Motives, what one thought and how one felt, let alone incidents, are difficult to recall with any degree of accuracy. Who is able to distinguish and give proper weight and place to the currents and influences that have made him what he is? And then, in the process of reconstructing the years gone by, with their achievements and failures, we have to reckon with three factors: the constant change in our sense of values; our natural ignorance of parallel and contemporaneous activities of others; and the reason or interest of the moment that may at any time betray us into confusing fact with fancy when we tell about what we have done.

Throughout his career John Wanamaker was daring and original. His business life was far longer than that of any other great American merchant. The revolutionary changes, in bringing about which he played a great part, marked a new era in retail merchandising. Up to the very end of his life he remained a pioneer and his own business was in crescendo. But imitators became competitors. It was natural

that his advertising should lay stress on Wanamaker pioneering, and that some of the statements made over his signature
were at times written by others.[1]   Keeping these considerations in mind, and with them the three factors mentioned
above, it has been necessary to scrutinize carefully the claims
of Wanamaker advertising and publications, and to study
the policies associated with John Wanamaker's name in the
light of what others were doing in his field at the same
period.   A history of the development of retail merchandising in the United States has yet to be written, and no
exhaustive or authoritative study of any American retail
merchant or his business has ever been published.   We have
had to go to original sources, therefore, in so far as they are
accessible.

In a speech in the 1894 congressional campaign Wanamaker said:

"There are certain classes of men that cannot exist without play for their invention and energy.   They must have
an individuality, as much as the painter or poet or artist.
They have to live in a swing.   Their nature requires that."

He was speaking of adventurers; and he was one of them.

Bethany was an adventure.   John Wanamaker had to
create his own sphere of religious activity in an atmosphere
of new ideas.   It was as an individualist and independent
that John Chambers had attracted the boy who was always
reaching out.   We have seen how he thought seriously of
the ministry.   But instinctively he had known that, while
he might be effective and happy as a layman in a church, he
would not be "in a swing" as the professional exponent of a
creed.   He sensed the fact that the business of retail sell-

[1] In the last ten years of his life, however, after he ceased his trips abroad,
which used to take him away months on end, John Wanamaker wrote in his
own hand everything that appeared over his signature in advertising, and he
never allowed anyone to substitute for him in the little rubric, in the upper
left-hand corner of the daily advertisement, which was called the "Store
editorial."

ing was in a chaotic state, drifting aimlessly in the current of changing conditions, and that it afforded a promising and fertile field for the man with the pioneer spirit. Hence the mad experiment of Oak Hall—another adventure.

Maintenance of the all-wool standard in men's clothing was the first distinctive policy of Wanamaker & Brown. It was resistance against an innovation rather than the making of one. The soaring price of wool after the start of the Civil War caused many reputable stores to yield to the temptation of offering fabrics mixed with cotton. In the autumn showings in 1861 they felt that customers would be attracted more by price than by quality. But John Wanamaker believed that for a new house, just breaking in, there was advertising value in offering nothing but all-wool, and he put out the slogan, "No shoddy sold here." In volume of business the result was at first disappointing, and had it not been for Houghton's popularity with many Market Street business men, it might have been disastrous. But the all-wool guaranty brought in customers that could be counted upon as permanent.

Sticking to this policy in the spring of 1862, when wholesalers' bargains were mostly in mixed goods, took all the courage the partners had. Wanamaker & Brown were unable to advertise, as they had done the first spring, a variety of offerings at low prices. In ready-made clothing virtually no bargains were to be had in which cotton did not enter. Throughout the Civil War the price of wool kept increasing. Wanamaker & Brown carried different grades of woolens to meet different purses; but they were all marked clearly with tickets in three colors, according to grade.

The all-wool guaranty, rash as it seemed, proved a blessing in disguise. It gave the firm a reputation among men seeking for the best, and many customers were gained who would not otherwise have thought of buying at Oak Hall.

It grounded John Wanamaker in building up his name and his advertising upon quality goods. The immediately important effect of the policy, however, was to make it a life-and-death matter to Wanamaker & Brown to devise new methods of doing business. Increases in contract work might yield profit, but retailing would never amount to anything if underpinned by this form of subsidy. Market Street competition could be met only by unconventional and original methods. Wanamaker was forced to study buying and advertising in a way that he might not have done had success come through the public's ready acceptance of his all-wool guaranty. He found that a frank and honest mercantile policy was not enough. Quality alone does not create customers. Prices had to be kept down. People had to be told that at Oak Hall there was a miraculous combination of quality and reasonable price. Even then the goods would not sell themselves. What else could be done to get the attention and the confidence of the people of Philadelphia?

The merchant of the 'sixties, if he hoped to change the conditions and standards of retailing, needed more than honesty and industry and selling skill, needed more than organizing ability, needed more than what is called business sense. Men far better established than John Wanamaker possessed some or all of those qualities. Where he differed from his contemporaries from the very beginning was in his willingness to look upon merchandising as a science that had to be studied. Oak Hall was to him a school, with daily lessons to be learned. Making a sale was in itself unimportant. Understanding the factors entering into making a sale was all important. It was not necessary to see this distinction to make money in retailing. Fortunes were coming to men uninspired and uninspiring, who stuck to the methods of the times. But the business adventurer would never have been satisfied to go along with the current, even to success.

The more Wanamaker was told that his all-wool guaranty, though admirable, was impracticable, the more the fun of seeing it through appealed to him. He determined to maintain the policy and find some way of competing with well-known stores that were selling mixed cloth.

He concentrated first on buying. The science of buying did not end with knowing goods and where to get them, sensing styles and patterns, and judging quantities. All this was essential, but the price had to be right. The all-wool guaranty could not be maintained unless there was a close margin in buying. The first move was to dispense with local jobbers and go directly to manufacturers and to the great wholesale houses in New York. He had already tried this as an emergency measure at the opening of the war, when he was seeking freshness and variety and credit. Now he decided to eliminate the middleman in order to get his all-wool goods at reasonable prices. Philadelphia jobbers and competitors immediately countered with the threat of boycotting houses that sold to Wanamaker & Brown. Upon the young man of twenty-four was imposed the task of convincing his sources of supplies that they would not lose out by dealing with Wanamaker & Brown. He had a momentary advantage in the purchasing power of cloth that his contract work gave him. But with the ready-made manufacturers the telling argument had to be large orders and cash payment.

How were they going to order goods to resell at retail on a large scale and pay for them? There was but one answer. The failure of the retail department seemed inevitable unless they were able to do a huge business and move stocks quickly during 1863. But that year, and also 1864, despite prognostications and although the war was raging bitterly and uncertainly, did not prove bad years for business in Philadelphia. The general prosperity affected favorably all lines of retail business. Wanamaker & Brown got along. The firm was putting more money than was justified by the profits of its retail business, however, into trying to attract the purchaser of a suit of clothes or an overcoat. The stock of men's furnishings first equaled and then surpassed Tower Hall, with the result that the expense of carrying it made a deficit in that department. Business was slowly growing, to be sure, and some benefit was coming in from energetic and generous advertising. But to prove the practicability of the merchandising ideas of John Wanamaker the retail business of Oak Hall had to grow rapidly and keep growing. The greatest danger was in being satisfied with making a little money.

Of course the firm could go into the wholesale business, and consider the store on the ground floor merely an adjunct, as was the common practice of the day. But if they were going to be large retailers, and stick to all-wool, which could be marketed at a profit only in large quantities, large orders could be placed and carried only if quickly marketed. The more rapid the turnover the larger the volume and variety of goods procurable, and the lower the price; for cash coming in before the end of the term meant the ability to discount and thus lessen the cost of goods.

Heretofore, only job lots and cheap goods had been sold in this fashion by single retailers. A man might be a bold and shrewd buyer—but if he bought only high-grade goods, and represented them honestly to the public, he would have to find some way of attracting purchasers in ever-increasing number. Wanamaker had learned that they would not come for quality alone, and now he was beginning to wonder whether they would come where both quality and price were right.

The purpose of the first advertisements of the new firm had been publicity for the name. Then they had aimed to

be known for quality. This appeal was limited. Next
Wanamaker & Brown advertised their ability to meet the
prices of competitors and still continue to offer better goods.
But that went only so far.

For two years longer Wanamaker literally lay awake
nights trying to think of a solution of this great problem.
The thought came to him—and it never left him as long as
he lived—that he must study the customer and find out
how merchandising could be made a public service. This
thought was the foundation of all the policies that he
adapted and originated in Oak Hall and in the great stores
that were to follow. "The merchant should seek to serve
the public," he said to himself. Upon that sentence he
built his life. By exemplifying it he created a new epoch in
retail merchandising.

It was the extension to the customer of an ideal that was
already being followed in regard to employees. Wanamaker & Brown had started business with revolutionary ideas
concerning the duty of employers to those who worked for
them. They paid spot cash to the people who made up their
clothing, which was a reform of the first order in the manufacturing business of Philadelphia,[1] and in 1862 they inaugurated shorter business days. But they were only groping
toward the big changes in merchandising policies. These
followed, sweeping and startling, when the young merchant
had a vision of a business inspired by studying the customer.

Up to the close of the Civil War, when Oak Hall announced that merchandising was a public service, belief in
the identity of interests between merchant and customer did
not exist. On the contrary, buying and selling at retail was

---

[1] Years later Wanamaker explained the custom prevalent in 1861 as follows: "Seldom was cash paid to the work people who made the clothing.
The general rule was fortnightly settlements in grocery, coal, or other orders,
on which the manufacturers had a percentage." This system is still in vogue
in the cotton-raising industry in some parts of the South.

as much pitting wit against wit as buying and selling at wholesale. Every sale was an argument. The customer had no confidence in the merchant, and had to trust his own shrewdness and knowledge as to quality and price. The merchant looked upon the customer as an enemy from whom tribute was to be exacted. The amount of profit depended upon cleverness in selling. The more ignorant or careless a customer, the more easily he was deceived. *Caveat emptor* (let the buyer beware) had persisted from Roman times as the expression of the natural relationship between merchant and customer.

By guaranteeing the quality of the goods and by ticketing grades of stocks the first step towards a revolutionary change in merchandising methods was made by John Wanamaker. When he stood against the rising tide of shoddy he started on a new path the end of which he himself did not see. Knowledge is progressive revelation. To friends Wanamaker often said that he had no preconceived ideas of how to do business. The formulas, the principles, of the early days of Oak Hall were originated and adopted to meet a challenge, to solve a problem. They were the result of study and experience. Study alone would not have discovered them, nor would experience. Study and experience together did. The ideas came to the young merchant. He had the vision to see that they were good and the boldness to put them into execution.

One day at a Fourth of July celebration in Fairmount Park, of which he was chairman of the committee, Wanamaker was watching the fireworks. There were rockets that burst, and then the diffused colors burst again after a time, and sent forth new bouquets. "That's how I learned about merchandising," he said to a friend. "It did not come all at once, but one thing after another, and each thing because of what had gone before."

Among the qualities of leadership patience needs careful definition. Some one has well said that genius is the infinite capacity for taking pains. But it is only a half-truth. Young Wanamaker could work long hours, master details, and practice rigid economy in his personal expenditures. He was a model of patience in those respects. But when a big idea came to him he had no patience at all with those who were reluctant to try it out. Here he was a born gambler. Every day was the day to seize, and his restless and fertile mind did not easily listen to words of caution. Oak Hall was a hard school, and if the business world had not been ripe for innovations and radical changes, John Wanamaker might easily have failed to make good. Nathan Brown was constantly distressed by his partner's boldness. John R. Houghton had profound misgivings, born of what the world calls "common sense." The saving grace of the senior partner in the early crises—and throughout his business career—was his willingness to study his own ideas and use his brains in applying them. Thoughtfulness is as much a quality of leadership as originality or enterprise.

The records of Oak Hall show that the business grew more rapidly in its early years than Wanamaker's recollections would indicate. A billhead, dated November 29, 1862, gives a picture of McNeille's Folly, showing the sign across the entire length of the Market Street front of the building and five windows down on Sixth Street, between the third and fourth stories, and also on the very top of the six-story building. Wanamaker & Brown called themselves "Wholesale and Retail Clothiers," and advertised "First-class ready-made clothing always on hand, and choice selections of piece goods for measure work, also gentlemen's furnishing goods. Terms: cash on delivery." The ability to go so far in eighteen months, which is conclusively established by this billhead, was of course possible only through the good fortune of contract work.

As we have already seen, however, it was a kind of business that did not appeal to Wanamaker's temperament and genius. The volume of business accruing from it, which resulted in substantial increase of capital and extension of credit facilities, meant to him only the underwriting of his experiment in retailing. It prevented Wanamaker & Brown from going under in their all-wool guaranty; it enabled them to enlarge their premises and put in sufficient stocks to compete with Tower Hall and other Market Street establishments; and it gave them money to use in advertising. Into the contract and wholesale field Oak Hall had to enter. But the dream of John Wanamaker was a great retail clothing store. Although there was probably a greater— or at least a surer—fortune to be made in wholesaling, it would not give scope to the pioneering ideas that were germinating in Wanamaker's mind.

So we see how Wanamaker came to make the "good landings," as he called them, by "swimming out" in 1865. These were "one price" and "money back." Taken together, they marked an epoch in the history of merchandising.

The all-wool guaranty did not have its inspiration in the inherent honesty of Wanamaker; for according to the standards of the time it was the buyer's responsibility to decide whether what was offered him was worth the price. Nor was it born of the idea of service. We have seen how the idea of service followed it. At the beginning it was simply something different—a policy advertised to attract attention to the new firm. Pride and the challenge of "It can't be done" spurred on its originator. In thinking how he could make good on this idea Wanamaker hit upon the prime importance of establishing a bond of confidence between merchant and customer. It was by following out a logical train of thought that Wanamaker went from guaranteeing the quality of goods to establishing one price for all; and then from announcing one price to demonstrating good faith by being willing to take back the goods and return the money. The customer had come to know that at Oak Hall he did not have to be expert in cloth to be sure of what he was buying. But how about price? Was there not some other way than the customer's bargaining ability to assure him that he was not paying too much? And how could he be sure that it was a fixed price unless he could return the purchase and get back his money?

In accounts of Wanamaker's life we find an anecdote which he told himself, of how, when he was a little boy, he bought a present for his mother, and as the salesman was wrapping it up John saw something else he liked better. But the salesman would not let him change his mind. A purchase was a purchase! From that moment, we are told, the boy decided that when he grew up and had a store he would let people bring back what they bought and get something else or their money. The anecdote is interesting, and it was undoubtedly told in good faith. But it cannot be used by the biographer to illustrate how the Wanamaker business policies originated. With all of us reminiscences of childhood are used *post factum* to explain achievements of later years.

The credit for having initiated the one-price system in retail merchandising has often been given to Wanamaker; but he himself wrote on March 2, 1907:

A. T. Stewart first began the one-price rule for dry goods, and our system carried it further than he did.

This generous attribution to another of the policy so

frequently attributed to him is backed by many authorities.[1]
But we find it advertised by other New York stores in 1841
and 1842.[2] It was claimed by Marshall Field in 1867.
Both in England and in France one price was made a drawing-card by merchants at least as early as we find it on this
side of the Atlantic. The Bon Marché advertised it in
1854, but did not claim to be the first in making the effort
to put a stop to haggling and bargaining in the retail trade.[3]
The earliest definite claim that we have been able to discover
is that of the great Newcastle merchant, Bainbridge, who
opened a shop in 1837 with "a definite fixed price, distinctly
marked on all goods, and to this custom he rigidly adhered."[4]

In writing about the one-price system at a considerably
later date Wanamaker said that it had been ostensibly
adopted by several other Philadelphia stores, but that there
were ways of getting around it. A varying scale of discounts
met almost any condition of customer; and, while in some

[1] In M. H. Smith's *Sunshine and Shadow in New York*, written in 1868,
it is stated that when A. T. Stewart was still at what is now 262 Broadway
he had a sale to meet a note falling due. "People crowded in. He presided
in person and took the cash. To all attempts to beat him down, he quietly
pointed to the plainly written price on each package." Stewart is given the
credit for the policy by Hartley Davis, *Everybody's*, September, 1907. See
also Nasmith's *Timothy Eaton*, page 100; the New York *World*, April 10,
1876; J. D. McCabe, Jr., *Great Fortunes: How They Were Made*, published
in 1870; and an editorial in *Dry Goods Economist*, November 4, 1899. We
have collected many statements that attribute the policy to John Wanamaker.
But the writers of these do not seem to be aware of the earlier history of
retail merchandising.

[2] The one-price system was advertised by Jacob Cogseell on May 17, 1841,
and by P. Gregory & Sons on March 26, 1842. On February 22, 1842,
Brown, Urquhart Co. advertised: "We pledge ourselves to conduct our business on the strictest system of one price. All goods will be found marked in
plain figures and no deviation under any circumstances will be allowed from
prices so marked." These three advertisements appeared in the New York
Tribune.

[3] Several French authorities cite instances of one-price merchants in Paris
shortly after the Restoration. Emile Zola, in *Au Bonheur des Dames*, states
that "*prix fixe*" was known, though not universally adopted, before 1850.

[4] *The House of Bainbridge*, Newcastle and Leeds, 1914, p. 7.

shops the marked price was paid, a cap, a pair of gloves or suspenders, collars, or sometimes only a handkerchief, was "thrown in." There were days when articles were lower than ticketed. It could happen conveniently to be the day on which a customer who insisted on bargaining was in the shop.

We know, too, that it was a long hard fight to get the buying public to understand that one price had come to stay. This is evident from the frequent announcement of the policy, and insistence on it, by other large establishments in Philadelphia and New York in the early 'seventies. Wanamaker reiterated it in 1871, and again in 1874, as a "cardinal point" of Wanamaker merchandising policy. As late as February 18, 1875, we find an advertisement of Oak Hall headed:

WANTED: A POCKET HANDKERCHIEF
CURIOSITIES OF TRADE

Then follows a dialogue between a customer and a clerk, the customer insisting that a twenty-five-cent handkerchief be thrown in with a twenty-dollar purchase. The clerk says:

You might as well ask me to give you one of the elephants out of the Zoölogical Gardens as to expect me to take a penny off the price marked on this coat, either by a reduction or as a gift of any kind.[1]

Where Wanamaker led the way in establishing one price as a business principle, later to be universally accepted in retailing, was by announcing in 1865 that the customer could return the article and get his money back. There were no strings to this offer (except, of course, that the article had not been used). We find nowhere that this policy had been

[1] Referring to the opening of the Grand Depot in 1876, Wanamaker said in an advertisement thirty years later (March 16, 1906): "One price of the shifting kind that prevailed in two or three places had to come out into the open, to meet our plain figures, unshifting, inflexible."

advertised before Oak Hall announced it. It was really the complement to one price. It gave the buyer faith in the genuineness of the claim that the price he paid was the same to all. Despite the many inconveniences and problems, which we shall mention later, attendant upon return of merchandise, it was a stroke of genius that revolutionized the American mercantile world of the post-Civil War period.

ONE PRICE was not invented by John Wanamaker either as a slogan or as a policy. MONEY BACK was; and it meant for Wanamaker & Brown the turning of the corner in their retail business.

At a recent convention of the Advertising Clubs of the World, at Dallas, Texas, a man went round among the delegates, handing out his visiting card, on which he had, after his name, the modest claim, "Highest paid writer in the world." He was a slogan-maker, and his claim—if inventing slogans constitute a writer—may have been true. The amusing incident gave rise to a discussion among clever delegates as to what slogan had made the most money for its inventor. One insisted that the three words, "His master's voice," could not be surpassed for financial return.

"I know two words that made far more money than that," said another.

"What?"

"John Wanamaker's 'Money back.' "

There was a chorus of, "You win!"

SHAKESPEARE ADVERTISEMENT FOR OAK HALL

CHAPTER XII

OAK HALL ADVERTISING

THERE are those who stoutly affirm that advertising is not necessary to success. He who indulges in it, they say, has something blatant in his fiber. If a man quietly pursues his work, with no thought of letting others know what he is doing, he will get to the top, provided he has it in him. They cite the old adage that the world makes a path to the great man's door. Does not merit invariably get its reward, sooner or later? They profess to believe that in the professional world only the charlatan attempts to sell his wares. They pity the merchant or manufacturer who is compelled to make his own name a trade mark. They assume to draw a sharp line of distinction between those engaged in trade, whose title to fame rests upon their own advertising, and statesmen, jurists, physicians, scientists, and authors, whose achievements they profess to believe, the world recognizes without having to be told about them.

The prejudice against merchants and the achievements of trade, like all prejudices, is based upon superficial distinctions, if not upon ignorance. It is contrary to the experience of mankind. Crying one's wares in newspapers and on billboards is only one form of advertising. Those who have "left their footprints on the sands of time," from Julius Cæsar to Calvin Coolidge, have almost without exception won the opportunity of doing great things by advertising themselves and allowing others to do it for them. The poet Grey has the monopoly of singing the praises of the other kind of folks. Margaret Ogilvie showed her keen insight into the *sine qua non* of success when she said of her son Barrie, "Speak gud o' the lad, speak ill o' him, but aye be speaking of him!" And Jean Ingelow delved further into one of the homely truths in life when she wrote: "A woman needs not only to be loved, but to be constantly told that she is loved."

When John Wanamaker went into business, the era of the small shopkeeper selling to his neighbors was coming to an end. The growth of cities and the increase of facilities of transportation and communication created the opportunity for a rapid evolution in retailing. The precedent of mammoth establishments, developing from specialty shops into general stores, was already set in London and Paris, whose merchants antedated by a few years Stewart, Wanamaker, and Field, precisely because concentration of population in great centers was an earlier phenomenon there than here. But in the field of advertising Americans were the unquestioned pioneers and originators. Here John Wanamaker led the others, and he continued to lead as long as he lived. As his business grew he employed able men to carry out his ideas; but he never relinquished the control of every detail of advertising. For over sixty years he studied advertising, which he regarded as the life blood of his business.

Oak Hall advertising, therefore, is an original source in the history of this essential auxiliary of the business man.

The young man did not have to learn the importance of advertising. The story of the first months at Oak Hall shows it. Wanamaker & Brown had to become known, and no sacrifice was too great to publish the fact that at the corner of Sixth and Market Streets the man who wanted an overcoat or suit of clothes would find it there. The new firm was stocked to fit everybody, and the prices were right. Wanamaker instinctively put good will as an asset on a footing with location, stocks, equipment, and efficient personnel.

This conception justified a larger outlay for advertising than a mere budget apportionment in the general expense of doing business. Nowadays investing initial capital in extensive advertising is universally accepted as good business when a new enterprise is being launched. It was rarely, if ever, so looked upon sixty-five years ago.

What constituted good will gradually took on new meaning to Wanamaker & Brown. They wanted customers to be satisfied, of course, so that they would return themselves and would recommend the store to others. In casting up the claims of a store to the patronage of the public the advertising set forth fair price, prompt delivery, variety of styles, and quality of goods. Then came the great idea of the merchant as a servant of the public. The advertising had to emphasize this. By doing so it created good will and was amply justified as a capital investment. Soon good will became the principal asset in the Wanamaker business. When John Wanamaker died, his name was worth far more than the land, buildings, equipment, and stocks of his two great stores and their machinery for doing business at home and abroad.

Wanamaker was in business only a few years when he said that every cent he had invested in advertising had created tangible assets that could at any time be converted into cash to yield a better return than other opportunities of investment he had had.

Along with his conception of advertising as a capital investment Wanamaker placed the necessity of having the goods to advertise. Here the buyer's knowledge, energy, and resourcefulness were the indispensable corollary of the advertiser. It was this belief that led him to New York to buy additional stocks the day after the store opened, and we note that the first advertisement announced the offering of a "new and complete stock of ready-made clothing" at bargain prices. Very early in his career he declared that advertising money was squandered unless the customers attracted by it could be held. Then it was that he added to buying ability deftness in salesmanship. In his first recorded talk to his staff he is reported to have said:

"I try my best to buy in falling markets. I manage to have the cash or get the credit to make the purchase. I buy only good and attractive stocks. Then I put more money than I have into advertising. But this does not complete the work. You must show the goods and sell them, and it isn't all right for me to have put out a lot of money in advertising just for that particular sale to that particular customer. You must make him want to come back."

All the while the buyer and advertiser kept a watchful eye over the selling force, and he spent most of his time on the floor. An employee of the early years says that Wanamaker helped with the selling at first, working side by side with his men. As the business increased, he got into the habit of standing by the front door, where he kept an eye on the work of the salesmen. When customers went out, he would ask if they had been suited, thank them, and invite them to come again. He never hesitated to hold up a sale if he thought the clothes did not fit. More than once he asked customers, when the purchases were completed, to go back to the salesman who had waited on them, and he helped them get a better fit. All the while, in the most kindly way, he would keep saying to the men on the floor:

"What we advertise we must do. Tell the customer the exact quality of the goods, if he does not know it, and don't let him be satisfied with a poor fit or with a style that is manifestly unbecoming. Don't you see that his women folk will make him dissatisfied? Then he won't come back. Why am I advertising?"

After the conception of advertising as an investment, because if the buying was able and the salesmanship deft it would enhance the good will asset of the firm, Wanamaker gave his attention to advertising methods and content. In both of these fields what he did at Oak Hall established innovations for which the business world is his debtor.

In advertising methods, being inexperienced, and enthusiastic, and bold, he was willing to try anything once. What were the best advertising mediums? He did not know. So he made experiments and studied them.

Where most men go wrong in advertising—as in everything else—is in refusing to believe that they can go wrong. If an advertising venture fails or does not yield the results expected of it, they think that the fault lies with some other person. Stubborn, they sometimes go on sinking money; or discouraged, they give up. In either case they have failed to retrieve the loss, which they might have done had they studied the failure and sought to find its reasons. Wanamaker was always willing to admit a wrong advertising investment, and because he never tried anything without watching it closely, he was quick in discovering failure. In this way he got out before the loss was serious. Generally there was no loss, because he had learned what not to do. The bull-headed man is almost always the fellow of limited intellect with few ideas. Wanamaker always had so many ideas that he could laugh at himself and go on to another idea when one exploded.

Illustrations of this are numerous. They go back to the first years of Oak Hall. He put a man in livery outside the door, but it did not take him long to discover that this gave a wrong impression to his Market Street trade. He overheard a man saying that the porter's livery and wages were paid by those who bought clothes in that place. The doorman disappeared, to bob up years later where women were delighted with his presence. A big gong was placed by the door, which was rung when the customer entered. Wanamaker thought that this would impress upon clients their importance and the desire to serve them immediately. But he found that it annoyed some and embarrassed others. The gong was taken out.

He was the first man in this country to try the mystery dodge. On boardings of vacant lots or where building was going on all over the city he got permission to have

W. & B.

painted in letters twelve feet high. That was the whole advertisement. Everybody in Philadelphia became curious to discover what the letters stood for. When he thought that all Philadelphia knew, he stopped short.

At county fairs around the city, which were important events in the 'sixties, handbills were distributed stating that Wanamaker & Brown specialized in out-of-town trade. Coaching had just become a fad of the rich. Wanamaker, to the disgust of the ultrafashionable set, got a coach with six horses—four was the usual number—and sent out Oak Hall employees, dressed as the smart coachers rigged themselves up, to "traverse the country in every direction, scattering advertising matter to the music of the horn," as Wanamaker put it in telling of this stunt. The handbills stated that balloons would be released from the roof of Oak Hall, and that whoever brought one back would receive a suit of clothes free. The balloons were twenty feet high, and were made right on the roof. Next came bigger balloons to write the invitation to Oak Hall against the sky. When these forms of attracting attention were no longer novel, Wanamaker distributed toy balloons to children who

CARL A. RUDISILL LIBRARY
LENOIR RHYNE COLLEGE

came to Oak Hall with their parents.[1] Then came Oak Hall slates and pencils and tracing books, and later the series of children's books with colored plates that are preserved in the Library of Congress as models of pioneering in this form of advertising.[2] We do not know whether Oak Hall originated picture postcards; but they were there before 1870, and were used with great effect at the Centennial Exhibition in 1876. The first artistic illustrating for mercantile advertising was done under Wanamaker's direction. Of its quality we are able to allow our readers to judge by reproductions from the Furness collection.[3] The Oak Hall advertisements were so popular that constant demand led Wanamaker & Brown to sell the right of reproduction, and a catalogue and price list of the drawings was published, a document unique in the annals of the history of advertising.

In 1864 a solicitor walked into Oak Hall one day and suggested that Wanamaker & Brown consider an advertisement in the City Directory. The custom of putting modest advertisements at the foot of the page on which the advertiser was listed had just come into vogue. In this way, the solicitor explained, attention was drawn immediately to "important establishments."

"How about the top of the page?" asked the young merchant.

"We have never done that, sir."

[1] The biographer's four children remind him at this point that the Paris *grands magasins* still stick to this delightful Wanamaker custom. There are balloons for kiddies at the Louvre and Printemps. Au Bon Marché they give out colored books like those of Oak Hall.

[2] According to Rev. S. T. Lowrie, the first Oak Hall booklet was called *Acorns*, and was edited by a Presbyterian clergyman who was glad to eke out his salary that way. This minister did several of the booklets. Dr. Lowrie says that Wanamaker was meticulously careful in seeing that text and illustrations were just right. We wonder whether Dr. Lowrie himself might not have been the editor.

[3] Dr. Horace Howard Furness, Jr., who is continuing his father's Shakespeare Variorum, kindly allowed the biographer to see the originals of the "Seven Ages of Man" and other pen-and-ink sketches made for Oak Hall, that were suggested by lines from Shakespeare.

"Well, what if I took the top of every page in the book?" The man was struck dumb.

"Have the publisher figure on that and let me know."

As the solicitor was leaving the little cubbyhole Wanamaker still used for his office, the young merchant added, "If I put in an order like this I shall expect also to have the cover page of the directory for a picture of our building."

The cost of the innovation was stiff. But Wanamaker paid it. The 1865 City Directory carried Oak Hall on the cover, and every time it was used the person finding a name had the merits of Wanamaker clothing staring him in the face. It did more to attract attention to Wanamaker & Brown than anything that had yet been attempted. John Wanamaker was finding his stride—and he had been in business less than four years.

Calendars were distributed. We find one in the private files, which announced that Wanamaker & Brown were "Clothiers to the People." Each month has a seasonable reference to Oak Hall clothing. What year this was started we do not know. Probably it was in 1866, for when the Directory innovation was being talked about it is recorded that Wanamaker said, "Now that they see where we are, no matter where they look in the Directory, we shall have to make them remember their clothing needs whenever they look at the calendar."

And then it occurred to him that people look more frequently at the clock than at the calendar. This led to a heavy investment in clocks—walnut-framed wall clocks, with the Wanamaker & Brown advertisement on the dial and a picture of Oak Hall etched in on the glass in front of the pendulum. These were put in public places and made a big hit, especially in the ferry-houses at the foot of Market Street. But when they began to keep poor time it was realized that the advertisement was "not so good," as Wanamaker ruefully put it, and he tried to call in all these clocks. With his love of punctuality and his daily plea that the public should not be deceived by merchants, the clocks soon became a sore point with him. He had learned what not to do!

Of the advertising features and innovations of the Grand Depot and of the Philadelphia and New York stores of later years we shall speak again. But it must be emphasized here that from the beginning of the Oak Hall venture John Wanamaker believed in daily newspaper advertising above all other forms of publicity. Signs on billboards and handbills he thought little of. Stunts of the kind that we have described were simply features that were being tried out from time to time. His investment in newspaper advertising was continuous, and increased steadily until it passed from hundreds of thousands to over the million dollar mark each year. Oak Hall kept taking more space and attained a full column in the Philadelphia dailies in the second decade of the Store's life. On September 26, 1874, appeared the first half-page mercantile advertisement ever published in a newspaper. It had the distinction, too, of being the first copyrighted advertisement. From this time on the newspaper advertising of John Wanamaker could not be missed even by the most casual reader of the daily press. It met his eye morning and evening.

Wanamaker was no less a pioneer in content of advertisements than in method of advertising. The full development of his powers in the field of writing advertisements, which the whole world studied and imitated, belongs to a later epoch. But the foundations for this creative work were laid when Wanamaker was in his twenties, experimenting with business policies at Oak Hall. Was it not because he had a story to tell that he conceived the idea that an advertisement was more than a mere announcement of the existence of a business house or of goods to sell?

Under the influence of the Tower Hall bard and the spirit of the day he floundered, like the rest of his contemporaries, for some years. Newspaper space, sparingly used at first, contained what we should regard as meaningless repetition of the same statement. For instance, WANA-MAKER & BROWN would head the advertisement, the name of the firm repeated in three lines; then the address three times; and the feature lines of the announcement occurring several times in the same advertisement. This was probably because newspapers had only two or three fonts, and repetition took the place of larger display type.

When newspapers increased in size and the volume of business made possible buying more space, Wanamaker used poetry and dialogues. Throughout his life he loved to rhyme words. It was a diversion, not always felicitous or with much meaning. The habit was formed in the early advertising days, when newspaper space was used for a jingle such as this:

> What a powerful agitation
> Now disturbs this Yankee nation
> On the subject of inflation.
> Folks of every rank and station,
> Folks in whom no perturbation
> Can be wakened in relation
> To the country's situation,
> Pending the consideration
> Of any other speculation
> Now display great indignation
> At the bare consideration
> Of the proposed application
> Of the plan in contemplation.
> To the financial situation
> We give little cogitation
> To the subject. If inflation

Suits the sages of the nation,
We give our approbation.
If contraction seem more ration-
Al to their deliberation
We'll contract, with resignation,
And will make this proclamation
To the whole male population
Of the land, in expectation
'Twill receive consideration.
Friends, this is an invitation
For you to make examination
Of our Spring Goods. Your admiration
We know sure our application
To well deserve your approbation
Has been assiduous. The foundation
Of it was nicest calculation
Of what would be the next sensation;
A thorough, strict investigation
Of coming styles, and meditation,
To put to your commendation
At very small remuneration;
So we invite a visitation
When we will make substantiation
Of all in this dissertation.

The dialogue was used first as a clever way of introducing price lists. For some time the column advertisement was headed: "What Jonas says." There would be conversation, changed every day, of which this is a sample:

WHAT JONAS SAYS

JONAS: I want to hand you, Neighbor Gates, something that will be of real interest, not only to you but to your boys.

NEIGHBOR GATES: Glad to get anything that has money in it.

JONAS: Well, I think you can certainly save money by consulting the list, which personal examination proves to be correct in every word and figure.

NEIGHBOR GATES: I saw a list of WANAMAKER & BROWN'S One-price Clothing last Saturday.

JONAS: Yes, but this is a new list, and it has a great deal more on it. The way business is done at Oak Hall is very gratifying. Every article is marked with its true name and price in plain figures, and no deviation. When anything does not suit the money is returned instanter. It is handy to get to OAK HALL, as the cars take you direct to WANAMAKER & BROWN'S, on the corner of SIXTH and MARKET.

After Jonas and Neighbor Gates finish talking would come the Wanamaker & Brown offerings, overcoats and combinations of coat, "pants" (yes, that was the word!); and vest.

When Wanamaker had a story to tell of new business principles faithfully adhered to by Oak Hall, jingles could not do this effectively, and fables proved inadequate because all the punch had to be put into the two or three lines of the "moral." He had to find some other way to popularize the new policies that were his drawing-card. The dialogue form was tried for telling anecdotes that would illustrate the fidelity of Wanamaker & Brown to one price and exchange of goods. The conversation would be between the doorkeeper or the salesman and a customer at first skeptical, then mystified, and ending up delighted with the new way of doing business that assured him a square deal and equal treatment.

It took years to convert the public to the unaccustomed methods and to convince the people of Philadelphia of Wanamaker & Brown's good faith and unswerving fidelity to one price and exchange of merchandise. This led Wanamaker to believe that his advertisements needed to do more than to announce stocks and prices and draw attention to Oak Hall. The dialogue form was not serious enough, he felt, to accomplish the educational work that was essential to the firm establishment of the new way of doing business.

As a complement to our historical statement of the origin of the one-price system we need to emphasize the credit due to Wanamaker for getting the buying public to accept the radical change in the relations between merchant and customer. It is a curious fact that the world is slow to seize upon innovations wholly to its advantage. We all know the story of the man who found that he could not give away genuine ten-dollars bills at the corner of Forty-second Street and Broadway. None would take what he offered. The feeling of a "nigger in the woodpile" is instinctive.

This quirk of human nature explains why in 1874, nine years after the first announcement of one price and money back, Wanamaker still had to make the content of his advertisements deal largely with the mercantile policies of which he had so long been the earnest advocate. Necessity led him into an unexplored field of advertising. It made him the pioneer in the bold use of an unprecedented amount of newspaper space to tell a story. His fight for better mercantile methods prompted him to create a new epoch in advertising by his copyrighted half-page of 1874, which was devoted, not to sounding the praises of Oak Hall merchandise, but to an announcement of how "the largest clothing concern in America now starts on a new career." He declared that the day of evasions was over, and that Wanamaker & Brown announced

FULL GUARANTEE
ONE PRICE
CASH PAYMENT
CASH RETURNED

as the "four cardinal points by which we will hereafter steer our craft." There followed an elaborate statement of these policies.

Despite the fact that it had become the largest business of the kind in the United States and was now known over a wide area outside of Philadelphia, a house that dealt exclusively in men's and boys' clothing could not revolutionize business methods even in one city. Having only one line of goods to offer, Wanamaker was limited in his influence in the general field of merchandising, and at the age of thirty-six he had well-nigh exhausted the possibilities of further development in the advertising of a clothing establishment. It was as far as he could go. Wanamaker did not realize this fact until the Centennial Exhibition opened his eyes to the wider field two years later. From the Grand Depot must be dated the beginning of a new stage in Wanamaker advertising. But upon the foundation of Oak Hall was built what was to follow.

"THEN, THE WHINING SCHOOLBOY....
CREEPING LIKE SNAIL, UNWILLINGLY TO SCHOOL

CHAPTER XIII

THE FIRST CHESTNUT STREET STORE

THE death of Nathan Brown seven years after the founding of Oak Hall deprived John Wanamaker of the partner whose loyalty and complete understanding had contributed inestimably to the success of the venture. He was an ideal associate, and his faith and zeal had made possible the great achievements of the 'sixties. In writing of these early years we must remember that Wanamaker's genius had not won immediate recognition. The unusual conditions created by the Civil War enabled many who were jealous of Oak Hall to explain its success by stating that its founders were children of fortune. Prosperity had come so quickly to Oak Hall that the easiest way to account for it was to attribute it to luck. It is only in view of the later career of Wanamaker that his achievements at this period have come to be recognized as marking a new era in the history of retail merchandising. Had he been the one who died, would his name be known to-day?

Faith is as great a virtue as vision, and deserves more credit, especially the faith of one in the vision of another. In the early years, when crisis after crisis arose, Brown stood by his impetuous brother-in-law. They were sailing on uncharted seas. Brown was an equal partner, and was frequently advised by his friends to "hold John in." He refused to prevent the full play of Wanamaker's new ideas. More than once he had been a balance wheel in times of stress. But he was not the brake to retard or stop the process of expansion. If we knew the inside history of partner-

13TH & CHESTNUT STREETS CORNER of GRAND DEPOT, PRIOR TO REBUILDING

ships, we should be able to note instances of the checked growth of men who, given free rein by their associates, might have created great enterprises.

Wanamaker was in a position to buy out the interest of his partner's estate. This he did. But affection and loyalty to the memory of Nathan Brown made him unwilling to change the name under which Oak Hall had started business. No trait was more characteristic of John Wanamaker than this. He went to other and greater undertakings. But he did not lose interest in Oak Hall. It remained a flourishing business, under his personal direction, and received its share of his attention, his talents, his ideas. A decade later it was to give new life to Oak Hall and to help his brothers that he first thought of Robert C. Ogden. It stands to-day on the original corner of Sixth and Market Streets, under the name of Wanamaker & Brown, still a men's and boys' clothing business.

For some years after Brown's death Oak Hall remained the principal asset of Wanamaker, and continued to grow. From it he gained the capital that enabled him to start the business upon which his fame rests. As we have seen, it was at Oak Hall that Wanamaker fought for new mercantile conditions in the early 'seventies and through its advertising he blazed a new trail. But his own name he gave to a new business on Chestnut Street, founded to enable him to work out ideas that did not fit in with the Market Street business. From the experiments in this Chestnut Street laboratory, rather than from Oak Hall, grew the great store some blocks further west that extends from Market Street to Chestnut Street.

John Wanamaker & Co. was established in 1869 on Chestnut Street between Eighth and Ninth, next door to the Continental Hotel, which was at that time the largest and most fashionable hostelry of Philadelphia. It was an expensive location—none in the city more expensive—and it was fitted up in a luxurious style that would have been out of place at Sixth and Market Streets.   Built with an open space in the center covered by a skylight, and with galleries for upper floors, it resembled on a small scale the great building of A. T. Stewart, at Ninth and Broadway, New York, which he greatly admired. Thick carpets were laid on the floors, and paintings and numerous gilt-framed mirrors covered the walls.   The man in livery at the door, banished from Oak Hall, made his reappearance in front of 818-20-22 Chestnut Street.

It was a setting that the young merchant had dreamed of for years, and he stocked the new store with clothing of a kind that he had always wanted to carry, but which would not have sold at Sixth and Market Streets, where the first advertised stock was at "three dollars a suit."   Custom trade was an important feature of the Chestnut Street store, and fifteen of the best cutters that could be found were employed to give personal attention to customers. The show windows, the upper part of which were of mediæval stained glass, were the sensation of the day; for the old conservative tailors of Philadelphia were opposed to display of any sort.

In the spring announcement of 1870, speaking of the first year, Wanamaker wrote:

We expected to have but a local trade; but we have been led, we might better say compelled, to do what we might also call a national business. In nearly every state we already have customers, with unlimited prospect of further expansion.

All this has greatly encouraged us, and nerved us to the determination to push our original design of establishing in Philadelphia a clothing house which shall be unrivaled in the country—a place where can be found a class of ready-made clothing such as can be had nowhere else, and where custom work of the highest order shall be done on a scale at once extensive and elevated.

A look at our west window will show you what we have done in this department. Such a display of gents' Furnishing Goods can be made by no other House; for the amount of capital we invested, and the time and care which we have bestowed, have secured to us a stock which is beyond rivalry. All the new importations, with some rich lines of goods, of which we have sole control for the supply of Philadelphia.

The announcement was on an engraved and colored card, with gilt edges, which invited the public to a reception on Tuesday, April 5. A newspaper account of the opening emphasizes the "impression of solid wealth and unstinted liberality," and declares that the "luxurious fittings and artistic decorations inside rival the appearance from the street."

Wanamaker & Brown, at Oak Hall, were at this time offering clothing "to meet the needs of every purse," and had become within ten years the largest retail clothing store in the United States. The goal of John Wanamaker & Co. was something entirely different. It was a Chestnut Street luxury shop, created to offer "the best that money can buy." Always fastidious in personal dress himself—an inherited trait—John Wanamaker wanted his name in merchandising to stand for elegance and good taste. He believed that Philadelphia was ready for this kind of establishment, and into its setting and its stock he put the ideas that had slowly been gathering in his mind and the knowledge of merchandise acquired by years of study, but based upon a background of innate good taste. It may have been of the Chestnut Street store and not of Oak Hall that A. T. Stewart, who died before the Grand Depot was fairly launched, was thinking when he told a friend that "over there in Philadelphia you have a young man named Wanamaker, who will bear watching."

Oak Hall in the early 'seventies had become an immense establishment, whose contract and wholesale departments on the upper floors manufactured clothing and shipped it all over the country. The business had gradually expanded until it occupied the whole of McNeille's Folly. But its retail department was inevitably becoming what Wanamaker did not want it to become, just a men's clothing store, different in policies, its owner believed, from those of other stores, but limited in its possibilities of development. The Chestnut Street store, on the other hand, enabled Wanamaker to experiment in drawing and building up a clientele that put service and quality above price—a clientele that Wanamaker could 'study. He allowed his associates to bother with problems of organization and meeting bills.[1] He himself did the buying and the advertising and set the stage.

We find that by 1874 there were six departments in the Chestnut Street store: gentlemen's ready-made clothing; youths' and boys' ready-made clothing; children's department; ladies' coats and habits; "bespoke" and measure goods; and fine haberdashery.

By this time the store was featuring silk-and-fur-lined overcoats and imported piece goods, and was carrying leather articles for travel in its "gentlemen's furnishings." This brought John Wanamaker into the market for lines outside of the usual clothing trade, and it was the first contact with women buying for themselves.

The best advertisements for John Wanamaker & Co. were the Chestnut Street windows and the location, facts which gave the owner furiously to think. The experiment of creating a luxurious interior proved, too, an excellent drawing-

---

[1] Isaac D. Shearer, who lived until the middle of March, 1926, was the cashier of John Wanamaker & Co. He told the biographer recently that John Wanamaker emancipated himself from worries over the machinery of his business and its finances before he was thirty, and that this was one of the principal reasons for Wanamaker's early and sweeping success. The young merchant had an amazing mastery of details and a penetrating eye that took in everything. But he knew what not to get wrought up over and expend his energy in. He used to tell his staff, even when he had only a few executives, that it was their business to attend to the machinery and the money. He refused to occupy himself with matters that others could manage.

card. Constant thought and study, and the changing tastes of the times, influenced Wanamaker to tone down the interior decorations and to concentrate more on the made-to-measure rooms. Here customers had to wait; and here piece goods were displayed, not in cases under glass and presided over by an alert salesman, but thrown out on tables with artistic carelessness. On the walls were paintings. The age-old look of the shop and the ubiquitous, obsequious salesman had been eliminated. On the tables Wanamaker placed suitings that he thought would sell themselves better than they could be sold to the particular clientele he was studying. The result exceeded his hopes. John Wanamaker & Co., by sheer merit of goods and by adroit display in the windows and within the store, were winning customers every day.

This did not mean that Wanamaker folded his hands and waited for the business to grow, or that he was satisfied with the sales records. Like Oak Hall, the Chestnut Street store was making strides forward because its proprietor was studying and working all the time. He enjoyed the effort. He once remarked that nervous troubles did not occur from overwork, but from the failure to strain every nerve all the time. "If you keep your nerves exercised," was the tenor of his thought (we have not the exact words), "they'll be like exercised muscles and bear well the unexpected load when it is thrust upon them."

John Wanamaker & Co. went out after trade, soliciting military and naval officers and clergymen by "special privilege cards," with the name of the recipient written on it. Whatever these "privileges" were, they extended to the whole family. But the advertising of the Chestnut Street store was more restrained than that of Oak Hall. The colored and engraved cards generally said nothing about clothing; and the booklets put out contained no word of advertising—simply the name: John Wanamaker & Co., as publishers, on the title page.

In the store book of Wanamaker & Brown, published in 1876, just before the Grand Depot opened, we read at the end, under the head of "postscript":

> The elegant Tailoring House of John Wanamaker & Co., on Chestnut Street, adjoining the Continental Hotel, is a part of the business of this House. The Merchant and Tailoring Department for making of goods to order has no superior in Paris, London, or America.

Oak Hall and the Grand Depot did not take all Wanamaker's time after 1876. Until he turned the store over to his brothers his interest in 818-20-22 Chestnut Street remained keen and vital, and in 1881 we find in his own handwriting figures to show that its business amounted to more than a million dollars a year. On the premises were 200 employees, and 600 more were in the workrooms. The Chestnut Street store was a triumph in merchandising ability. Among Philadelphians it established, as Oak Hall could never have done, John Wanamaker's reputation for taste and quality of merchandise, and in the merchant's own brain it planted the idea and gave the inspiration for the "new kind of store."

CHAPTER XIV

THE FIRST TRIP ABROAD

IN 1869 Wanamaker wrote that he had had no vacation since he went into business for himself. That was eight years before. Going back three years earlier still, to 1858, it seemed as if he had been strenuously at it for eleven years, in Philadelphia all the time, Sundays and week-days, with the exception of buying trips to New York and the occasional Y. M. C. A. conventions, at New Orleans in 1860, at New York City in 1861, at Saratoga Springs in 1863, and at Buffalo in 1868. For one who had experienced pioneer life in Indiana as a boy and who had had an unusual glimpse of his country in the Western trip when he was twenty, the close application to work from the age of twenty to thirty-three is an indication of its absorbing interest even more than of the man's industry.

If he had not enjoyed his adventures in building up a Sunday school and a business he would have not stuck to them the way he did. Only a distorted and superficial view of life makes it possible for men to extol the virtue of enduring hardness as the transcendent factor in success. Finding congenial work and having a zest for it are more important than industry. The spur to getting ahead in the world is dissatisfaction with one's own achievements and not with the work to which one has put his hand. Out of the joy he had in Bethany and Oak Hall, John Wanamaker found health and strength. He looked upon shouldering burdens, overcoming obstacles, and facing and solving problems as adventures. The shadows make the sunshine pleasant.

Wanamaker himself used to say this at Bethany, using the old illustration of the blackboard and chalk.

The first decade of business, as we have seen, took the young merchant through the Civil War and its aftermath of prosperity, culminating in the launching of the Chestnut Street store. He had passed through periods of anxiety and perplexity in his business, and had weathered the loss of his partner and the financial crisis precipitated by Jay Gould's Black Friday. He had suffered the personal humiliation of rejection from military service when shouldering a musket seemed to him the first duty of every young man. During the last year of the war his third son, Horace, died in infancy; and his oldest daughter, Hattie, was taken at the age of five in 1870. Intimate friends of John Wanamaker and his wife say that they never recovered from the loss of this child. There were two sons before Horace, and two daughters after Hattie. But parents know what we mean. Battles of the soul were fought, leaving memories that blessed and burned.[1]

Wanamaker's ambition to become a master merchant, leading the field because of the unsurpassed quality of the goods he offered for sale, demanded better acquaintance with woolens and a more thorough study of them than he had yet made. After opening the Chestnut Street store personal acquaintance with English markets became imperative. A large measure of his success lay in the fact that he was his own buyer, and he knew that the next step was a trip to Europe. He did not see how he could take the time. No man running a business ever does! But could he keep the place he had won as a seller of men's clothing, and go ahead

---

[1] The Presbyterian Church at Jenkintown was erected as a memorial to her, and bears a tablet inscribed: "In Loving Memory of Harriet Erringer Wanamaker Aged Five Years. 1865-1870. A Little Child Shall Lead Them."

to bigger things, unless he added to his activities periodical visits to the centers that set the standards for qualities and styles in his line of merchandising? It was the logical answer to this question, and not the desire or need of a vacation, that started him across the Atlantic and made ocean voyages a part of his life for forty years.

The first trip to Europe came after an experience that should be recorded at this point; for it indicates the importance he attached to English woolens in the success of his Chestnut Street business, and gives us an intimate glimpse of his daring and vision, and of the risks he took to make the Chestnut Street store the leading Philadelphia establishment in quality goods.

Shortly after he branched out to Chestnut Street, Wanamaker was offered by A. T. Stewart & Co. English woolens manufactured in America. Stewart was sales agent for a firm that had come over from England, bringing its machinery and weavers, and had set up a factory that was turning out a higher grade of American-made cloth than had ever before been on the market. Wanamaker promptly decided to take all the goods this factory produced, giving Stewart notes falling due in from six months to two years. When the time was approaching for the first of these notes to be met, he realized that he was not going to have the cash in hand. He was told that A. T. Stewart & Co. were alarmed about the account, and were quietly investigating his business, the expansion of which they believed to be unsound. The strain of setting up the new venture and of Hattie's illness had told on Wanamaker, and he wrote a letter that drew forth a remarkable answer.

The response of A. T. Stewart's partner tells its own story:

MY DEAR WANAMAKER:——

Your letter of the 30th ult. gave me quite a surprise this morning. After I had read it, I said to myself "what a serious friend this is. I wish he had twenty-five years more of battle for credit and position on his head. Then he could join me in my laugh."

My good fellow, you must have worked hard last week, and Saturday night is a very bad time to write a letter. You will feel more cool and independent on Monday morning, and I do not doubt, will tell John Wanamaker, if you know him, that you do not care a fig for A. T. Stewart and Co. or anybody else, that your credit is good enough, that you are able to take care of it, in spite of all the lies that the devil may get into line to do their dirty work under his generalship. Now, friend John, to reply to your standpoint, firstly, A. T. Stewart & Co. *have not requested any* investigation into the matter you refer to, *do not know anything about* it, *and do not care particularly anything about it so far as they are concerned,* and you should feel the same way. It is about time that John Wanamaker should laugh at all and every of these stories, be they *true* or *false,* either ought not to make any difference to him; if your stout heart and strong arm (under God's providence) has placed you where you are you need not let such trifles trouble you NOW. There are two classes of equally dangerous and annoying kinds of vagabonds, that we have to daily come in contact with. Those who spend all their time, generally stealing it from somebody, to tattle the little lies that the old devil makes sure that they are kept supplied with. The other a class of goodly persons who are simple hearted and believe all the tattle they hear, and confidentially go around to unburden themselves and load up those that the devil can tempt to waste their time upon them. They both come under the classes of the knaves and fools. The first robs you in cold blood, the other sets your house on fire and says he did it only in sport; don't waste any time on either. It's my way with all such. I generally ask them be so kind as to write me a letter covering all the points and which as you may judge I never get, as such people seldom dare to write what they are very willing to tell, as in the one case they could lie out of it and in the other they would find their signature against them.

In regard to your obligations, I do not know whether you owe us six thousand or sixteen thousand and it makes no difference which. I was not advised that any of your goods were undelivered. The last I knew about a large purchase made some time since was that they were to be stored in Philadelphia subject to your orders. Be assured, my friend, on all these matters and keep quiet.

Yours very truly,

WILLIAM LIBBEY.

Libbey was as good as his word. Wanamaker's notes were carried without question. A. T. Stewart & Co. backed him to the limit, then and later, never questioning his standing, even during the panic of 1873.[1]

Among his papers we have found a minute and vivid account of the traveler's first experiences in Europe, which we must resist the temptation to quote. It shows a marked improvement in literary style over the letters written from the Middle West fourteen years earlier. But it contains the same indication that Wanamaker thought more of the coming of the Kingdom of God than of business. His traveling companion was the Rev. Samuel T. Lowrie, who had been for three years the pastor of Bethany Church. On the steamer daily prayer-meetings were held, and the high lights of the summer abroad seemed to be meeting Horatius Bonar, the hymn-writer of Edinburgh, and George Williams, founder of the Y. M. C. A., in London; and hearing Charles Spurgeon preach on "Christ Is All and in All," at the Metropolitan Tabernacle.[2] John Wanamaker, merchant, did not forget that he was John Wanamaker, Sunday-school superintendent, and his buying included presents for every associate and scholar at Bethany.

[1] One of the sons of William Libbey has given us a letter to his father in Wanamaker's handwriting, written on January 24, 1874, when Oak Hall, having weathered the panic year, was sending out an ambitious announcement of expansion. Addressing Libbey as "my long and true and much valued friend," he wrote: "The first of the printed letters as enclosed is mailed *to you* and I feel sure of the smile of satisfaction and pleasure it will give to one who had so much faith in 'the lad' when there were so many unbelievers."

[2] Copies of this and other Spurgeon sermons published by the Tabernacle are in the private files.

The 1871 trip was made on the Cunarder *Scotia*, an old side-wheeler, which was as different from the palatial steamers of to-day as Oak Hall was different from what every one in Philadelphia calls simply "Wanamaker's." Many Philadelphians were on board. Professor T. W. Hunt of Princeton University, accompanying William Libbey's two sons as tutor, and later to be the beloved English teacher of Woodrow Wilson and John Wanamaker's sons, was a fellow-passenger. He comes in to see us as we are writing this chapter, and tells us that Wanamaker was "the life of the ship." None resented the prayer-meetings. All hands attended; and the tall Philadelphia merchant, away from men's clothing, proved that he could play as well as he prayed. He was interested in everybody, and no child was too small to claim his full attention or too bashful to be won by him.

We have a letter to one of his sisters, written from the Langham Hotel, London, on August 14, full of brotherly affection, in which he says:

Just as a little love token, I send you a little twig of the famous never fading Holly, in which England abounds. I plucked it at the Crystal Palace grounds on Saturday, and I can assure you that all we have seen in pictures or print does not surpass this wonderful work of art and skill. On Thursday last I visited Windsor Palace and Grounds, the home of good Queen Victoria, and it would take a week to go all over the vast and magnificent buildings and even longer to tell you of them—the rarest pictures, furniture, carvings and luxuries that one who does not see only dreams of. Still I think they are no happier than we who never know aught of their splendor.

This morning I breakfast out with Mr. Shipton, my friend, and afterwards call on His Lordship the Earl of Shaftesbury.

Will you please kiss dear Mother for me and tell her I never forget her and that I love her more and more every day of her life, and only wish I was a better son. God bless and keep you all! With kindest remembrances to all my dear Bethany friends who ask for me.

But business had not been forgotten. Leeds was the first stop after landing at Liverpool, where Wanamaker and Lowrie were guests of woolen manufacturers, who took them through the mill district. It was an historic occasion in the Wanamaker business, for it marked the first direct purchase abroad. Fifty thousand dollars was put into fine tweeds, which Wanamaker took back with him. Placed on sale at the fall opening of the Chestnut Street store, the offering of these goods was the beginning of a new era in John Wanamaker's career.

After Edinburgh and Glasgow came London. The continental part of the tour was *via* Ostend to Cologne, the Rhine, and Switzerland. Paris, with the dazzling vista it opened up to the American merchant, was to come later.

CHAPTER XV

CLOSED DOORS AND THE OPEN ONE

THE rise and rapid growth of general stores offering for
sale under one roof and management a wide variety of
merchandise was the phenomenon of the evolution of retailing in the last quarter of the nineteenth century. The so-
called department stores were first in evidence in Paris,
where the Bon Marché and the Grands Magasins du Louvre
were already attracting attention in the last brilliant decade
of the Second Empire. They were important enough in the
social and economic life of the city to be the theme of one of
Zola's realistic novels of the epoch before 1870.[1] London,
while clinging tenaciously to specialty shops, had one outstanding exception in William Whiteley, whose title of
"universal provider" revealed the catholic scope of his mercantile conception. On the whole, however, the general
store in Europe, as in America, was still only a big dry-
goods shop as late as 1876. The great American establishments of the present day, which boast of an earlier origin,
were, with the single exception of Wanamaker's, shops for
women's wear, and carried only piece goods, trimmings, rib-
bons, and notions to meet the needs of the age when clothes
and hats were still mostly made at home.

As manufacturing in large quantities began to replace
articles made by hand, the merchandise gradually became
more diversified, and the necessity of carrying large stocks
to fit all sizes of customers demanded bigger establishments
and greater capital. We have seen how wholesaling and

[1] *Au Bonheur des Dames.*

124

contract work were the underpinning of the Oak Hall retail trade. It was the same with A. T. Stewart & Co. and Field, Leiter & Co. At this period, Marshall Field drew most of his profit from lot sales to country merchants. Stewart loved retailing, and opened in 1863 a retail store ahead of anything else in the United States; but he, too, depended somewhat upon his wholesale trade. There were two tendencies —towards the general store, transplanting to the city the old country store and towards larger specialty shops, depending for their growth upon reaching a wider circle of customers than could be counted upon in the keen competition of city mercantile life.

For some years Wanamaker followed the latter road. In a decade he had built up at Oak Hall the greatest retail clothing business in the United States, and had opened a quality shop, which was proving an unqualified success, to cater in his own line to a limited class. But his ambition did not stop there. The first European trip had brought him into contact with the interesting experiment of Whiteley, which was only eight years old when he saw it. Whiteley was as yet doing a general business only in a small way. The Paris general stores of Boucicaut and Chauchard had begun to branch out into upholstery, housefurnishings, and toilet articles, when Wanamaker first visited them.

In London he talked with George Williams, who was head of a large wholesale house, about these tendencies in retailing. He expressed the opinion that if merchants became jacks-of-all-trades they incurred the danger of being masters of none. He saw the possibilities—the unlimited possibilities—of general stores, but he feared that they would become glorified auction rooms or clearing-houses for handling manufacturers' job lots, with no sense of responsibility for the quality of the goods passing through their hands. He told Williams how, even in his clothing business, turning over bargain lots was a frequent temptation, which, if yielded to, might quickly destroy the reputation and good will a merchant was trying to build up. The unique importance of London and Paris in their respective countries had also been noted as a reason for not making an analogy between merchandising conditions and possibilities in those cities and the widely scattered centers of population in the New World, none of which could be regarded as more than *prima inter pares*.

But Wanamaker's keen mind was searching for every form of merchandising that was being tried out to meet the new conditions of concentrated city population and mass production. Notes made in 1871 and 1874 prove that he foresaw a time when merchants would be asked for goods for which the manufacturer had created a demand by advertising his products, protected by a trade mark. Would the specialty shopkeeper have to become an agent for nationally advertised brands, the prices of which he could not control and stocks of which he would be unable to buy in the open market? Or would there be composite stores to meet this kind of demand?

Some writers believe that the department store had its origin in the Equitable Pioneers' Society, Ltd., which started its first store in Rochdale, Lancashire, 1844. In 1871 Wanamaker made an exhaustive study of the Rochdale enterprise, and brought back from London a member's book and rules of 1870.[1] With these books, in the private files, the biographer found copious notes in John Wanamaker's own hand, with figures, showing that he had studied in detail the running of the system, and the comments indicate that he had

---

[1] Book No. 1756 of 1863 and No. 2145 of 1870, in the names of John Tweedale and John Ashworth, respectively. The inscription on the fly leaf of the book of rules states that John Wanamaker got it in London in 1871. The fly leaves and the back paper cover of the Rochdale pamphlet are covered with figures and comments.

Pennsylvania Railroad Freight Sheds from City Hall Square, Prior to 1876

visited a Rochdale establishment. He had noted the community features in the Rochdale shops; the fact that there
were thirty-three different departments; that "stores closed
at 2 P.M. on Tuesdays for a holiday for all employees,"
and he commented: "The whole depends on people sticking
together—the harder the region where difficulties are to be
surmounted, the most successful. That is a mighty big
fact!"

After the first trip abroad Wanamaker's restlessness was
more noticeable than at any subsequent period of his career,
which is saying a good deal. He had outgrown Oak Hall.
And yet every bit of McNeille's Folly was in his hands. He
had bought out more than fifty other tenants, and was using
two acres of floor space. An adjoining property had been
acquired for hats. Further expansion for retailing was
blocked by the inability to acquire more property on Market
Street. The Chestnut Street store, success that it was, did
not keep pace with his ambition. And he was eager as a
child to carry the gospel of "one price" and "money back"
to a wider field than he had yet reached. On him was the
urge of other worlds to conquer.

Wanamaker & Brown had for several years been doing
business in semi-fit clothing through agents, mostly postmasters. Suits and overcoats were offered unfinished, a local
tailor to do the final fitting. Where there was much trade to
be had, tailors in small cities were appointed agents. They
would take measurements, send them in to Oak Hall, get
the partly made garment, and do the finishing. From this
to self-measurement and direct order, or order of ready-
made clothing on approval, was only a step.

Wanamaker came close to founding the pioneer mail-
order house. He did not follow up this lead energetically,
because business by correspondence was too impersonal. He

wanted the pleasure of displaying his goods and seeing customers come in and buy them.

At the end of 1871 Wanamaker & Brown had a surplus
in certain cheaper lines, due to widespread unemployment.
It was one of the few times in his career that he was
heavily overstocked. Studying the situation, he learned
that there were good times in the Pittsburgh steel business,
where all the mills were working to capacity rolling steel
rails. Promptly he shipped the surplus stock to Pittsburgh,
and opened a store on Fifth Avenue, advertising the Wanamaker principles. Washington and Richmond stores came
next, and then branches in Middle Western cities. It was
a great field, and if he had followed it out Wanamaker
would have become the originator of the first chain store
system in America. The opportunity was within his grasp.

The door was closed, partly by circumstances and partly
by his own choice. The failure of Jay Cooke in September,
1873, precipitated a national panic, which started in Philadelphia. It made business men cautious. Wanamaker did
not want to invest heavily in stocks in other cities unless he
had the opportunity to study local conditions first hand. He
found, too, that it was impossible successfully to delegate
authority. Some of the men he sent out were fine and upright salesmen, who understood and believed in the Wanamaker principles. Others needed constant watching, not only
to make the business a success, but also to be sure that the
quality of the merchandise and the methods of selling it
were worthy of Oak Hall. This meant that the head of the
business would have to travel—and keep traveling. Wanamaker could not bring himself to give up Bethany. Nor
would he jeopardize the reputation of Oak Hall, which
was growing throughout the country. He went suddenly
to the Washington store one day, and on the next to Richmond. In neither place were things the way he wanted

them. This influenced him to give up the chain-store idea and to concentrate on forward progress in Philadelphia. He closed the branch stores, and he decided that Wanamaker & Brown, in their wholesaling, would give only commercial credits and not tie up capital by letting small stores have terms that amounted to the wholesale house becoming a silent partner in local business ventures.

Having arrived at this conclusion, Wanamaker began once more to try to get possession of adjoining Market Street properties for the expansion of the retail floors of Oak Hall. It must be remembered that in the 'seventies a store could grow only laterally. There were no basements. Elevators were primitive and slow-running; and most people were afraid to get into them. Customers did most of their shopping on the ground floor, and could not easily be induced to climb more than one flight of stairs.

But when the ambitious merchant figured out satisfying tenants and added to the cost of evacuating premises, the high prices demanded for freehold or long leases, he realized that the expenditure would be justified only if the clothing trade held up in the region of Oak Hall. Of this he was far from being convinced. The more he thought of it, the more he felt that it would be foolish to pay top prices for buildings on Market Street below Sixth. The country trade, especially that of New Jersey, seemed likely to continue indefinitely to be served there. But Philadelphia was growing westward. The choice of the square at the intersection of Market and Broad Streets for the new public buildings—at that time the most ambitious project of the time ever planned in the United States—led him to cast about for a new location in that region.

During his thirteen years in business he had consistently set aside a portion of his earnings for investment in his own building. He believed in this policy fully as much as in

investing in advertising. He reasoned that working for a
landlord was sheer folly for the business man. If the business prospered that very fact enhanced the value of the
property occupied by it. Why should a landlord have an
unearned increment? The policy of ownership of premises
was followed throughout Wanamaker's long life. Where
he could not purchase a freehold, as in the case of the land
for the New York store, he secured a leasehold whose
length made it virtually a purchase. When the opportunity
came, the same policy was followed in London and Paris as
in Philadelphia and New York. Wanamaker protected
himself from being penalized for his success. He took
care that all the increment in land values should accrue to
his own business.

On October 6, 1874, the Franklin Institute held a fair in
the freight depot of the Pennsylvania Railroad at Thirteenth and Market Streets. This unsightly group of buildings, a four-story office and sheds and tracks, with temporary
storage space ranged along the landing platforms, had been
abandoned by the railroad when the decision to put the new
city hall at the intersection of Broad and Market Streets
cut off the railroad's right of way. The interior of the sheds
was made over into booths to exhibit the progress of mechanics and engineering during the first half century of the
Institute. Wanamaker was deeply interested in inventions,
and he was just launching the movement to begin tangible
preparations for the Centennial Exhibition. He visited the
Franklin Institute Fair several times, and the idea came
to him that this might be the site for a new Oak Hall.[1]   If
he could get an entrance through to Chestnut Street, it might

[1] We find in a letter written by an old employee, on the occasion of the
Silver Anniversary in 1901, the following sentence, which indicates that
Wanamaker & Brown had an exhibit at the Franklin Institute Fair: "I well
remember the Fair held in 1874 in the old Freight Depot when you were
promised a space 12 x 20 feet for the Oak Hall exhibit, and it was cut down
to 12 X 10."

Old Pennsylvania Railroad Freight Depot

be possible to move both of his stores to this place. He went to see Thomas A. Scott, president of the Pennsylvania Railroad, and secured an option on the property for half a million dollars. It seemed too big for his purposes. But he felt that he would have no difficulty in subleasing what he did not need of it, and thus bring other lines of business into the new locality.

Before the purchase was concluded, Wanamaker took his family for their first trip abroad, going again on the *Scotia*. It was the last trip of the Cunard paddle-wheeler. Steamship building, too, was passing into a new era, when greater speed with less coal was being obtained by the use of propellers. Once more London was visited, and there were further talks with Williams. Whiteley had made great strides in four years. Paris was recovering from the Prussian defeat. In 1875, the Louvre, under Hériot & Chauchard, was doing an annual volume of business of forty million francs. Aristide Boucicaut had completed his great building on the Rue de Sèvres. The Bon Marché's business amounted to over sixty million francs a year, done entirely on the one-price principle and a cash basis, with a merchandise guaranty, and exchange of goods. Boucicaut had not, however, yet come to Wanamaker's "money back." The great Paris merchants ran what were still essentially dry-goods stores. But they did business on a mammoth scale; they knew how to display their goods; and in treatment of employees and customers, they were developing along the same lines as Wanamaker.

As far as the principles of merchandising went Wanamaker found little in his study of French retailing that he had not thought of. But he was impressed with the immensity of the business done in the Paris stores, and he was inspired by the way goods were displayed.

When he returned to Philadelphia in September his mind

was fully made up to take title to the freight-depot lot.   As to the next step, he kept an open mind.   One door after another closed.   But he was going to find the open one by thinking and trying.   All the while it is probable that influences of which he was not aware were working subconsciously to point the way.

MOODY AND SANKEY IN PHILADELPHIA—OUTSIDE THE BUILDING.—[From a Sketch by Theo. R. Davis.]

CHAPTER XVI

THE MOODY AND SANKEY REVIVAL

A BIT of cardboard, faded and very much worn, was one of John Wanamaker's most prized possessions. It was his usher's card at the Moody and Sankey meetings which were held in the Pennsylvania Railroad Freight Station from November 21, 1875, to January 21, 1876. No memory of his crowded life was more precious to the great merchant than this revival. No event had a more far-reaching effect upon his business and religious activities, always so closely interwoven. The great revival was held on his property, and the ushering was largely done by salesmen from Oak Hall, each of whom gave three evenings a week to this work.

Wanamaker had first heard Moody in the pulpit of an Albany church at a Y. M. C. A. convention eight years before. The man's fervor carried him away, but not so completely that he did not record his amazement at Moody's lack of grammar. He wrote home that "Dwight L. Moody murdered the King's English." It was an indication that when he was still in his twenties Wanamaker realized the importance of speaking and writing correctly. He himself had to struggle under the handicap of his own deficiencies in education. In preparing for Bethany and in writing advertisements he kept a dictionary at hand, and was constantly studying and practicing to acquire a good English style. He envied Lincoln's facility in English expression. Lincoln's model was his own, and if he did not achieve Lincoln's success from daily contact with the Bible, it was

133

not because he did not try. When Moody first visited Philadelphia in 1871 he was a guest in Wanamaker's home. By this time Wanamaker had come to agree with George H. Stuart, who said that he "cared little or nothing about Moody's grammar so long as he brought sinners to Christ."

Wanamaker had long been under the spell of Sankey's Gospel Hymns, many of which remained dear to him throughout his life. He told his Bethany scholars once that he would have given all his worldly wealth to have been present at Edinburgh the night that Ira D. Sankey, placing before him verses torn from a newspaper, improvised on the organ at a great meeting, singing the words as he played, "There were ninety-and-nine that safely lay."

Wanamaker was in Europe when a committee of Philadelphia business men, headed by Joshua L. Bailey, George H. Stuart, and Alexander Whilldin, decided to invite Moody and Sankey to conduct a revival in Philadelphia. Casting around for a place large enough to hold the meeting, they hit upon the freight depot of the Pennsylvania Railroad, which was not being used. The municipality had started to build a City Hall on the square at the intersection of Market and Broad Streets. Trains were no longer being run on Market Street from the Delaware, and the projected building cut off the railroad's access to Thirteenth and Market Streets from the Schuylkill. When they approached the Pennsylvania officials they discovered, to their astonishment, that John Wanamaker had an option on the property. They cabled him. He replied that he was soon leaving for home, and was heart and soul in any plans they decided upon. He arrived from Liverpool at the end of September, completed the purchase of the buildings and yards, and immediately turned the property over to the committee. Not only did he offer it rent free, but he took an active part in arranging the great shed for the meetings.

The tracks were taken up and a board floor put down. A great platform rising in tiers was erected at the end of the shed, and entrances were arranged on Market Street and Thirteenth Street. Stuart ordered all the chairs that the building could hold—8,900 for the main floor, and 1,300 for the platform.

"Add eight more to the order and we'll squeeze them in somehow," said Wanamaker.

"Why?" answered Stuart, puzzled over this request.

"Exact numbers always make a bigger impression than round numbers," was Wanamaker's reason. "If we tell the newspapers that we have 8,904 for the audience, and 1,304 for the speakers and choir, people will remember the figures."

Forty thousand dollars was raised, and a generous part of it went into advertising. The evangelists took no money for their own services. This was their invariable rule, and they did not believe in the collections for expenses that marred the closing days of later revivals. Sankey was John F. Keene's guest, and Moody was entertained for a second time in the Wanamaker home. All the expenses of the evangelists were met by these two men. A piano dealer, William G. Fischer, who, like Sankey, was writing hymns that were to live, gathered and drilled a volunteer choir of three hundred members, many of whom came from Bethany and were in Wanamaker's employ. Wanamaker used to attend rehearsals, and chose as the opening hymns "For you I am praying" and "I love to tell the story." [1]

Moody arrived some days before the opening, and gathered together some of the leading men of Philadelphia who had consented to be the workers in the aisles, watching for converts and leading them to the front. Several New

---

[1] Sankey had composed the music of the former and Fischer that of the latter. Wanamaker always knew how to compliment and encourage those who were working with him, when they had something of merit to contribute.

York business men, who had been helping Moody and Sankey in the Brooklyn revival just closed, came with him, and among these was Robert C. Ogden. He loved to tell a story on his future partner that we cannot refrain from repeating. One day Moody was exhorting the little group of about twenty-five, which included Jay Cooke and A. J. Drexel, the bankers; George W. Childs, who ran the *Public Ledger;* and others of prominence in the social and business life of the city. He told them that if they hoped to lead sinners to Christ, they must be ready themselves to meet their Maker. He called them by name asking each one, "Are you ready?" The tension was great. But it was broken when he said, "John Wanamaker, are you ready?" and the clothing merchant (whose advertisements at that time were instructing the public that they did not need to have their suits made to order) responded, "Yes, ready-made." [1] Wanamaker's sense of humor was sometimes irresistible, making him a delightful *enfant terrible.* It was a safety valve for pent-up emotions. At times of stress, he was gay, not tragic; and by not taking himself too seriously he forestalled getting wrought up.

Wanamaker could have his laugh at Moody. But he was none the less the devoted helper. He did not miss a service during the two months except on Sundays, when he conducted the young men's overflow meeting in the new Methodist church at Broad and Arch Streets, and then hurried to Bethany for the round of duties that were to occupy his Sunday hours for nearly fifty years longer.

The Moody and Sankey meetings were unique in the annals of Philadelphia. From the very first day there was a tremendous pressure for tickets, and rain or shine, for two months, week days and Sundays, crowds found their way to

---

[1] This story was communicated to us by P. W. Wilson, biographer of Robert C. Ogden.

John Wanamaker and Jay Cooke, the Eminent Philadelphia Banker and Financier of the Civil War

Thirteenth and Market Streets the like of which had never before been seen in the city. The street-car lines revised their schedules and put on extra cars to take care of the traffic. Straight through the Christmas holidays the audiences kept coming. It was distinctively a laymen's movement, in which virtually all men of note participated. So thoroughly stirred was the community that the judges of the Supreme Court attended in a body, and President Grant and most of his Cabinet came from Washington, as guests of George W. Childs, to hear Moody preach and Sankey sing.

From the newspapers of the day we learn that, once they were admitted to the building, the crowds were handled admirably. In the first place the floor rose gradually so that all could see the speaker and the choir. A wide vestibule ran around three sides of the building. The acoustics were so good that even those who were unable to get seats could hear from the corridor. In addition to the entrances on Thirteenth Street and Market Street, a wide thoroughfare had been put through from Juniper Street. Inside were four main aisles and four cross aisles. Wanamaker had speaking tubes installed so that the chief usher could direct his three hundred assistants. The auditorium was well heated, and was ventilated and lighted by skylights. At night a thousand gas burners, with reflectors in front of the platform, established a new era in lighting. Against emergency a telegraph wire ran to the central police station.

Revivals, like wars and panics, come in cycles, and have much the same features. Other evangelists, though not many, have shown the power of Moody on the platform. Other revivals, though not many, have been as carefully staged as the one in the Pennsylvania Railroad freight shed. But never before or after has there been so skillful a combination of exhorting and singing and bringing penitents into the fold as during the two months in Philadelphia at the end of 1875. The arrangement of the building was just right. Workers, stationed in the aisles, could lead inquirers quickly to the three large rooms at the back and on the sides of the auditorium. There laymen and ministers, and the specially trained assistants of the evangelists, were waiting to give individual attention to all who came. With emotions stirred by Moody's message and Sankey's rich pleading voice, almost everybody felt himself to be a sinner and wanted to turn over a new leaf. Of course they took the pencils and signed the cards that were put before them in the inquiry rooms. The cards, passed out to the platform, were held up in triumph. God's spirit was present! He had blessed the preaching! Hallelujah! Brother Sankey, have you a message?

Brother Sankey to the organ. And then with the lilt of a love ballad, came

"There were ninety-and-nine that safely lay
Within the Saviour's breast
But one was lost and far away. . . ."

The hundredth sheep couldn't stand it any longer. Narrowly looked for, if he showed signs that the song had got him, he was pounced upon and led out. Professor Fischer allowed the spell to last just long enough, and then waved to his choir. They stood attention while Sankey changed his ballad to a crooning prayer. The choir was ready for the chorus:

"For you I am praying,
For you I am praying,
I'm pray-ay-ing for you!"

It is human nature to revel in religion. Gospel hymns and crowds and eloquent preaching and being singled out by workers and repenting are an emotional experience that cannot be surpassed. Irresistible, too. Those who came to scoff did stay to pray. And because most of the workers were men of deep conviction and intelligence who worshiped God "not only with their lips, but in their lives," and because the pastors of churches co-operated wholeheartedly with the evangelists, the Moody and Sankey meetings did much permanent good. There are many ways of reaching people, and none that succeeds is to be held lightly. Moody's method of appealing to his audience, like his grammar, was not the important consideration.

Wanamaker's activity as a worker in the meetings and his keen enjoyment of the revival do not call for comment. His religious convictions were no deeper and no more openly displayed than those of Philadelphians far more prominent than he in the business and public life of the city in the early 'seventies. What singled him out from the others was the part he played in organizing and directing the revival, and the fact that the scene of the Moody and Sankey preaching and singing was to be Wanamaker's new store.

Attracted by the publicity given the revival and the fact that it was a big enough attraction for the President of the United States to come and see, visitors poured in from the surrounding country. Few who had not tickets were able to get inside, but their attention was inevitably drawn to the place where the meetings were being held. Every day the newspapers carried columns of what was going on at Thirteenth and Market Streets. Everybody in Philadelphia came to know that John Wanamaker owned the building, and that after the revival he intended to roof over the whole plot for a new kind of clothing store. Everybody came to identify, too, the young proprietor of Oak Hall and the store by the Continental Hotel with the superin-

tendent of a Sunday school that was having phenomenal
growth and in which new ideas were being tried out.

Moody's last sermon was preached on Sunday evening,
January 21. The next morning Wanamaker started to
carry out his plans for the Grand Depot, which was to be
ready when the Centennial Exposition opened.

The site of the venture had been criticized and ridiculed. What sane merchant would think of opening a
store on a large scale so far from the shopping center of
the city? If Wanamaker had any doubt on this score, it
was removed when he saw how easily the people found
their way to the Moody and Sankey meetings. Afterwards
it was charged that he had brought Moody and Sankey to
Philadelphia to advertise the location of his third venture
in merchandising. The facts do not bear out this accusation. We have seen that he selected the block by the new
City Hall before the revival committee was formed, and
that its members had picked the old freight depot while
he was in Europe and when they were still ignorant of his
intentions.

But the Moody and Sankey meetings had taught Philadelphians the way to Thirteenth and Market Streets.

CHAPTER XVII

THE GRAND DEPOT

THE Moody and Sankey revival contributed powerfully to advertise the opening of the Grand Depot, and to make Wanamaker better known to his fellow-Philadelphians. But it was neither by design nor by luck that it happened that way. The first opportunity that he had had of meeting leading business men was in connection with a revival. While still in his teens he distinguished himself by his zeal and energy in the revival of 1857. At that time he was simply a clerk in a Market Street clothing store, unknown and without capital or credit. He had not decided what he was going to be. The creation of a great business had not entered even into his dreams. It was as an ardent member of John Chambers' church, taught by his pastor that it was his duty to win souls to Christ, that he had participated in the revival. He frankly enjoyed it. He enjoyed the revival of 1875 still more. He continued to be a revival supporter throughout his life, sponsoring and working with Billy Sunday in his seventies as he had sponsored and worked with Dwight L. Moody in his thirties.

That Wanamaker planned to have his new store running when the Centennial opened was known to his friends, although, like all successful men, he did not tell other people what he was thinking about. The habit of secretiveness worried his family. They did not relish not being able to say anything definite when others asked them what John was scheming. "Why don't you tell us what you are going to do at Thirteenth and Market Streets?" said one of them during the revival meetings. "Too busy, and, anyway, I don't know," answered John. Only his wife knew that it was the truth, and not an excuse or explanation. Of course he would not have told had he known, but he was very much at sea, thinking hard every day about the immediate future. Wanamaker did not mind taking risks, and his faith in the new site was unbounded. But was it not possible to go after the bird in the bush without sacrificing those in the hand?

As he was helping Moody and Sankey, however, the thought must have come into his mind that he was shaving the time pretty close if the Grand Depot was to be opened and in smooth running order before the Centennial visitors began flocking to the city. The committee wondered whether they might not be imposing upon Wanamaker. They came to him after the first month. The meetings were going strong and would certainly be demanded through the holidays. After that, could he wait any longer to start upon his new store? "The Lord's work must not be hurried," was the laconic response. So the revival continued for three more weeks in January.

"A small army of workmen was ready to begin as soon as the last hymn was sung," Wanamaker afterwards said. But he himself was not ready. He had acquired the option fifteen months earlier, and had completed the purchase of the entire block from Thirteenth Street to Juniper Street, adjoining the new City Hall, two months before the revival started. The old freight depot ran back to Kelly Street. Between Kelly and Chestnut Streets was a row of houses, most of them still used as residences. Wanamaker needed one of these for an entrance through from Chestnut Street, but the purchase had not yet been completed. Upon whether the negotiations turned out successfully would depend the planning of the aisles in the new store.[1]

Wanamaker's first idea had been to move the two existing stores, and consolidate them on the new site. The lower Chestnut Street store, in its choice location, had a heavy overhead, and it proved impossible for him to expand his retail selling space at Sixth and Market Streets. Exorbitant prices were asked for adjoining properties. He could not utilize the upper floors of Oak Hall for retailing because at that time elevators were not in common use. He said to a reporter twelve years later:

"The idea came to me that it was the greatest situation for a large store, but I was perplexed and frightened at making such a purchase. I could afford it, but with our Pennsylvania caution it seemed like almost a reckless thing to do. What am I to do with my two other stores? I thought; and then it occurred to me that at my place at Chelten Hills I had once planted, after removal, a line of trees, and that two of them died because they were too old to transplant. I thought to myself that perhaps the business places I have are too old to transplant, and I let them stay and took up the new undertaking as a third operation. There began my establishment. The ground cost me upward of $500,000." [2]

It is certain, however, that even while the Moody and

[1] On March 11, 1901, Robert H. Hinckley, who was Wanamaker's lawyer in 1876, wrote a letter of congratulations on the twenty-fifth anniversary of the Grand Depot. He said:
"I well remember the urgency of getting title to the first Chestnut Street front, when Kelly Street ran along the southern line of the Depot property. It was material for you to have the title at a certain day, so that the aisles of the Grand Depot might be arranged; and I remember very well how glad I felt, when within the given time I was able to hand you the key to the property and finish the conveyancing."
[2] When he was figuring on the improvements of the Pennsylvania freight depot lot, on February 29, 1876, Wanamaker drew up a statement of the assets of Wanamaker & Brown. They amounted to $2,003,799.16. John F. Hillman's interest was very small—only a few thousand dollars.

Sankey meetings were in progress the merchant had not yet finally decided upon the practicability of three clothing stores. In preparation for the Centennial visitors he got out a booklet of which one million copies were printed. In this the stores were spoken of as one undertaking, and the first letterheads, as well as the great sign on the outside of the new store, gave the business at Thirteenth and Market Streets as Wanamaker & Brown. The term "Grand Depot" was considered an advertising slogan. Later in 1876 the name was changed to "Wanamaker's New Establishment."

In February, 1876, while the alterations on the freight depot site were in progress, Wanamaker thought that he might persuade other merchants to take a portion of the new location. These negotiations mostly fell through. This fact, and the difficulty about getting title to a Chestnut Street property, held up the final decision as to the new building and the arrangement of the floor space. Correspondence and notes in the private files indicate that Wanamaker's plans were in the experimental stage not only up to the time of the opening of the Grand Depot but for some months after that.

Undaunted by the failure to work out the ideas that had come to him as a result of his own change of plans, he adjusted with lightning rapidity the new undertaking to Centennial conditions. He felt that he would not need to worry about the additional business necessary to make a third store a financial success during its first summer and autumn. The hordes of visitors attracted by the Centennial would take care of that problem. He seized the opportunity to make his Grand Depot an annex to the exhibition in Fairmount Park. It would be a great advertisement for Oak Hall, and he would create a startling educational demonstration of his new principles of merchandising for the whole nation.

When we look at the stately building that covers the entire block from Chestnut to Market and from Thirteenth to Juniper, it is hard to realize that it is the result of thirty-five years of almost constant reconstruction. From the day the Grand Depot opened in 1876 until President Taft dedicated the new building in 1911, changes were being made while business went on, an improvement, a development, here and there, all the time. Wanamaker was always in a labyrinth, seeking a way to the center, and he had a lot of fun in doing it. The business was an adventure when he had millions fully as much as when his capital was less than two thousand dollars. That is why it grew. And that is why the great merchant in his apogee kept the open mind of the boy who founded Oak Hall.

Speaking of the Grand Depot at the Silver Anniversary in 1901, Wanamaker referred to it as an "old one-story shack." At another time he said that it was "no more than a glorified shed." Use was made, as far as possible, of the existing structures on the property. Only in one corner of the lot was excavating for the basement completed. The rest was simply boarded over. Wanamaker had learned a lot about temporary buildings and attractive façades in his work for the Centennial Exhibition. This knowledge he used in making the Grand Depot attractive without committing himself too far in permanent construction. The Kelly Street corners were used for tailoring and shipping. In the center came the entrance through from Chestnut Street. Three-quarters of the selling space was devoted to clothing and the other quarter to men's furnishings and hats. On every pillar were clover leaves, announcing the "four cardinal principles" of the Wanamaker policy. There were large windows on the Market Street side. From the roof flag poles arose, flying pennants.

We have mentioned R. S. Walton, the young hatter,

whose prayer-meeting talk in 1855 brought about Wanamaker's conversion. For nearly twenty years Walton had
been the friend and associate of Wanamaker at Bethany
when he was asked to open a hat store in the new establishment. He accepted the proposition, and his "Rookery," as
it was called, in the Market and Juniper corner, was opened
on April 10, 1876. Walton remained in association with
Wanamaker until his death, and endowed Bethany College.[1]
Wanamaker had secured the exclusive agency for the Lincoln Bennett hats, worn by the Prince of Wales, and they
were on display at the opening. As all Philadelphians know,
hats are still being sold in the same corner of Wanamaker's,
fifty years later. It is interesting to record that the first
"go off," as General Grant put it, was the purchase of a
hat, and that the first day's business amounted to $100. It
took several weeks longer to get the clothing stock in order,
and during that time 1321 Chestnut Street finally came into
Wanamaker's hands, and the entrance through to the new
store on the Kelly Street side was completed within a fortnight.

The Grand Depot was formally opened on May 6 of the
Centennial year, with two acres of aisles and tables and show
cases. An initial stock of half a million dollars, equaling
the value of the land, was announced, and Wanamaker was
able to advertise:

There is no store in the United States that covers so much ground floor
space as our single establishment at Thirteenth and Market, and such a
busy scene as it presents is well worth going a long distance to see. Some
of our employees are especially detailed to show visitors around who wish
only to look, not to buy.

The genius for display, always so marked in Wanamaker,
had its first full swing in the Grand Depot. There was

[1] Walton left $200,000 to this institution, which now bears Wanamaker's
name. See vol. ii, pp. 290-94.

elbow room, so much of it that the owner himself was a bit dismayed, though he never confessed it. With a stock consisting exclusively of articles for men's wear, and mostly clothing, it is difficult to imagine how the display was made impressive. But there is no doubt that Wanamaker captured the imagination of Philadelphians, and Centennial visitors as well. Everyone was thinking in terms of vistas and space and exhibits. People were out to see novelties. When we consider the limited character of the stock—male feathers are drab at the best—we cannot think that Wanamaker had a fair chance in the original Grand Depot to demonstrate his talent for display or that the building itself and its stock were sufficiently attractive to make the lasting impression that the Grand Depot, in its first year, certainly did make upon all who entered its doors. We do not rely upon later advertisements of the Wanamaker business, but upon numerous eye witnesses, to establish the fact that the Grand Depot was regarded by all who came to the Centennial as a side-show that they never forgot.

Only seven years later, Wanamaker wrote:

Perhaps you saw the store during the Centennial Year. To have seen it then was one thing; indeed, to have seen it any year since, is quite a different thing, but to see it now is quite a different thing still.

In the Centennial Year it was simply an overgrown clothing store, full of men's and boys' garments, and the workmen who cut and made the goods.

Now the clothing is relegated to its old quarters in the big clothing houses of Oak Hall, at Sixth and Market, and the large establishment adjoining the Continental Hotel on Chestnut Street, and here only a small section remains of what was seen at the Centennial time.

Then there was a single floor; now it is skirted with galleries on all sides, and since they have gone up to the third story, elevators have had to be put in to carry the people up.

Then there was no opening through to Chestnut Street, and now ten stores have been taken in the Chestnut Street end, so that the block from

Chestnut to Market and from Thirteenth to Juniper, or East Broad, is practically one property.[1]

It is hard for parents to bring back the pictures of their own children of a few years earlier. During the period of growth we accustom ourselves to the gradual changes. Nothing is more difficult, in fact, than to recall out of our own past the physical aspect of the places in which we live. The constant sight of things as they are virtually obliterates the past. Because there were no large stores in 1876, the Grand Depot, ungainly as it must have been with only men's clothing in it, was striking visually simply because it was something new. The spell of anything "big" is potent to Americans.

But there was more to the Grand Depot than what the eye saw. Undoubtedly the deep impression that it made was largely due to the new methods of business. In a few cities one price was not unknown, and money back already had its imitators. But to most Centennial visitors, who had not seen or paid attention to the advertisements of Oak Hall and a few other establishments in New York, Philadelphia, and Chicago, the "four cardinal principles" of the Wanamaker business on the clover leaves in the Grand Depot were a revelation. Seeing them carried out and practiced was more of a revelation still. Never before had they thought of merchandising as a service to customers. And never before had they been in a store that was manifestly a show place, where they could look around without being importuned to buy, and where they could feel as much at ease as if they were strolling down the street. It was a unique experience, too, to find a store in which there was a place to sit down and write letters. Of course they all sent

[1] In the *Philadelphia Store News*, September, 1883, page 4. The statement, "Then there was no opening through to Chestnut Street," must mean that the main aisle could not be extended straight through until after more than the one Chestnut Street property had been acquired.

home postcards, furnished free, with a picture of the Grand
Depot, one of the features of the Centennial. Along with
the guide books and pamphlets purchased or handed out to
them at Fairmount Park they put among their souvenirs of
the World's Fair the "Wanamaker Store Book," which
explained the new mercantile policies, and described the
magnitude of the Wanamaker clothing business.

From this "Store Book" we get an idea of the difficulties
of transportation in the Centennial year, and realize the
courage and vision of John Wanamaker in the Thirteenth
and Market Streets operation. A page is headed, "How to
get to this store." It shows that there were eight railroad
stations in Philadelphia in 1876, and that not one of them
was near the Grand Depot. Horse cars had to be taken
from all of them, and from some one had either to exchange to other lines or walk several blocks. The New
York and Belvidere divisions of the Pennsylvania Railroad
had their terminal at Thirty-second and Market Streets, a
long distance in those days, and some of the trains came
only as far as Kensington, a full hour and a quarter from
town. One had to cross the Schuylkill, too, to find the
stations for the South and West. The Reading lines came
to two terminals on Third and Ninth Streets, many blocks
north of Market Street. Now the two great terminals
serving all the lines entering Philadelphia are within a
stone's throw of Wanamaker's.

For the benefit of visitors the first Store Book published
also eight rules for the guidance of the employees of
Wanamaker & Brown, 650 of whom we are told were in
the Grand Depot. It is stated that John Wanamaker "employs only competent persons, at fixed salaries," that they
receive "no uncertain percentages," that "politeness must
be observed with all," and that "undue persuasion and

overtalking are prohibited." One of the curious rules is No. 6; "The use of paper to light gas is not allowed." A dining room was provided "with cooking apparatus for such use as may be desired."

During the 159 days of the Centennial Exhibition more than seven and a half million admissions, exclusive of the free list, were recorded. It is estimated that 800,000 of the visitors had never before been to Philadelphia. They came from all over the United States and Canada. How many of them found their way to the Grand Depot it is impossible to state. But we do know that the new store was always crowded, and did a volume of business that enabled Wanamaker to do far more advertising than he had planned and to come out handsomely on the venture. And his principles of merchandising and methods of running the store were so new to the vast majority of the visitors that he won the reputation of being the pioneer in the new era of retailing and advertising that was dawning throughout the country.

The significance of the Centennial Exhibition in the career of John Wanamaker, however, is not to be estimated by the success and fame of the Grand Depot. Had he not been a vigilant observer and a thinker, the summer of 1876 might easily have proved ruinous to him. It is dangerous for a man to accept the world's valuation of himself. Unless vanity has clouded our judgment we know our weak points and the glaring imperfections of our own work.

Once the Exhibition was over, with Oak Hall and the Chestnut Street store, each with its special field, and both on a solid foundation, Wanamaker knew that he would be competing only with himself if he insisted in carrying on at the Grand Depot a mammoth clothing store. Wisely looking forward to the lull in trade that would follow the

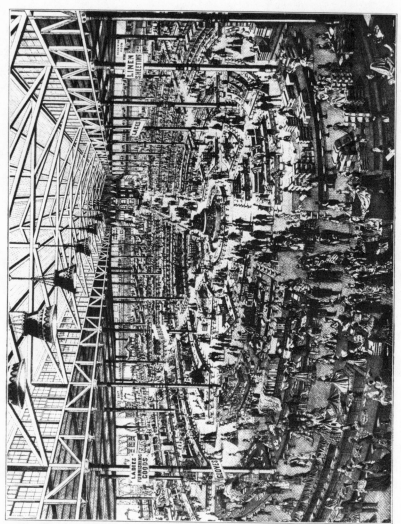

INTERIOR OF THE GRAND DEPOT

closing of the Exhibition, he tried hard to get other merchants interested in subletting space in the Grand Depot.
Right in the midst of the dazzling success of the summer
of 1876 he refused to be deceived, and knew that he had
to cast an anchor to the windward.

What was he to do?   To sell outright, or to lease independently, any part of the land would be interpreted as a
confession of failure.   The alternative was to acquire a solid
Chestnut Street frontage and establish under one roof and
general management a number of specialty shops, in which
men's and boys' clothing, hats, and haberdashery would
form units of moderate dimensions.

The time was ripe for such an undertaking.   He had seen
general stores in Paris and London.   The idea had come
into his mind several years before, but he had rejected it,
because he had thought that the future of merchandising
in America lay in combined wholesaling and retailing within
special lines.   The reasoning had seemed sound.   A. T.
Stewart had done this in New York, and Field, Leiter &
Co. were doing it in Chicago, in the dry-goods trade.   His
own success had been conspicuous in the clothing trade.   Up
to 1876 Wanamaker had been convinced that no American
city could hope to become the retail market that Paris and
London were.   These two capitals were the shopping centers for the whole of France and England.   But America
would always have the "magnificent distances" that made
a similar evolution impossible.

Here his open mind and his constant study of conditions
saved him.   Long before Grover Cleveland, he knew what
it was to have a condition, not a theory, confronting him.
The Grand Depot had opened in glory.   He owned the
land.   That it would soon become the heart of Philadelphia
he did not doubt.   Wanamaker did not have the foolish idea

that one should always control circumstances.   So he became
a general merchant.   What he had accomplished in 1876
was not the beginning of a new epoch, but the ending of an
old one.   The turning-point in the Wanamaker business
came in 1877.

Copyright 1906

The Grand Depot in 1902

CHAPTER XVIII

THE CENTENNIAL EXHIBITION

THE Sanitary Fair in Logan Square intrigued Wanamaker. He discovered how much he liked to get people together for a show, and it was his first lesson in combining selling with educational exhibits and amusements. Dr. Lowrie said that he was "like a child" at the Crystal Palace in London in 1871. It inspired him with the desire to build something similar in Philadelphia. The day after visiting the Crystal Palace he wrote to one of his sisters, "Why didn't I make this trip two years earlier when they had the World's Fair in Paris?" A big organ and a big crowd singing, exhibits of pictures and textiles and pottery, the latest inventions in machinery, cruising in a small boat on an artificial lake brilliantly lighted up, and razzle-dazzling in an amusement park thriller, made for him a perfect day. He could not go off with Henry M. Stanley to find Livingstone in Darkest Africa, but there was compensation in seeing the world's oddities and achievements and "the wealth of Ormus and of Ind" housed in stucco buildings surmounted with gay pennants, with a band playing outside.

We have seen how the revival in the old freight shed was the precursor of the Grand Depot, but his life-long interest in revivals proved that this activity in 1875 was no advertising scheme. Similarly, the great part he played in the Centennial Exhibition had in it no selfish thought, although it turned out to have a vital bearing on his business fortunes just as the Moody and Sankey meetings had done. The Centennial opened up the vision of "the new kind of store."

And yet, he had been working tirelessly for the Centennial long before he thought of Thirteenth and Market Streets and of what he might do there.

World's fairs were in the air, and he was one of the first in Philadelphia to hail the project of celebrating the one-hundredth anniversary of the signing of the Declaration of Independence by a monster show, to which the world would be invited. It was the first time that the United States would serve as host to other nations—and Wanamaker was a great fellow for "firsts." The idea appealed to his national and civic pride as well as to his liking for show. His family had been much too rigid and unworldly to indulge children in circuses; but he must have had Toby Tyler thoughts when Barnum was in the offing.

In the last New-Year's editorial he was to pen, on January 1, 1922, he said:

The writer trusts he will be forgiven if it be a fault to refer here to the enterprise and zeal of our city in 1876, when the population was less than 700,000, and it undertook to celebrate the Centennial and gathered the world in Fairmount Park, where the Memorial Hall and Horticultural Hall remain as permanent exhibits of the public spirit, pride and enterprise of its citizenship of that time.

He was the only surviving member of the Centennial Commission when he wrote those words, and he was looking forward with eagerness to the Philadelphia Sesquicentennial of 1926. How he must have been reviving the memories of the years of opposition and discouragement that preceded the earlier undertaking! There was the same opposition to meet, the same indifference to overcome, the same unwillingness to underwrite the proposition of 1922 that there had been fifty years earlier. Wanamaker's faith and persistence did much to save the Centennial. It was his first great service to his native city. Its place in his life is important not only because of the impetus the Centennial gave

MEMBERS OF CENTENNIAL EXPOSITION, BOARD OF FINANCE—1876

Top row (left to right)—John Baird, John Wanamaker and Thomas Cochran.

Second row, standing (left to right)—Nathan Parker Shortridge, Clement M. Biddle, Daniel M. Fox, Amos R. Little, Joseph Patterson and William Sellers.

Third row, sitting (left to right)—Thomas H. Dudley, John Welsh, John S. Barbour, Frederick Fraley, Henry Winsor and James N. Robb.

Fourth row, sitting (left to right)—John Price Wetherill and Edwin H. Fitler

to the development of the Wanamaker business, but also because it shows the man's grit and his devotion to Philadelphia.

The Exhibition was made a national undertaking by Congress. President Grant signed the bill on March 3, 1871, and appointed commissioners from all the states. They assembled in Philadelphia just a year and a day later —an impressive gathering representing twenty-four states, three territories, and the District of Columbia. There was much talk, and it was decided to choose a site offered in Fairmount Park overlooking the Schuylkill. But there were no funds. Discussion was lively as to who should give the money and how it should be raised. John Welsh declared that it was a national undertaking, under the sponsorship of the government, to commemorate a great national event, and that the Federal government and the states should provide the funds. In this contention he was ably seconded by John Wanamaker, who spoke for the first time before a representative national gathering that was not religious.

But others felt that the Exhibition was in its essence a commercial proposition, for the benefit of Philadelphia, and that Philadelphia should raise the funds. It had taken a year to get the Commission together, and then it was discovered that everybody was willing to say, "Let George do it." Had not a small group of Philadelphians been determined to go ahead, the project would have been abandoned there. Washington was appealed to, and a new Centennial Exhibition Act was passed, which the President signed on June 3, 1872. Under its provisions the Centennial Board of Finance was created a body corporate, with an authorized capital of ten million dollars, divided into shares of ten dollars each. To this stock the Secretary of the Treasury was directed to subscribe for the government $1,500,000.

The President visited Philadelphia on the Fourth of July, 1873, and was received at Independence Hall, together with his Cabinet and the Governors of several states, by the fifteen members of the Board of Finance. President Grant had appointed Philadelphians, and among the fifteen was John Wanamaker. The party rode to Fairmount Park to view the site, and then attended a banquet, at which many fine speeches were made. The work was yet to be done! The sum to be raised was stupendous; there was little interest or good will anywhere; and the financial panic came at an opportune moment for the opponents of the scheme to point out that the idea was foolish and ought to be abandoned.

The first crisis had to be met right at home. The Philadelphia Councils refused to appropriate $75,000, sorely needed for the organization of the subscription campaign. Representative women stepped into the breach, and the newspapers gave a hand. Petitions were circulated in every part of the city, and on the morning the ordinance was up for reconsideration wheelbarrows and carts loaded with petitions cluttered up the street in front of the Council Chamber. To this pressure the city fathers yielded. Later, under the influence of public sentiment, the city voted $500,000 for Memorial Hall and $1,000,000 for Machinery and Horticultural Halls, with the stipulation that these buildings were to be erected as permanent structures of Fairmount Park, and to be turned over to the city at the close of the Centennial. One million dollars was appropriated by the State of Pennsylvania. But the stock had yet to be sold, and a world's fair on a large scale could not be undertaken without millions of dollars collected from private individuals.

Shortly before his death Wanamaker was shown a photograph of the Centennial Board of Finance. Standing in the middle of the back row, he was the only young-looking man of the group. He had outlived them all. Pointing to John Welsh, seated in the center, he said:

"There is the one man who made the Centennial Exhibition a success. He never told us what to do, but what not to do. We would go to him downcast, but in his inimitable way he would iron out things. He made the exhibition. He seemed never, never to tire, and would greet us with a cheery smile that gave new hope and energy."[1]

Wanamaker refrained from mentioning his own vital part in the work, and did not say that Welsh got into the habit of referring the perplexing details—and questions of policy as well—to the enthusiastic youngest member. Other splendid men there were on the Board, names illustrious in Philadelphia history. But the young clothing merchant, who was thought to be sufficiently rewarded by the honor of being in such company, did most of the work. Just as the original high-sounding "Citizens' Centennial Finance Committee of Three Hundred," of November, 1872, had simmered down to fifteen in six months, so within another year—and two years before the Exhibition opened—the Board of Finance had an inside "finance committee" of three, of which John Wanamaker was the chairman. He was also the leading spirit in the "bureau of subscriptions" of five in 1874, and was chairman of the "bureau of revenue" and also of the "press committee" in 1875.

The papers in the private files give eloquent witness to the inside story of the Board's activities. Wanamaker directed the nation-wide press campaign; he wrote and saw to the printing of the stock certificates; he handled the subscription books; he solicited subscriptions personally and

[1] Wanamaker contributed to the fund raised to endow a chair of English at the University of Pennsylvania in memory of John Welsh's work for the Centennial Exhibition.

by letter; he devised schemes for awakening enthusiasm and raising money; he carried on the correspondence with individuals and officials in other cities and states; and we even find the plans and estimates for the buildings, and a lot of correspondence, addressed to him, up to the very opening of the Fair, by contractors and concessionaires. When we consider that during the same year he was enlarging Oak Hall and the Chestnut Street Store, establishing buying contacts abroad, putting the Philadelphia Y. M. C. A. on a sound basis and supervising its expansion, running the *Sunday School Times* and Bethany, founding a printing establishment, participating in the Moody and Sankey revival, and doing all the work for the opening of the Grand Depot simultaneously with the preparation for the Centennial, we realize his unlimited capacity for work. His was the genius of instantly mastering details, of making up his mind on the spot, of instinctive good judgment, and of getting recreation and fun out of keeping everlastingly at half a dozen things at the same time.

From the mass of papers we have picked out a striking illustration of his determined spirit and the magnitude of the difficulties ahead of the Board—the notes of a speech delivered before the Board in the spring of 1874. These notes are on the inside of a torn half sheet of paper, and are headed, "My duty—Jno. Wanamaker." They are simply the key thoughts of his paragraphs, but they present a graphic picture of his own activities and his conception of the work to be done.

Survey present situation. More than 12 months ago nearly one million raised. Board of Finance elected. Secured plans. Spread information. Canvassed our own state. Mass. R. I. Me. N. Y. N. J. Del. Md. Ga. Al. Cal. Mo. Ill. Iowa. Ind. Wis. Ore. Miss. Amount of labor needed—wrong impressions—must educate people. Whilst all this—not unmindful of universal character. Must get our own country before others.

Must begin work. This brings us to present hour—press and people clamoring for Board to make contracts. Called you together to say that there are about 700 working days—not an hour to lose. The need is for one million to start the buildings—needed now—no certain way of getting it quickly—the great mass of people have no conception. In other states we know that many of the commissioners have not acted. Also— citizens doubted. What was thought to be a gift, is not. We have done nobly but this shall not deter us from doing more than our whole duty.

To get the building started Wanamaker wrote out in his own hand petitions to be signed, pledges of contributions in cash, and offers of labor, the object being to get everyone in Philadelphia to volunteer two days of free labor "for the purpose of having the Centennial buildings commenced at once." He appealed especially for men with picks and shovels and with their own horses and wagons to go out to Fairmount Park and start to dig. The effect was great, and acted as a stimulus to raising money. Wanamaker headed the first Philadelphia subscription list with $17,500, and he got a number of $10,000, $5,000, $2,000, and $1,000 pledges. This original book is among his papers. Another book gives the smaller subscriptions—171 pages of them— which he also headed with $100. This is how the buildings were actually started—with over $1,000,000 in cash and free labor for excavation raised by Wanamaker himself. The three large permanent buildings, as we have seen, were voted by the city. With the government and the state appropriations the work began to be pushed. But it needed the personal effort that Wanamaker gave.

As chairman of the Finance Committee and of the Press Committee, Wanamaker tried for nation-wide subscriptions, and originated, through Peaslee & Co. of Boston, a form of high-pressure collection of small sums in New England and New York which was the forerunner of the contemporary "drive." Asked by Peaslee if the Board would countenance "lady collectors," Wanamaker responded, "Why not?" Other states, too, were canvassed for stock subscriptions by professionals. But Wanamaker drew up the rules for canvassers, and gave them hints as to their "selling talk."

When the Exhibition opened, Wanamaker's work was done. The Centennial was a success. People came from all over the United States in larger number than had been attracted to one city in the history of the nation. Others managed the first American world's fair and got the credit for it. Wanamaker, busy and happy in his Grand Depot, effaced himself from the picture. He had had his day when the prospect was uncertain. The joy of the venture was in its making. But he used with decisive effect his influence in the inner circle to keep the gates rigorously closed on Sundays, despite powerful pressure.

John Welsh did not overlook giving public recognition to what his lieutenant had done. He appointed John Wanamaker chairman of the celebration at Independence Hall. On July 4, 1876, on the spot where the Declaration of Independence had been signed one hundred years earlier, a young clothing merchant introduced the distinguished speakers. It was a great moment for him when he stood in the place of honor in his own city before people gathered from all over the world. Only fifteen years had passed since the "country boy," somewhere in the crowd, had heard Abraham Lincoln speak on that same spot on the eve of the Civil War.

CHAPTER XIX

THE NEW KIND OF STORE

AFTER the Centennial Exhibition closed, John Wanamaker began making preparations to develop the
space that seemed so vast for a clothing store into a merchandising enterprise which could utilize it.   In its first
form, his conception of "the new kind of store," as he called
it, was to bring into close association a group of merchants,
each a specialist in his line to conduct separate shops under
one roof and one management.   The purpose of the association was a double one: to decrease overhead by a common use
of one establishment, pooling the expenses of organization
and advertising; and to operate the business in which they
were associated along the lines of the merchandising principles and policies that Wanamaker had originated and developed at Oak Hall.

The idea was a brilliant one, and had his invitation been
accepted by the outstanding merchants he wanted to get
in dry-goods and house-furnishing lines, there might have
been a different development of retail merchandising from
that which our generation has known.   Speculation as to
what might have happened is hardly worth while, however,
because it did not happen, and Wanamaker himself was
quick to recognize that the type of merchant whom he
wanted to go along with him could not be persuaded to do
it.   Strong and gifted men, who had the vision to see what
the Wanamaker merchandising policies and advertising were
leading to, decided to try them out for themselves.   They
were not attracted by the limited share of the profits or the

limited glory that co-operation with a dominant merchant like Wanamaker would mean. Men of rare ability and experience in merchandising he could and did get, and they helped materially to make Wanamaker's what it is. But to Wanamaker they left the responsibility, the risks, the leadership. Philadelphia retailers of commanding personality stuck to their specialty shops under their own name or developed general stores themselves.

When Wanamaker discovered that others were not willing to go in with him, he was disappointed but not dismayed. Oak Hall and the Chestnut Street store were doing splendidly. He had built up an efficient and devoted personnel. Behind him were fifteen years of successful development in store management and in knowledge of advertising, and he had learned that his name was now well enough and favorably enough known to make possible putting out commercial paper on a large scale. He had his own printing establishment. Most important of all, he had faith in the new principles and methods of merchandising for which he had been valiantly contending. Might it not, after all, be easier for him to extend their application to other lines of retailing by being in sole control than by enlisting the co-operation of other merchants? He did not know the French motto, *qui se fait payer se fait commander,* but the truth expressed in it had not escaped him. The fight to place retail business upon a basis of square dealing had not yet been won. It was better that there be only subordinates in the new venture.

We have given the reasons that held Wanamaker back from entering the new department-store field. He was wrong in assuming that the success of the Paris general stores, and of those that were beginning to spring up on a much smaller scale in London, might be attributed to the fact that those cities were marts for whole nations, which

American cities could not become. We see now that because of changing conditions the rise and development of this form of retail merchandising was inevitable. But no man at the end of 1876 could have foreseen the revolutionary changes brought about by electricity in illumination, ventilation, and power; the new economic conditions created by intensive manufacturing and rapid growth of cities; and the effect upon the mercantile world of the universal adoption of Wanamaker's own policies. These all came with a rush during the years immediately following 1876. In one sense John Wanamaker was the child of fortune both as to his choice of the career of a general merchant and the hour of making it; but we must not forget that his own efforts of fifteen years had contributed powerfully to pave the way for what followed.

When Wanamaker, with a great plot of land on his hands, decided to become a general merchant, a one-story building, with galleries, not extending far back, was the only feasible structure for retail selling. Light had to come from above, as the central part of the building was too far from the windows. Gas was dangerous, with so much inflammable material around, and if used too extensively it made the air bad. Judging colors by gas was difficult. A basement floor was impracticable, with gas for illumination, because it could not be ventilated. The fire risk also was enormous. Upper selling floors in a large building would cut off the light entirely from part of the ground floor, and women dislike climbing stairs.

These facts may be obvious, but it is necessary to emphasize them in order to show how essential to the growth of department stores electricity has been. Incandescent lighting, invented by Edison and used by Wanamaker the same year; electrical suction apparatus for ventilation; and elevators—all made commercially workable during the first five years of the Grand Depot—were the prerequisites of the great retail store. The first electric railway of full size was constructed in 1879. It is electricity that has made possible the maintenance of a concentrated shopping district as cities have grown.[1] So vital have been the exploitations of these inventions that we can safely say that the great stores of our day could never have developed without them. It might be added that the ability to reach the buying public every morning through newspapers, from both the manufacturing and the distribution viewpoints, is due to electricity. Big retail business is a child of the electrical era.

Intensive manufacturing is another indispensable factor of the success of department stores. It has enabled them to procure uninterruptedly the great stocks that their volume of business requires; and it has brought into urban centers an ever-increasing population, thus creating the clientele for the stores. During the half-century since the Grand Depot was founded no American city has experienced the benefit of this circle (which is by no means vicious) more than Philadelphia, and the stores to which Philadelphia's workers go have always been able to supply their needs largely from the produce of their own work.[2]

The relation between good will and advertising, which makes advertising an investment, we have already discussed. That this powerful factor in the development of general stores was a unique contribution of John Wanamaker none will question. When his advertising became educational,

[1] Without the trolley, superseding the horse car, and followed and supplemented by the subways and tubes under rivers, department stores could not have benefited by the enormous growth of cities.

[2] During the dull times of 1894, Wanamaker advertised: "We have put our organization at the disposal of Philadelphia manufacturers to distribute Philadelphia-made goods of the grades we sell, whenever we can get back their cost." This offer was of course immediately matched by the other great stores of the city. The stimulation of trade that followed showed the extent of home consumption of home production, and was a revelation in the variety of Philadelphia manufacturing.

and was pressed in the interest of his mercantile policies, he was unconsciously laying the foundations upon which the general stores rest. The customer's confidence and interest were built up. It paid to advertise because honest goods were offered at an honest price, the same for everybody. The store's good faith was proved by its willingness to take back the purchase and refund the money. The salesman had no incentive to overtalk his goods or indulge in sharp practices. Then, too, without the one-price rule rigidly adhered to, it would have been impossible to have run a general store successfully, with great diversity of merchandise and a large and necessarily changing sales force. Only in the specialty shop, where the seller knows the minimum and maximum prices and has acquired the art of being at the selling end of bargaining, is the policy of "the best price you can get" practicable. Until the general public became trained to buy at sight on faith and for a fixed price, it can readily be seen that there would be chaos and the risk of heavy losses in general storekeeping as we understand that term in our generation.

Wanamaker did not foresee, because he could not have foreseen, the unlimited future ahead of the general store in American cities, but his instinctive fear that great establishments, doing a varied business, would have difficulty in keeping up in all lines of merchandise a uniformly high standard, was well founded. Because his business experience of fifteen years had had to do with men's wear exclusively, he realized the danger more clearly than other merchants of his time whose general stores evolved from the varied business of dry-goods and notions and women's wear. He had bought haberdashery for Tower Hall. He had been his own buyer at home and abroad for Oak Hall and the Chestnut Street store. He had studied styles as well as materials, and had become a potent influence in taste in clothes in Philadelphia. Could he hope to extend his field to women's wear and house furnishings and still keep the name of Wanamaker a guaranty for the quality and a guide for the style of everything offered for sale in a vast emporium with diversified stock?

This was his problem. It was the cause of his reluctance to engage in general storekeeping. The man's boldness in financing—a boldness that verged on recklessness—and his unbounded faith in the drawing power of advertising and of catering to customers make it difficult to believe that the principal motive of his plan to get other merchants to cooperate with him was to have others share in the capital outlay and the risks of stocking the Grand Depot. Was it not rather his respect for the knowledge and experience requisite to honest and judicious buying? One man might be a great financier and organizer and advertiser, and be endowed with the genius for display and the insight into the customer's point of view. But could one man be a master buyer in many lines, unerring in his knowledge of the goods and a profound student of style and taste and the demand of the public for all sorts of things?

Because he was a great merchant, ready to risk everything on his own judgment when he knew he was on solid ground, and at the same time recognizing his own limitations, Wanamaker determined to go into general storekeeping with his original conception unmodified in so far as it looked forward to gathering distinctive specialty shops under one roof, with a common administrative organization, but with the buying in charge of highly trained specialists each of whom had proved his worth in the particular line he had to do with. He had no intention of creating a department store. The name was always abhorrent to him. He never used it, and throughout his life he stoutly maintained what he announced at the beginning of the experiment, that Wanamaker's was "a new kind of store"—new not only in the cardinal points of merchandising policy upon which it was founded, but new also in the conception of offering shoppers the convenience of making their purchases in specialty stores, grouped in one establishment.

Initiating this policy and maintaining it throughout his life made him at times seem churlish and lacking in the spirit of *camaraderie* in what came to be considered a new classification of retail merchandising.[1] It led him occasionally in his advertising into what competitors believed to be hair-splitting, if not extravagant, claims. It brought down upon his head the condemnation of merchants who stuck to their special lines, and did not win him the friendship of most of those who went along with him into the wider field or who followed and imitated him. On the other hand, the results amply prove that there was nothing quixotic about the conception, and there can be no doubt that it became—and remained until his death—the greatest single factor in establishing the success of the general stores of to-day.

Alexander T. Stewart and Rowland H. Macy died at the moment of the radical transformation of retail merchandising, and the dry-goods stores they founded passed into other hands, Wanamaker himself finally becoming the successor of Stewart in New York.

[1] When asked to serve on the Department and Chain Stores Committee for the Third Liberty Loan by Governor Passmore of the Federal Reserve Bank, Wanamaker replied on September 19, 1918:

I appreciate your desire to make me Chairman of the Department and Chain Stores Committee, but I would feel myself out of place, for the reason that the A. T. Stewart store in New York and the Marshall Field store in Chicago were never classed as department stores, and the Wanamaker store is no more a department store than the Tiffany or the Bailey, Banks & Biddle stores, with their numerous sections. But beyond this fact, I think perhaps I can be of better service in working in the same way I have done for the three previous loans.

When the new store buildings were going up in Philadelphia and New York, it is evident from documents in the files that Wanamaker thought for a time of calling his business "The Wanamaker Composite Stores." He never used the term "department store," and was consistent throughout his career in believing that and asserting that he was not in the department-store business.

Marshall Field divided his time and talents between the wholesale and retail business, and he always had partners. Virtually all the department stores of Paris, London, New York, Philadelphia, Chicago, Boston, and other cities became stock companies or went to the public for capital with huge bond issues. For nearly half a century John Wanamaker personally directed the enterprise that he had founded and owned, imposing upon himself a life-long sentence of hard labor as a first-hand student of merchandising materials and policies and of the psychology of advertising and the buying public. This is the significance of "the new kind of store."

When he had squarely before him the two facts, that he must enter the dry-goods business in order to make a success of the Grand Depot, and that he could not hope to get other merchants, masters in their lines, to associate with him in the new enterprise, Wanamaker looked for men who had been in business for themselves, but who had failed to prosper for reasons other than a lack of knowledge of materials and markets. Retail selling is a risky venture at the best, and the ablest merchants frequently fail or do not go ahead. They may not be good financiers or organizers, or they may have played into ill luck. Or, as is the case with most people (witness the success of our great corporations), the best qualities are called forth in association with others and under the direction of a master mind. For each line that he proposed to carry John Wanamaker found men who could be depended upon to buy only goods worthy of the Wana-

maker guaranty and to keep their stocks up to a high standard in quantity, quality, and variety of styles. To these
department heads he first gave the name of section chief,
when speaking of them in the store, but to the public they
were "merchants," and later the term "buyer" became the
usage. As the business developed, most of them—their
number was being added to each year—found a larger and
more lucrative field at Wanamaker's than when they had
been in business for themselves.

After the Centennial Exhibition closed, and while Wanamaker was quietly studying conditions and seeking his buyers, a beginning was made of catering to women. Women's
and misses' shoes were advertised, and a few weeks later
rubber coats.[1] These were the only innovations up to the
opening of "the new kind of store," which was first announced by a double-column advertisement in the Philadelphia papers on March 3, 1877. On Monday, March 12,
"the new kind of store" was launched. This date, and not
that of the opening of the Grand Depot in 1876, marks the
new departure, and is the turning-point in the merchant's
career.

Before the opening, Wanamaker gathered his staff of
nearly a thousand around him, and talked to them in his
homely fashion. He asked them to look at the design of
the store, aisles, and circles, each one larger, until the outer
one touched the four great entrances, and eight vertical
aisles, leading from the center, and cutting through the five

[1] Mr. Isaac D. Shearer, who went from Oak Hall to the Chestnut Street
store in 1869, and who later became a partner in the business when John
Wanamaker retired from the active management of John Wanamaker & Co.,
says that Wanamaker's first experience in women's wear was at the lower
Chestnut Street store about 1870. He opened a department for women's
riding habits to measure, and offered the first imported women's sports clothing
ever sold in this country (to Mr. Shearer's knowledge). Despite attractive
stocks and salesrooms, the department did not take on well because women had
not yet become accustomed to shop where men did. In 1870 a bit of the
harem idea seemed still to be found in the United States.

circles. "It is a wheel," he said, "and each of you is a spoke. I am the motive power, and I shall see that the wheel keeps moving. But you must each be in your place at all times, and do your duty, or I can accomplish nothing. But if we all do our part, this wheel will keep on revolving, and it will become the largest and best of its kind in the world." Throughout that first day Wanamaker remained on the floor, making the rounds of the departments, and studying the wheel which he had put in motion. Taking a trick from the World's Fair, he had doormen to count those who entered. On that first day seventy thousand people came to see "the new kind of store." [1] It was claimed to be a "world's record."

We can give no better description of the Grand Depot of 1877 than to quote what George W. Childs wrote in the *Public Ledger:*

Mr. John Wanamaker has converted his immense establishment at Thirteenth and Market Streets into a retail dry goods store, and will open it for business today. The interior has been remodeled to accommodate the new trade, and is very attractive and convenient. In the center of the building is a circular counter, ninety feet in circumference, which is devoted to the sale of silks.

In the space enclosed by this circle is an elegantly carpeted 'dark room,' lighted only by gas, to be used for showing silks for evening dresses. Radiating from the central counter are aisles 196 feet in length. These are intersected by other aisles running between the concentric circles of the counters, on which are exhibited all sorts of articles that go to make up a large and complete stock of dry goods.

There are thirty-three blocks of counters, numbering 129 in all, and aggregating two-thirds of a mile in length, and in front of which are 1400 stools for the convenience of shoppers. There are elegantly fitted rooms for such goods as ladies' finished suits, and other departments,

---

[1] "Seventy thousand one hundred and six visited the establishment yesterday. The building was so jammed at one time that Mr. Wanamaker seriously contemplated closing the doors and allowing only a limited number in at one time. There were 654 employees in the building yesterday, and only by the most assiduous industry were they able to wait on all the customers."

besides parlors, retiring rooms, etc., for the comfort of customers. The store, No. 1313 Chestnut street, has been purchased by Mr. Wanamaker and entirely demolished in order to make room for a beautiful arcade, leading from Chestnut street into his great store. The entrance is handsomely ornamented, and the arcade is tiled with marble and lighted by day by means of stained glass skylights, and by night by elaborate chandeliers.

The one thing that might have proved fatal then, or later, to a store covering two acres of floor space, and visited by a mob of people, many of whom were simply sightseers, would have been undue delay in getting waited on, and, once the purchase was made, in completing the transaction. After half a century is not this still the partially unsolved problem of our mammoth stores? Wanamaker studied it all his life, bringing his fertile imagination constantly to bear upon how to speed up a sale without mistakes at the cashier's desk and in the delivery department. His first sale slip is worth examining. The date of the purchase was rubber stamped. The amount, and the numbers of the package clerk and salesman, were entered on it. The customer was told to "keep this." While he was waiting for his package, he had time to study "our compass" in the corner, whose "cardinal points" were: one price, full guaranty, cash payment, and cash returned. At the bottom was the statement:

Determined that Philadelphia shall have not only the largest but best of business houses in the world, we ask each of our customers to aid us by promptly reporting, for correction, any mistakes of our Salespeople, Clerks or Porters. Every person who approves the system under which we do business, as set forth in the "Guarantee" (see other side), will please recommend the House. The more goods sold, the Lower the Prices. John Wanamaker. Dry Goods, Clothing, Hats and Caps, Boots and Shoes, etc.

When the store was in its second week, five columns were taken in the newspapers to advertising the "floor plan of the Wanamaker Dry Goods Emporium, covering the entire block on Market, Thirteenth, off Broad, and through to Chestnut Street." The diagram indicates that when "the new kind of a store" started, it carried dry-goods and notions "and all things for the ready-dress needs of the people." There was a counter for toilet articles, and a department in three sections for table linens, bedding, and "upholstering goods." At the entrance at the end of the Chestnut Street arcade was a reading room, and, at the right, ladies' dressing rooms. These were distinct innovations. Very soon were added women's coats; trunks and leather goods; hosiery; and gloves. Three months after the opening there were sixteen departments designated by letters from A to P, and in the autumn of 1877 we find that the number of salesmen and clerks had been increased to 1,250.

Thirty years later, on the anniversary of the opening of his general store, Wanamaker said:

"There are none who can say that there ever was in this or any other city a store like the one we established on the twelfth day of March, 1877.

"There seems to be an electric wire running through the years to where I stand that gives to me a sensation of mental and bodily vigor. I can see a white lantern swinging before me. The broad principle underlying the foundation of this New Kind of Store has become the American system of Commercial Life applicable to all business as well as that of retailing. It is a system that recognizes and stands for the rights of buyers not waived by the payment and delivery of the article purchased.

"And further, it grants a title to all employees to fair wages and an adjustment at regular intervals upon value of work done. Further, still, it insures education and practice to enable the earnest and diligent to rise in their positions."

Wanamaker was looking back over a generation of

achievement. He did not know that within a few months, as we shall see later, he was to pass through the dangerous days of the financial crisis of the autumn of 1907. But he must have had in mind, although he did not mention it, the great battle he fought during the first year of "the new kind of store." It was an experiment of faith, just as Oak Hall had been, undertaken against the advice of friends; and their voices were no more silent than those of his enemies when he was passing through deep waters. It would be giving a false impression to picture Wanamaker going from one success to another, all bright sunshine. Only fiction is like that. There were shadows in the picture. Wanamaker was no wizard, no Ali Baba provided with an open sesame. For great men and successful men, just as for lesser mortals, there is the arduous traveling along a precipitous route where a misstep may prove fatal.

During the initial year of "the new kind of store," if we had only advertising and reminiscences to go by, we might be deceived into thinking that whatever Wanamaker undertook turned to gold just because he touched it. But the private files tell a different story—a story of dark days boldly faced, a story of pluck and endurance. Wanamaker succeeded because he knew how to stand the gaff. Without the aid that he had first counted upon, as we have explained, he plunged into a new enterprise. The pack tried to howl him down, as they had done before, and at the beginning of the first autumn of his general storekeeping the merchant was expected to fail. The rumors reached his old friend, Samuel T. Lowrie, then a professor in the Western Theological Seminary at Pittsburgh, who wrote to him on October 13, 1877:

I have been wanting very much to write to you ever since I came home. . . . The trouble is to know what to write. My desire to write arises solely from my concern about you in the trials that now encompass your business life. Of course, I know nothing exactly about them. But from what all are saying, I can only apprehend that they are very great, and that even your whole fortune may be imperiled.

You are much spoken against, and in addition to the common risks of business at this time, you have to contend against verbal, perhaps actual, conspiracy to ruin you financially. Almost everything I know about your difficulties comes from yourself, either directly or through Mrs. Lowrie. How my heart aches at the thought of what a trial this experience must be to you, and I suffer with you every day.

If your present venture in the Grand Depot should fail, it will have this advantage, that you will be free to lay hold on all the consolations that are so rich to God's children in times of trial and defeat. One of the precious consolations is that you may rely on God himself to make evident in due time the purity of your motives, and the simplicity and guiltlessness of your life.

If the combination referred to has actually brought your business to a condition that places your whole fortune in risk, I can easily sympathize with the keenness of your regrets. I say regrets, because you will already have been brought where it was your purpose not to be. I have known your aim has been to put your business on a solid foundation and to conduct it with the guarantee of safe continuance that might challenge comparison with any other business in the world. I believed that you had attained that position with full assurance years ago. Of course, you have meant to maintain the happy eminence you reached at Oak Hall. The many fortunes that have become involved in yours all call upon you to do this, and no one would feel the call more than you.

If then your present situation is that of actual risk and possible loss of all, I know that you already suffer a sense of loss far greater than most men would feel at the actual disaster of fortune and business all in ruins, no matter if in the end you come out successful or not. . . . But I cannot contemplate the likelihood of disaster in your business; for besides having got to believe in you, I am still more used to expecting God's blessing upon your business and that He will use you and it to bless men, and to show how good it is to trust in Him. But it is quite consistent with both of these latter convictions to fear that you may have come to a situation where all you have may be in peril. . . .

If you are tempted to think that men and even friends are turning their backs on you, do not yield to it. Do not even interpret the silence of friends in that way. If you knew with how much shrinking I write this letter in spite of my repeated promptings to write it, you would not do so, for I am strangely withheld from it by the thought that you may think what I am saying quite superfluous. It will be a holiday with me when I know that your ship has weathered this storm, and, with all on board, is sailing in an even sea, under a serene sky, like the old Scotia when fairly past the Banks and the icebergs.

A letter like this must have been a great comfort, even though it was not needed. In moments of crisis, when rumors fly thick and fast, the "silence of friends," as Dr. Lowrie put it, is difficult to gauge. Friends are between Scylla and Charybdis. If they say anything, they may be seeming to doubt; if they refrain from speaking, silence may be interpreted as indifference.

On Wanamaker's side, the correspondence reveals the difficulties he was facing, but at the same time shows that his faith in his star did not waver. Three letters of this period, written to William Libbey, of A. T. Stewart and Co., show that Wanamaker was not disheartened. But they give a vivid picture of the situation in his own words. On September 3, 1877, he wrote from "Wanamaker's New Establishment":

Thank you from the bottom of my heart for proving to me that there was one man in New York who believed in me. Though I am brave as a lion and strong as a mule and just as tough, yet I can pull better and stand up longer if I can hear one manly man give a cheer.

Your letter set me up for a week at least and came when I needed it most. This village has been like a heated furnace for a week past and New York must have caught the blaze. But I believe the thing has burnt itself out. The open boast is made and has been made here (by Dry Goods people that you know) for weeks past that they would spend fabulous sums "to run John Wanamaker out" and every lie that could be concocted has gone the rounds thoroughly.

I have my coat off and am at it night and day—my confidence in the Grand Depot to distribute 5 millions is unshaken and as you have so grandly stood by me, when I fail to stick by you my name will no longer be

Yours gratefully

JNO WANAMAKER.

The very next day he wrote to Libbey:

The enclosed is to prove that the howl is not over. It was sent me this morning from New York by a party to whom it was sent from here and I learned from other sources that a large number of these advertisements were sent to the Importers and large houses of your city.

A gentleman here who took pains quietly to trace up who owned electric pens in this city (with which the writing was done) fastens the infamous thing pretty close upon ——————. There is, as you see, the most determined effort to cripple me and prevent me getting goods.

McCreery sent the few goods Hafleigh selected "as novelties."

Jaffray hung fire and Arnold Constable's came along.

Full of hope and determination to win with God's blessing.

Yours as ever

JNO WANAMAKER.

His courage is strikingly revealed, just a fortnight before the Lowrie letter, when a late warm spell retarded the fall sales, just when he needed money to meet his bills. On October 1, he told Libbey:

As one warm day after another has slipped away and my receipts have disappointed me and the remittances that I promised myself to make to you had to be withheld I felt I ought to write you to be patient for a few days longer.

The fact is I have paid off nearly all that I owe to others that is overdue and when I get a few goods out of the Customs House that I was foolish enough to have bought abroad I shall have little to do but to pay you. I know I can pay all the money I owe you but I never expect to get out of debt to you what I owe you for kindnesses which I hope soon to talk over with you.

I am glad to fling into some people's faces that you and your house are the exception in dunning me for payments. I mean to have it remain so by pouring money in to you soon.

Rumors of a crash not only passed from mouth to mouth during the summer of 1877, but they got into the type of newspaper that used to exist a generation ago but which has long passed into history. The newspapers that lived by scandal and blackmail Wanamaker never advertised in. This was their opportunity. The new enterprise was at first ridiculed, and when financial circles began to speak of Wanamaker's difficulties several Philadelphia papers, which have long since disappeared, so their names have no interest to us, made the most of the critical situation. In one of these, on August 31, 1877, we find:

There's trouble in the big Market Street Wigwam. Protests, extensions, unpaid employes, etc., etc. Not long ago, we predicted that somebody would soon meet the fate of the overambitious frog in the fable, which tried and tried to swell itself up to the size of an ox, and busted itself. Somebody has been trying to swell himself up to the mercantile dimensions of the late A. T. Stewart, and an explosion is imminent. " 'Twas ever thus!" But, there has been something more than foolish ambition and imprudence in this case. There has been a greedy, grasping and godless spirit at work in the mind of somebody, prompting him to break down other business and absorb almost every branch of mercantile business in his own establishment. Herein crops out, in a very offensive form, the ambition to imitate A. T. Stewart, who was one of the meanest men and merchants that ever lived. He squelched hundreds of smaller dealers without compunction and ground his employes into the very dust of humiliation and impecuniosity; and his ambitious Philadelphia prototype on a smaller scale, has been trying to play the same heartless game. But, this Philadelphia merchant has had to cope with some very solid business men, and he has found that he has been butting his poor head against some very stubborn stone walls. He's in danger. He is walking on the thin crust of a volcano which threatens to blow him and his wigwam sky-high, scattering hats and haberdashery, shoes and chemisettes, collars and cuffs, trunks and teapots, lawns and lines, boots and broadcloth, furs and flannels to the four winds.

The ill will and active hostility of Philadelphia merchants had been incurred for two reasons: The first was the fear that the general store would prove to be an octopus, stretching out its tentacles in all directions and strangling the small shopkeepers, who could not meet the competitive prices, the advantages and attractions, and the advertising offensive, of large establishments. Retail merchandising had always been carried on by specialty shops. Men with ideas like Wanamaker's were a subversive influence, menacing the existing structure of the business world. The second was that the Wanamaker policy, begun in the "Opportunity Sale" of April, 1877, and followed by "Partial Inventory," "Midsummer" and "Early Fall" sales in the first six months of "the new kind of store," of clearing at a sacrifice existing stocks that had not moved quickly, made a radical change in the existing methods of retailing to which specialty shops found difficulty in adjusting themselves. This had already happened in Paris, and it was upsetting the business world in New York and Chicago as well as in Philadelphia.

Seeking a personal devil whom they might blame for their own failure to read the trend of the times, the small merchants concentrated their animus on Wanamaker. They could not see that he was not personally responsible for the changed conditions in merchandising. What happened in Philadelphia was happening in all large cities. Wanamaker was simply the interpreter of the spirit of the age. His genius and industry and faith were enabling him to meet the new conditions that had arisen. He was leading in the way that all merchants would have to follow, willy-nilly, if they were to continue to be successful in retailing. The day had gone when styles of men's and women's wear, and of house furnishings, and when the quality of goods offered to the public, were to be regulated by the conditions of existing stocks. In the new competition no merchant, overloaded with certain goods, could any longer sell them as fresh and of the latest style. Merchants would have to study the markets and the styles, and take their losses when they over-stocked. Moreover, they would have to adopt the Wana-maker policies, make their stores attractive, offer service to the buying public, and render the working conditions of their personnel more tolerable. With the advent of "the new kind of store" in Philadelphia, there was no reason why specialty shops should not continue to thrive.[1] But retailing was to become a science, and the successful merchant and his staff would have to make up their minds to go to school all their lives.

The trying months of October and November were safely weathered. As at Oak Hall, Wanamaker proved himself to be a bold advertiser, and he knew how to make low prices yield a rich profit by quick turnover and by increasing the volume of sales in every department. In this way he met his bills, got new credits, and then concentrated on the first Christmas.

Shortly after Thanksgiving the Christmas sale began. Merchandise was displayed in a novel way. Lists of sug-gestions for gifts at varying prices were published. Decora-tive lighting arrangements were installed, and a band was engaged to play every evening. The crush on the first day of the Christmas sale was so great that the police department had to be summoned to close the doors. Before Christmas the serious question was not how to attract the people, but how to get the goods to keep the departments stocked.

The last months of the first year were marked by an unemployment crisis. Philadelphia was a manufacturing city, and there was overproduction throughout the country. Most merchants felt that it was prudent to retrench. Wana-maker's policy, on the other hand, was to stimulate buying.

[1] In his *Annals of the Wanamaker Business*, in 1899, Wanamaker wrote: "It was said that the store would break up the other stores, and yet every one of the old stores still exists, and is doubled or quadrupled, while hun-dreds if not thousands of new stores have been planted since this store began.

With a boldness that equaled anything he had yet done, he decided to put in a basement floor, taking advantage of the new experiments in ventilation, and he began to get options on the Chestnut Street properties between Thirteenth Street and Juniper Street. He redoubled his advertising efforts.

On the first anniversary of "the new kind of store" he announced in the newspapers that "the business done at the Grand Depot during the year just closed fully confirms our expectations and settles to the complete satisfaction of the writer all doubts of its success, the facts proving beyond question that never before in one year were so many goods retailed in Philadelphia by one house." He went on to say:

Our great faith in the future of Philadelphia made it very easy to make our plans on a large scale, and there is, so far, no reason yet, nor do we expect there will be, to be disappointed.

We labor to increase the importance of the city, to add to its employments, and increase the conveniences of shopping to the 817,000 of her residents, and the 800,000 more whose homes are in the outlying towns and villages, to whom Philadelphia ought to be an attractive resort. The floating population that made our streets so lively and our stores so busy during 1876 may become permanent by due enterprise and joint action of Philadelphia business men.

No city in the Union has so large a body of trained, industrious and worthy workmen and workwomen as Philadelphia, and their idleness and consequent removal to other cities can be averted only by enterprises that will give work and bring people to the city. These, while benefiting the city at large, will also benefit those who judiciously invest their capital.

CHAPTER XX

THE NEW KIND OF SUNDAY SCHOOL

WANAMAKER would not have been himself had he neglected Bethany for his business or any other demand of his worldly career; nor would he have been himself had he failed to use in his Sunday-school work the pioneering instinct, the fertile imagination, and the methods he employed in his storekeeping. Bethany, as we have already emphasized, antedated Oak Hall by more than three years. Up to the opening of the Grand Depot we find a surprisingly large number of his business associates aiding him in his religious activities, and most of these were connected with Bethany Church or Sunday School. After the new departure in merchandising was made, and the Wanamaker employees increased from hundreds to thousands, the "store family," as its head loved to call it, naturally became a cross-section of Philadelphia life, its members coming from all parts of the city and the suburbs and representing all forms of religious belief. Although proportionately the Bethany contingent was no longer marked, numerically it did not diminish. Throughout his life some of Wanamaker's closest business associates were coworkers at Bethany.

Some men make a virtue of not mixing their religion and their business. Wanamaker could not have made this boast had he wanted to. He carried his religion into his business from the time he was a boy at Tower Hall, and his first experience in business, where he had a chance to show initiative and assume responsibility, was in the parallel enterprises of the Philadelphia Y. M. C. A. and Bethany Mission. If his Sunday school enjoyed great benefits, financially and in the direction of its activities and in the prominence it gained, from the success of Wanamaker as a merchant, it is equally true that in his business development he was under constant obligation to contacts made through his religious work and especially to his Bethany training. Prominent men became interested in the confidence thus won that secured for him financial backing and a circle of acquaintances in the business world unusual for a merchant in his twenties.

Not as the proprietor of the largest clothing house in the United States, but as the first Y. M. C. A. secretary and as Bethany's guiding genius had he come into contact with the English merchant, George Williams, founder of the Y. M. C. A., in his European trips in 1871 and 1875. It was Williams who had first taken him to Whiteley's, who had furnished him with the data concerning the Rochdale movement, and who had been his guest and sympathetic adviser in Philadelphia in the Centennial year. It was at Bethany that he acquired his style of speaking and writing, essential to the success of his store talks to employees and to the drafting of advertisements. It is not too much to say that in the formative years of his career he was thinking business at Bethany just as he thought Bethany at business. Evidence of this turns up in the anniversary program of Bethany Sunday School, where we find that the idea of the general store was in his mind in 1874.[1]

[1] This was the program for the sixteenth anniversary, and was called "To-night's Doings." One of the events on the program was called "Sweet Sixteen in Our Bethany Home," where children were dressed up to represent different articles. Among them were drugs and chemicals, stationery, hardware, hats and caps, dry goods, and groceries. Hymns are interspersed between. A considerably earlier example of his tendency to express moral truths in business language can be cited. In teaching the Sunday School lesson in 1863 he brought out the idea of the birthright sale by exhibiting on the blackboard a receipted bill in the following form, executed in large letters with colored crayons:

What more natural, then, that "a new kind of Sunday school" should have preceded—or at least paralleled—"a new kind of store"? And it is not without significance that Centennial visitors to Philadelphia "took in" Bethany Sunday School on a Sabbath afternoon as one of the sights of their trip to Philadelphia, just as they "took in" the Grand Depot on a week-day.

In the private files, in juxtaposition to the charter of the Rochdale Equitable Pioneers' Society, Limited, which had started its general store system in 1844, we find the Constitution and By-Laws of the Judean Sunday School Society, founded in Philadelphia in 1830. Both bear evidence of careful study. Wanamaker was no more satisfied with the old system of religious education than he was with the old mercantile system. He believed that there was the same opportunity for the Sunday school as for the store to serve the community by developing along progressive and efficient lines. We remember that his first budget for Bethany in 1858 carried a large item for advertising. He saw the problem confronting the superintendent launching a new Sunday school in the same light as the merchant launching a new store. First, the enterprise had to be made known, and then, when it was noticed, it had to be made attractive and serviceable. New methods had to be devised, and a competent personnel created whose devotion had to be won and held by leadership. In founding and developing Bethany, Wanamaker was the gifted organizer, the earnest student, and the fearless innovator, who cast aside the traditional methods

---

BEERSHEBA, 2208.

JACOB *Bought of* ESAU:

1 Birthright $\begin{cases} \text{Head of family,} \\ \text{Double portion of land,} \\ \text{Right to act as priest,} \end{cases}$ for 1 meal.

Received payment in one plate of pottage,

ESAU.

of doing things because he had it in him to establish a better tradition of his own.

The story of how Bethany was founded and of how quickly the young superintendent, who had no money in those days, financed and constructed a building, has already been told. Young pastors of to-day, in far more promising neighborhoods and devoting all their time to the work, would be proud of creating in one year a solidly constructed new mission chapel out of local contributions and a Sunday school of 17 teachers and 275 scholars. If in seven years their mission had developed into a church of a hundred members, with a Sunday school of 900 members, and with a larger lot acquired and plans under way for an ambitious church and Sunday-school building, they would consider themselves in line for a big pastorate. And yet this is what Wanamaker accomplished before his twenty-eighth birthday, in addition to his Y. M. C. A. and war work, the establishment of a flourishing business, and getting married and having three children.

How did he do it? Infinite capacity for work, a fertile imagination, genius for organization, and unlimited faith might account for the business success. But in the section of Philadelphia where Bethany was founded, genius and industry—with courage thrown in—are not enough to explain Bethany Sunday School. Much has been written about the early days at Bethany, and the contemporary records and reminiscences of old Bethany people are numerous. But the whole story is summed up in a sentence in one of the numerous articles we have read. In the *Home Herald* of October 21, 1908, Jane A. Stewart tells how Wanamaker got the children:

Between 1858 and 1865 the young man had gone in and out among those people, encouraging them, bringing comfort in their sickness, washing the faces of the youngsters, bearing up the infirm, and gaining a hold which he has never shaken on the affections of the whole district.

Keeping in touch with his staff and his scholars was many times given by John Wanamaker as the prerequisite to success in running a Sunday school. He believed that there was no vital and lasting influence of the Sunday-school superintendent unless the "eager upturned faces" he was addressing were the faces of friends. "Christianity is a friendly religion," he said when he was a very young man, "and you can't do much with it unless those to whom you give the message know that you are really their friend." Not long after he said the same thing about relations with employees. "No man can be expected to work with a whole heart except for his friend. A business man will not get very far in insuring the safeguarding of his interests by those who work for him merely with salary checks. He has to be their friend and associate, and he must conduct himself in such a way that they will know it."

Since there was nothing mournful or austere in Wanamaker's conception of religion, like his grandfather he had a good time at it. He enjoyed Bethany Sundays more than most people enjoy what he called "Worldly Amusements." It was his recreation. Why shouldn't it be? The thought was well expressed in a hymn that he loved:

> "We shall be happy in Jesus
> All the day long."

It was for this reason that he made much of music at Bethany. From the earliest days he was on the lookout for tuneful songs rather than old-fashioned dirges. He introduced Gospel Hymns that the children enjoyed singing. Of course the words were sometimes almost inane. He was nobody's fool, and recognized that fact. But he did not hesitate long if the tune was a good one. "After all, if it makes them happy, it's all right," he would say philosophically. He was careful, however, to exclude what he believed to be false doctrine or harmful sentiments. Just the accusation that a Gospel Hymn was poor verse or a jingle did not bother Wanamaker. Always ready with an answer. to an objection, he would point out that children love jingles, witness Mother Goose.

In the early days of Bethany, when even organs were looked at askance in the churches, he got a cornet and a violin, and by 1866 there was an orchestra at Bethany. Taking his cue from the evangelistic campaigners whom he loved, he enlisted the services of a professional choir leader, and made Bethany music, in the Sunday school as well as in the church, a matter of careful training and preparation.

In following the development of Bethany Sunday School during the 'sixties we find the youthful superintendent constantly telling his teachers that Sunday-school work demanded organization and preparation just as much as business. He created a machinery at Bethany, and asked everyone associated with him to be thinking all the time about making it more efficient. He originated and developed an amazing variety of organizations within the Sunday school to help along its work. Scholars were carefully graded, from infant school through junior, intermediate, and senior departments, up to adults' Bible classes. His conception of the Sunday school was not limited to children. "We need Bible study when we are grown up just the same as when we are children," was the way he put it.

An orderly form of service, varied from time to time, was one of his earliest innovations. As soon as he could afford it he began to have the Bethany "order of worship" printed.

On the sixty-second anniversary, February 1, 1920, the first of these, which was "used some time in the 1860's," was reproduced. It has twenty-eight numbers, and shows that in the earliest years, when the school was still comparatively small, John Wanamaker knew how to prepare an attractive service. The order opened with half a dozen Scripture sentences recited responsively. Then there was a chant, the creed, the catechism question and answer of the day, followed by hymns, prayers, Bible reading, lesson study, and the superintendent's review. After another hymn and notices came the closing sentences, the last song, the Lord's Prayer, and the recessional. Before 1870 instrumental selections and choir singing were added. These printed forms were multiplied, and before 1876 a dozen were in use, all of which had been prepared personally by the superintendent.

On the tenth anniversary, February 16, 1868, Bethany Sunday School marched from South Street to the corner of Twenty-second and Bainbridge Streets, and held a service in the unfinished building—the first of the group of buildings still in use. On that same day a doorman's association was founded.[1]

So rapidly did the school and church grow in the first half of the seventies that a new building for the Sunday school was required. The building of 1868-70 was made over for the church, and the Sunday school was housed in a structure unique in American religious life, which was completed in 1875. From the dedication program we take the following:

---

[1] When it held its jubilee celebration in 1918, only the president, John Wanamaker, and one of its members were still alive. The member was George W. Cromwell, who had been standing at the same door on Bainbridge Street for half a century.

DESCRIPTION OF THE NEW HALL

of the

BETHANY SABBATH SCHOOL

ACCOMMODATION, 3,000   NUMBER OF ROOMS, 42

This structure covers the whole of the western end of the block on Twenty-second Street, from Bainbridge Street to Pemberton Street. The front is circular in form, rising 3 stories, with bell tower and projected spire, 105 feet high.

The style of architecture is Scandinavian, and is quaint and picturesque, without being costly. Although the edifice may be considered a new one, yet the walls and floors of the old building, which occupied half the lot, were utilized.

The building proper is 138 feet 6 inches by 106 feet. From the Superintendent's stand, 42 feet from the south wall, on a platform, 42 feet long and 12 feet wide, the best view and description of the building can be had. In front is the general school room, 63 feet by 58 feet, with gradually rising floor, and a series of radiating rooms for adult classes, separated from the main hall by glass sash. To the right is the chapel for male infant scholars; to the left, the chapel for the female infant scholars; on the north, the adult class rooms, 13 in number, on the first floor. On the south, to the rear of the platform, is the Lecture Room, with graceful gallery, accommodating 350 persons, and separated from the main hall by huge glass sash. A Visitors' Gallery runs around the east, north and west sides of the building, reached by distinct entrances at the north-east and north-west angles of the building. Adjoining the main entrances, and on the first floor, on east and west sides of the building, are provided Ladies' and Gentlemen's Cloak Rooms, with wash basins, etc. The entrance halls to the building, 4 in number, permit separate and distinct entrance to each class room.

The south-west corner of the building, fronting on Pemberton Street, is 4 stories in height and contains Kitchen, Church, Parlor, Mothers' Meeting Room, Band of Hope Room, and the Bible and Book Room. Under the elevated floor of the Lecture Room is a fine hall for Young People's Association and Athletic Society. In the south-east wing of the building, is located Superintendent's Room, Secretaries' Room, Parish School Room, Social Room, and Committee Room. The floor of the main hall, rising at a grade of 1 inch to the foot, admits an extra story at the front on

BETHANY

Bainbridge Street, where 3 large rooms are located with fine front entrances intended respectively for neighborhood Library, Dispensary, and
Evening Conversation and Amusement Room; wide staircases lead to the
2d floor, where are a series of radiating Class Rooms, 5 in number, and
adjoining over main entrance halls 2 large rooms for Class Prayer Meetings, while 2 small rooms are arranged in the Towers.

The Ceiling of the main Hall is broken up in panels and two-thirds of
it of glass, part of which is simply decorated.

Abundant attention has been paid to ventilation, and the building is
bright and cheerful.

RECAPITULATION

	Seats
Main Hall for Junior Department	620
18 Adult Class Rooms	900
Teachers' Chairs	94
Infant Chapel	300
Primary Chapel	300
Lecture Room	356
Visitors' Galleries	350
Platform	80
Seating Capacity of Building	3,000

It is important for the biographer of Wanamaker to
emphasize the fact that "the new kind of Sunday school"
antedated "the new kind of store" by two years, and the
Grand Depot by more than a year, just as the Bethany
enterprise was originally founded three years before Oak
Hall. Too many who have written about Bethany—and
virtually all the visitors of later years—have assumed, by
implication at least, that Wanamaker's prosperity as a merchant explained the prosperity of Bethany, and that the
enormous size of the Sunday school was due to the merchant's success in creating a mammoth store. Quite the
reverse is true. It throws significant light upon the life and
genius of the man to be able to demonstrate that he built

up the greatest Sunday school in America before he originated the "new kind of store."

The picture would be incomplete were we to leave it here.
We have indicated the work of a pioneer, a promoter, an
organizer, an advertiser, and a zealous Christian, endowed
with magnetic personality and a love for intimate contact
with his fellow-beings. But we must go further and show
how Bethany fulfilled the purpose for which it was founded.
In business and Sunday-school work alike Wanamaker possessed the talent of developing on a grandiose scale, of doing
everything in a big way, of making what he created attractive. But in storekeeping the basis of it all was the high
quality of the merchandise offered for sale and its adaptabil-
ity to the changing needs of those who bought. Similarly,
the great building, filled with people of all ages, was the
result of illuminating and inspiring teaching of the Bible.

In studying how to make his Sunday school an effective
organization, from the very first days Wanamaker subordi-
nated everything to adequate preparation on the part of
superintendent and teachers for the lesson of the day. His
distaste for having things done in a haphazard way was
instinctive and violent. None was more kindly in dealing
with the mistakes due to inexperience and zeal. But mud-
dling through or bungling he regarded as dishonesty. "The
man cheats who does not give the best that is in him, and
how can one give his best who does not prepare and study?"
was his philosophy of life. He put this question to his
Sunday-school teachers. He stoutly affirmed that the Lord's
business was as important as their worldly affairs, and he
wanted no casually minded teachers in his Sunday school.
Throughout his life he devoted Saturday evenings to thorough preparation for Bethany, and he expected all the
teachers to do the same. If it wasn't Saturday night it must
be some other time.

INTERIOR OF BETHANY SUNDAY SCHOOL

But he had not been a Sunday-school superintendent long before he discovered the difficulties in the way of adequate preparation. His staff were not trained teachers. They were simply earnest men and women, most of whom were limited in their opportunities for getting a proper grasp of the lesson. They needed interpretation, suggestions of illustrations, hints as to methods. Where were these to be found? The lack of teachers' helps had long been recognized in the Sunday-school world, but it had not been met. There were no reviews of the lesson in the newspapers, and the religious press was inadequate. Popular Bible commentaries were few in number, and not within the reach of most of the teachers. Wanamaker was deeply interested in the series of commentaries by Albert Barnes, pastor of the old First Presbyterian Church in Philadelphia. He used these, and bought several sets for the Sunday school. For years he had a teachers' class to prepare for the lesson. But he could not keep this up.

After the revival of 1858 the American Sunday School Union started a weekly, the *Sunday School Times*, to fill the need which was so keenly felt by the young Bethany superintendent. The principal of the Central High School, John S. Hart, was impressed with the unique opportunity in religious education afforded by the new venture, and resigned his position to become its editor. The general failure to recognize the importance of the field covered by the new weekly, however, retarded its growth and influence. In 1871 the Union was on the point of suspending publication when Wanamaker stepped in and bought the *Sunday School Times* in order to save it.

With all his other irons in the fire he gave time and money to making the paper what he realized, from his Bethany experience, it could become. If the teaching staff of Bethany sorely needed a paper devoted to the pedagogi-

cal problems of the Sunday school and the weekly exposition of the lesson, it must be equally needed throughout the
country. Wanamaker put the *Sunday School Times* on a
solid business basis, and in order to lessen the cost of publication he founded the Times Printing House, to which he
gave all the printing of Oak Hall and the Chestnut Street
store. So it happened that he was the first merchant in
America—perhaps in the world—to have his own printing
plant. In four years the little paper grew in circulation
from a few thousand to seventeen thousand, and became a
substantial weekly of sixteen pages.

When Dr. Hart resigned in 1875, Wanamaker brought
Henry Clay Trumbull and John D. Wattles to Philadelphia
as editor and business manager of his paper, and helpers in
the Bethany Sunday School. Dr. Trumbull had been his
friend for fifteen years, and had become the outstanding
figure in Sunday-school work in the United States. Around
the new editor Wanamaker gathered a strong and active
committee of clergymen and laymen, which included his
old friends George H. Stuart and George W. Childs, and
the bankers, C. H. Clark, B. B. Comegys, and A. J. Drexel.
Elaborate preparations were made to take advantage of the
Centennial Exhibition to advertise the *Times*. Wanamaker
secured a letter of indorsement in President Grant's own
hand, written from the White House, which was reproduced
in facsimile on the cover. This issue, June 6, 1876, was
distributed to all Centennial visitors who showed interest in
Sunday-school work, accompanied by a subscription blank.
The feat established the *Sunday School Times* as a national
institution among Protestant churches, and Wanamaker
lived to see the circulation pass the half-million mark. The
next year, having put the paper on a good foundation, he
sold it to Trumbull and Wattles, upon their assurance that
they would consecrate their lives to it.

Not content with stimulating the study of the Sunday-school lesson by means of a weekly newspaper for teachers, Wanamaker conceived the idea of a publication for scholars, produced so cheaply that it would be within the reach of all. At the Times Printing House his men went into the problem of costs, and the result was *The Scholars' Quarterly*, offered at 25 cents a year, or 7 cents a copy. This marked a new era in scholars' helps, and led to a vast improvement in lesson leaves, which affected all Protestant Sunday schools between 1876 and 1880. *The Scholars' Quarterly* contained Wanamaker's idea of what he wanted his Bethany children to have—a book with the lessons for thirteen weeks, review exercises, order of service, a map, and a Bible dictionary of places and glossary of unusual words. For more than two years most of what went into *The Scholars' Quarterly* was prepared by Wanamaker himself.

Thorough preparation, mastery of the lesson of the day, and having in mind always what was to follow, made Wanamaker a new kind of Sunday-school superintendent as well as superintendent of a new kind of Sunday school. His pastor, Dr. A. T. Pearson, once described Wanamaker as "a cross between a Presbyterian and a Methodist, with a sprinkle of independency, who would run a Sunday school by wind, water, and steam—all at once—anything to make it go."

Visited as the Grand Depot was by many thousands during the Centennial, Bethany and its superintendent leading the exercises and reviewing the lesson formed an exhibit that influenced the development of the Sunday school in the United States. In the new West a number of Sunday schools took the Bethany name. The *Sunday School Times* remained a strong and abiding educational and inspirational influence for teachers long after most of those who came to the Centennial were dead.

Like the "new kind of store," the "new kind of Sunday school" had come to stay. A new era was opening in church work throughout the world. No more than he was the one merchant of his time was John Wanamaker the one Sunday-school superintendent. In both fields others were working along the same lines, adapting their storekeeping and Sunday-school teaching to the changed conditions. But no man of the new era was as fertile in ideas and as successful in carrying them out as Wanamaker, and none other was destined to father the children of his faith with undiminished devotion for more than sixty years.

CHAPTER XXI

BOOKISH ADVENTURES

THE importance Wanamaker attached to studying the Sunday-school lesson before it was taught is shown by his venture as publisher of the *Sunday School Times.* He did not go into it half-heartedly, and he did not give it up because he wanted to. Trumbull and Wattles were making a success of the paper. His own affairs, as we have seen, were in a critical state in 1877. He was unwilling to have what was essentially a religious enterprise dependent upon his business fortunes and involved in his business risks. With the men he had picked making good, and a healthy and increasing circulation for the *Sunday School Times* after the Centennial, there was no longer need for him to remain at the helm.

Wanamaker loved the smell of printer's ink, and if the Landreth Sunday School superintendent who got him his first job had had friends among newspaper men instead of among lawyers and merchants, he might have become a dominant figure in American journalism. Buried in men's clothing and Bethany, he had little time for books for books' sake, and his reading during the formative years of a man's literary tastes was almost wholly the Bible, Bible commentaries, and tracts.

Tracts! The little paper-covered (if covered at all) four to sixteen page pamphlets, in a type so small that few eyes of the electrical era can read them, are so nearly forgotten in this generation that we must remind the reader that the tract is a story of religious experience, piously told, and gen-

erally ending in a moral.   How Wanamaker loved tracts!
He used to carry a pocketful, and handing out a tract was
his way of driving home a homily.   The twenty-year-old
John got the habit at Jaynes Hall in 1858.   He studied the
tracts—and had his A, B, C, D, E, and F to meet the
particular need of the inquirer.   It was easy to get tracts.
Several dear old Quakers in Philadelphia invested large
sums annually in having them printed, and they were delighted to find discriminating distributors for this form of
carrying the Gospel message.   We cannot give it as a fact, but
we have been told that when Oak Hall was being launched,
and Wanamaker & Brown were having a hard time getting
goods on credit, there was a peremptory refusal on the part
of a big wholesaler.   As young John was dejectedly turning away, the Quaker, to whom his name meant nothing,
suddenly recognized him.   "Ah!" he exclaimed "Thee is
the lad who comes for tracts.   Woolens, too, thee can have."

When he got a little money Wanamaker himself became
a publisher of tracts.   It is on a pamphlet (price one cent),
called "A B C of Christian Faith," with a question and
answer under each letter of the alphabet, that we find for
the first time JOHN WANAMAKER—PUBLISHER.   And the
second booklet bearing his imprint is a collection of Gospel
Hymns.[1]   He carried on his tract enterprise under the name

[1] We have reason to believe that he subsidized several collections of Gospel
Hymns, with music, in the period from 1870 to 1890.   John R. Sweney,
writer of many successful hymns and promoter of others, was the Bethany
Sunday School choirmaster.   Among the copyrights owned by John Wana-
maker were such familiar hymns as "Showers of Blessing," "Tell Me the
Story of Jesus," "Faithful Unto Death," "While the Years are Rolling On,"
"There Is Sunshine in My Soul To-day," "I Will Shout His Praise and
Glory," and "Since I Found My Saviour."   The copyright dates are from
1875 to 1898.   In the last years of his life, Wanamaker financed Bentley
Ackley, Billy Sunday's former song leader, in the hymn-publishing business.
On May 28, 1919, he suggested that Ackley make the following statement
in his advertising: "D. L. Moody greatly urged praise worship.   His old
friend, John Wanamaker, believing in singing churches, established Sunday-
school orders of worship sixty years ago full of hymns.   He helped to make
Hymns of Blessing, and uses it in Brotherhood and Sunday School."

of Bethany Tract Repository. The private files reveal early tracts of a totally different kind from those issued by the Quakers and from those brought back from England after the 1871 trip. First comes an attractive cover and attractive title, and then display type and different colored ink. Very soon the form of the tract was changed to resemble something familiar. We have before us, for instance, a "Trip Pass Good for One Continuous Passage on the Red Line Railway from Earth to Heaven. Subject to Conditions on the Other Side. This Road Has No Connection With Any Other Line." Turning to the other side, one finds that the red represents Christ's redeeming blood. The message is striking. It shows how Wanamaker, in his religious work, discarded old methods and was constantly seeking for the novel thing that would drive home a lesson.

But if we are to trust Wanamaker's memory, his first publication was *Everybody's Journal*, which he brought out when he was "a boy." Diligent search yields no trace of this early paper, its nature, or the circumstances surrounding its publication. We wonder whether, as is the case with most juvenile efforts, it was not simply a sheet printed by hand and passed out to friends. What matters is the title. The boy who thought of that was giving early promise of what came afterwards. We first find *Everybody's Journal* as a publication of Oak Hall, which contained four pages of anecdotes, different in content but written in the style of the tracts, and brief comment on matters of current interest, interspersed with the advice to go to Wanamaker & 'Brown for the best clothing. The *Journal*, when Oak Hall became a big organization, was changed into a store paper, with news of the activities of employees. After the New York store was founded, *Everybody's* was converted into a general magazine which quickly gained great vogue. Wanamaker and his associate, Robert C. Ogden, had sensed the demand for an illustrated magazine at a popular price, made possible by the new era of national advertising. *Everybody's* was one of the first of the ten-cent magazines, and before the end of 1900 it had attained a circulation of over 100,000.[1]

Another publication which was a pioneer in its field and which attained national fame and influence was started by Wanamaker in 1877. Oak Hall did a great business among farmers, and how best to reach them was a problem Wanamaker was constantly studying. When he was contemplating turning the Grand Depot into a general store, a young newspaper man, Wilmer Atkinson, who had been publishing in Wilmington, Delaware, a daily newspaper that had failed, proposed to Wanamaker the publication of a monthly for farmers, which would circulate in the counties surrounding Philadelphia. *The Farm Journal*, now a paper whose circulation has passed the million mark, was launched in March, 1877, in the Grand Depot. Twenty-five thousand copies of an eight-page paper were printed, containing a full-page announcement of "a great event near at hand, when the door of the Grand Depot at Thirteenth and Market will spring open to welcome ladies." For seven years Wanamaker stood behind the *Farm Journal*. In view of the fact that under Wilmer Atkinson the *Farm Journal* became one of the greatest periodicals published in Philadelphia, it is interesting to reproduce a letter, dated April 30, 1920, written by Wanamaker to Atkinson. It reads:

You will remember that I began the publication of the *Farm Journal* in the old Grand Depot, in 1877. You were my Editor until the little *Journal* had so grown that I felt the object I had in starting it was accom-

[1] After the retirement of Robert C. Ogden and Thomas B. Wanamaker in 1907, when John Wanamaker found himself under the necessity of shouldering once more the entire responsibility of his two great stores, he sold *Everybody's*. In the issue for June, 1911, we find the statement, "This is the twelfth year since Mr. Wanamaker founded the magazine."

plished and turned the paper over to you without any price on it except your agreement to see that all its subscribers had my contract fully carried out for the subscriptions they had paid, which I think were twenty-five cents a year.

I have been very proud of the little paper and of your skilful and intelligent management of it, and I am glad that it has prospered and been beneficial to our agricultural and other friends.

It is a great pleasure, I assure you, dear Mr. Atkinson, to extend felicitations and good wishes to you, my longtime friend, and to wish for the *Journal* which reflects your perseverance and personality, greater success in the years to come than it has ever enjoyed.

As requested, I am sending you one of my earlier photographs, though not so far back as the beginning of this business.

In 1879 *The Ladies' Journal* was launched to attract the new clientèle. It was an eight-page paper, three columns to the page, publishing poems and signed articles, and was called "a woman's paper devoted to fashions, business, society, and home interests." A professional editor was secured, and it contained very little advertising—just a hint here and there in the reading matter. The make-up and contents are surprisingly good for the period. In the *Philadelphia Times* we find that the second number, August, 1879, was commented upon in the periodical column:

It is superior, in most respects, to many papers sold at a high price. It is well written, original, bright, and will be an undoubted authority on all things pertaining to fashions.

One remarkable feature of the *Ladies' Journal* was its report of the latest fashions abroad. The fall openings in Paris were described, and the winter styles forecast by a Wanamaker buyer.[1] As the paper was printed at the Grand Depot "for gratuitous distribution" it was, of course, solely

---

[1] This distinctive Wanamaker custom did not lapse with the suspension of the *Ladies' Journal*. It was continued in newspaper advertisements and in later store publications. The Wanamaker fashion news was eventually published by the stores in French in a periodical called, *La Dernière Heure à Paris.* This paper got a "scoop" on the pictures of Rostand's "Chantecler," which it published in February, 1910, a month before the play was put on the stage.

an advertisement. But it contained an idea which later made the fortune of more than one publisher.

Wanamaker was also the originator of the periodicals, so distressingly numerous now, devoted to book reviews. The first issue of the *Book News Monthly* was published on August 30, 1882. The beginning was modest, of course, but the mistake of "gratuitous circulation," which placed the *Ladies' Journal* definitely in the category of advertising, was not repeated. The *Book News Monthly* built up a paid subscription list, and solicited advertisements in the book trade. It was published uninterruptedly until 1918.[1]

The early love of writing and publishing inevitably took the form of advertising his business and promoting the interests of Bethany. There are limits to the capacity of the most gifted men. Wanamaker had to be content to express himself and to give substance to his fertile imagination, in the early and middle periods of his life, to the two great fields in which he lived and worked. Vistas of national influence opened up to John Wanamaker through the publications he launched. But he had to resist the temptation to follow them. In his self-circumscribed sphere, however, he managed to get all the pleasure of adventure that a busi-

[1] In 1906, when the success of *Everybody's* had intrigued him and when books had become one of the principal interests of his life, Wanamaker, dissatisfied with the modest rôle of the *Book News Monthly*, decided to give it his personal attention. Articles from prominent writers were secured and popular book reviews were introduced. The magazine grew by leaps and bounds, and became the only American publication that attempted to cover the entire literary output of the English-speaking world. As many as five hundred reviews and notices were published in a single number. Fiction and serials were added. Wanamaker introduced the work of Arnold Bennett in this country, and published Ezra Pound's first poem. In each issue was the sketch of a living author. There was a section devoted to drama. When he took the magazine under his personal wing, Wanamaker wrote to his son Thomas: "I may find it necessary to stop *Book News* at the end of one or two years, but I will make the best effort I can with it." What he did accomplish with the magazine for more than a decade until the World War and Liberty Loans claimed all his attention, demonstrates the fact that success in any undertaking comes from the man and not from the material with which he works.

ness man and Sunday-school superintendent could. His periodical enterprises he passed on to others. But he continued to study the best ways of reaching customers with the goods he had to sell and the plain people of south-eastern Philadelphia with the Gospel message. Advertising was his outlet for literary expression.

In compiling our bibliography it was our hope to list and examine all the publications of the Wanamaker stores and of Bethany Church. We discovered that there were more than fifty periodicals and thousands of booklets of every conceivable kind between 1858 and 1922. All bear witness to the fact that Wanamaker found his greatest pleasure in creating reading matter. The store was constantly putting out periodicals and illustrated books. Every organization at Bethany had its own paper.

This output became so voluminous, even before the Grand Depot, that it was good business policy to create a printing establishment. In the Philadelphia directory for 1874 we find the Times Printing House at Sixth and Chestnut Streets. The name was taken from the *Sunday School Times*, but it was wholly independent of that paper. A certain amount of job work was done, but with the growth of the store and Bethany, and with the various periodicals that had to be taken care of from time to time, the Printing House soon found its hands full in taking care of Wanamaker's own enterprises. Its capacity as early as 1876 is indicated by the fact that the million copies of the Centennial booklet were "printed at our own steam-power printing office" which was able at the same time to take care of the weekly issue of the *Sunday School Times*. When that publication was sold, "the new kind of store" began printing the *Philadelphia Store News* and the *Bethany Gleaner*. Then came the *Book News Monthly*. By running his own plant Wanamaker not only got instant service, impossible to secure elsewhere, and a substantial decrease in cost, but he was also able to smell printer's ink and to watch the presses working for him. Although the Times Printing House did not solicit outside work, more always came in than could be handled. For fifty years it kept abreast, and frequently ahead, of the times in its system, its machinery, and its styles.

It was natural that the man who loved to print and publish should have a passion for books. In September, 1877, the book stock of "the new kind of store" was valued at ten dollars, in children's books, and two months later at the first Christmas season, there was a special book counter with juvenile books. In January, 1879, a single copy of Taine's *History of English Literature* was offered for sale. This was the beginning of the book department, which grew so rapidly that a thousand dollars' worth of books were sold in a single day in the Christmas season of the same year. In 1880 Bibles were added, and two years later the Wanamaker Book Store was opened on the ground floor of the Philadelphia store. The next year the importation of French books was begun—a distinct innovation in American book retailing, and by 1887 Wanamaker was doing the largest retail book business in the United States. This success was attained by a revolutionary change in the methods of bookselling. Years later Wanamaker said:

"When we started selling books there were four separate discounts allowed by the bookstores: A trade discount to booksellers; a movable discount to their best customers and neighbors; a discount to clergymen and college professors; while they were known to take almost any price that was offered by a missionary.

"It is a matter of record that we had a long running fight for six months in the *Publishers' Circular* of the booksellers. It was a bitter strife. But inasmuch as the basis of fixing

prices of this Store was to fix them at the lowest at which
the goods were ever sold by anybody, our prices were naturally always the lowest.   We saw to it that this was the case
by making constant comparisons."

There soon came an opportunity to render another service to book-buyers, which, owing to the unusual circumstances, had great influence in breaking up a custom from
which the country was suffering.   General Grant's death,
before his *Memoirs* was ready for publication, had added
to the interest in them.   But the publishers had planned to
sell them only by subscription through agents.   Wanamaker
got hold of a large quantity of the books, and on the morning of publication, May 13, 1886, in a column announcement in the Philadelphia papers, he offered them for sale
at a price considerably below what the agents were to ask.
He said:

> The publishers meant to keep these books, in which the American
> people take so deep an interest, out of the bookstores.   They intended
> that you should open your door to whatever book peddler happened to
> pull your bell or go without the *Memoirs* of General Grant.   We hold
> it hostile to public and private interests that this constraint should be put
> on the sale of a book of such a character.   That is why we put it in our
> bookstore—to give it a market without reproach.

Then followed a keen analysis of the evils of book-peddling.   Wanamaker declared that the books sold by book
agents "are not made to read.   They are made to sell to
people who have learned their letters and very little beyond that.   Big, thick books; big letters far apart; thick
paper; pictures; plenty of gilt on the covers; the subject—
no matter; the author—no matter."   He drew a vigorous
comparison between the English newsstand with its spread
of "orderly publications fit for a civilized people" and the
low type of books offered to the American public.   He said
that the stuff peddled around the country makes "a library of

ignorance vulgarly bound." He charged "almost the whole subscription business" with being "based on books that serve no useful purpose at prices too high for good ones." He protested against the "unreasonably high" price of the *Memoirs*, marketed in this way, as well as against the insult to General Grant's memory. He expressed the belief that "the family of General Grant is a loser through the restrictions put upon the sale of the book." And then he announced his merchandising policy in regard to books:

We have a rare opportunity to say a word in behalf of what appears to us good policy in publishing as well as in other business. Isn't it better to publish a popular book at a popular price? Let us say nothing of what is fair to the public. Isn't it wise in money-wisdom to sell a book that millions want at a price at which millions can buy it? Are not the profits that come from the trade of the millions more than the profits that come from the trade of the upper ten thousands?

Throughout his life Wanamaker fought to keep book prices down. He felt that books were a reflection of as well as an influence upon the civilization of the country, and that publishers had no more right than public service corporations to retard the progress of the country. Frequently he classed reading matter with the mails, the telegraph, and transportation facilities as public necessities. He contended that by virtue of their wares publishers had an obligation to the public greater than that of most business men.

But he was careful to emphasize the distinction between book-peddling and legitimate subscription business. He said:

Great undertakings, involving costs too great and profits too little for individual publishers, must be helped along by those who want them accomplished. There is a work in preparation in Germany on which four hundred eminent scholars have been writing for many years already with many more years before them. The Encyclopedia Britannica is being rewritten at the rate of two volumes a year—a work of twelve or fifteen years. Such works must be helped along. But the subscription method they call for is directly opposed to that of the book-peddler.

Three years later an American reprint of the Encyclopedia Britannica appeared, set up and published in this country by John Wanamaker. This was the beginning of a reprint business in sets of worth-while authors, sold by mail as well as to the stores in Philadelphia and New York, which made Wanamaker a heavy advertiser in periodicals of national circulation. A new style of writing book advertisements was developed by a feature writer on the New York *Herald*, under Wanamaker's guidance.[1]

But the greatest change in bookselling methods brought by Wanamaker was his insistence that the old-fashioned booksellers should "accept their responsibilities as merchants," which he defined as "either to have books in stock or to know what they were and where they were and to get them promptly." He spent a great deal of time in his bookstore, training its staff in this new way of handling customers. When a book was asked for it was the clerk's business to get the book without asking questions. And if the book-buyer did not know the exact title or wanted advice on a book dealing with any subject, it was still the clerk's business to supply the book—quickly and without questions. As in any other branch of merchandising, Wanamaker believed that it was possible to gauge the demand in books, to keep stocks, and to know about the merchandise. After all, it was only treating books like other lines. Instead of bankrupting the merchant, as was prophesied, giving service to customers increased the volume of business so rapidly that ten years after the first children's books appeared on the corner of the counter the buyer of the book department was able one

[1] This was Clinton T. Brainard, who succeeded George Harvey as president of Harper and Brothers; and who is owner and manager of the McClure and Wheeler newspaper syndicates.

evening in the Christmas season to report sales for the day of $10,000, about a tenth of the total for the whole store.

The files contain more notes in the merchant's own handwriting about books and music and art than for any other departments of the business. The notes show the infinite pains that he took and the constant thought extending over nearly half a century with unflagging zeal to make his bookselling what he honestly believed that it was—an educational service. Scarcely a day passed without his morning visit to the book department. He was constantly suggesting reclassifications and new methods of display. We find, for instance, this note:

Take up to-day question of special book room—with the books of last month and up to the last 24 hours—and the reviews in scrap books for the customers to consult. Having special saleswoman as guide to contents of new books.

The advertising given to a book that he liked delighted publisher and author. There were times when he ordered that a Chestnut Street window in the holiday season be devoted to the display of a single book, with originals of the illustrations, against the background of decorations and art objects indicative of the favorite's contents. His people sometimes mildly demurred. No matter how good a book and how large the sales, the profit, he was reminded, did not justify a window. This did not deter him, however, and the idea was copied by other general stores.

Before he left Tower Hall, Wanamaker was a member of a group that used to meet for discussion of books in a second-story room on Chestnut Street above Seventeenth. Little is known of this organization but the name, the Henry Clay Literary Club. There are references to it in letters of reminiscence of early days written to Wanamaker by old friends as late as the year before his death. Boys who had scant opportunity of an education, like himself, found in reading their equivalent of college. In one of the earliest sketches of his life Wanamaker is spoken of as having tried to make up for the lack of educational opportunities by "daily and systematic reading" which "enriched his thought, trained his mind, enlarged his sympathies, broadened his outlook, and widened his horizon."

More than once he said that without access to books and a good pair of eyes he would never have been "anything but an ignoramus." After the Centennial Exhibition—scarcely at all before that—we begin to find allusions in his Bethany talks and in his advertising to historical and geographical facts, to philosophical sentiments, and to characters of literature that a man who lacked schooling could have acquired only by diligent reading. His choice of books and his taste in books were not always those of a cultivated man. He was an incurable sentimentalist. But before he had passed middle age his close application and wide scope of reading, and his innate keenness, enabled him to distinguish fairly well between what was scholarly and what was not and between pseudo-scientific speculation and solid fact. Had we the space to make extensive quotations from his speeches and writings we could demonstrate a mental development through reading that put him far ahead of college men who did not follow books after graduation.

Once he had entered and elected to dwell in the world that the reading of books opens to a man, Wanamaker not only kept himself surrounded with the latest books, but he made them his favorite gift.[1] He became what might be

---

[1] He used to keep in his office to give away several hundred copies of a book he thought would prove helpful to friends. He would get a copy of a book he was especially interested in, write his autograph in it, and hand it to a visitor. Special editions of books were printed for Grand Army days and for the Lincoln memorial dinners. There are thousands of letters from people in all ranks of life, thanking him for books. It was his custom to give books

called a propagandist in trying to broaden the horizon of others, as his was being broadened, by constant reading. More as an educationalist than as a merchant was his interest aroused in the wide dissemination of reading matter. It was the motive that led him to try to keep the price of good books down, and to use the power his enormous book business gave him to make uniform and stabilize fiction prices and prevent the publication of books that ought to have a wide circulation at prices prohibitive to the purses of those who needed them most.

His growing interest in books led him to give frequent advice about reading to his Bethany and store people. We find him protesting against the grotesque idea that a man could become a master of English style simply through the Bible. To him the Bible was a devotional book. It might help others, as it had helped Lincoln, to acquire a knowledge of and taste for good English. But that was not the reason for reading it! And the Bible alone was not enough for the man who wanted to express himself correctly and forcibly. He felt that language was not a static medium, and that every generation had a right to its own form of expression. We first find this idea in his defense of Gospel Hymns, but he greatly extended it, and once said that the world we live in had to be interpreted by living men. Contemporary

---

to Bethany children and to send them to people he met in his travels—from the age of seventy to seven! A collection of these letters would form an interesting contemporary estimate of books that appeared from 1887 to the end of his life. To illustrate:

My Dear Friend Mr. Wanamaker. I have not got either of those books you spoke of this morning in the Brotherhood. Do you mind letting me have these two? You gave me *The Heart of Nan Rutledge*. I have read it three times. I love Lincoln very much, but I never read about him before I got that book, and I want so much *The Man for the Ages*.

books, therefore, compelled our attention if we were to keep pace with the thought of our times.

All that was notable in biography intrigued him; but he liked best autobiography or "lives and letters," where the letters and extracts from diaries formed the principal part of the text. He was more interested in what men said about themselves than in what others told of them or thought of them. He traveled the world over in books about other lands. Here, too, we find the personal form of narrative most attractive to him. The reactions to themselves in things that they saw were what he wanted of explorers and adventurers. The historical or the factual form of travel writing quickly tired him. This we discover from the number of pages he cut in a volume! When he was voyaging, as well as when he was at his town or country home, he revealed himself as the faithful reader of books light and serious. Especially on shipboard was his diary full of books. It was natural that books should fill the pages of an indefatigible letter-writer on long ocean stretches.[1]

It must be stated that while Wanamaker's taste in books improved, and while he kept abreast of the times in non-fiction, he was never a discriminating reader of novels and poetry. Did we not say that he was a sentimentalist? The passages of Dickens at which we smile were the ones his memory loved to cherish. James Whitcomb Riley was his favorite poet—and then Tennyson. The books of Florence Barclay were his delight. He professed admiration for Ralph Connor, and invited him to preach at Bethany. Pastor Wagner's *Simple Life* he liked, but never really understood. His own devotion to his mother made him give an honored place

---

[1] To illustrate: "I read to-day 'According to St. John' by Amélie Rives and shall throw it overboard;" "I am now on 'Wee MacGregor,' of which 100,000 have been sold in Scotland, and have started 'Mlle. de Lespinasse.' This closeth the second day of the home stretch;" "I have just finished a book of travel that I would like you to read. It is Caroline Kirkland's 'Some African Highways.' It is very readable."

to Barrie's *Margaret Ogilvie*. *Pollyanna* he adored—the
word is not too strong. He stood behind the story and
watched the progress of its sale, getting reports from both
bookstores on it.[1] Similarly, he had a daily report on
Florence Barclay's *The Rosary*. Although we doubt whether
he read every word of it, he sometimes called *Les Misérables*
his favorite book of fiction. And he would couple with it
Zona Gale's *The Loves of Pelléas and Etarre*. Books of
pure adventure he called boring, because life was more thrill-
ing than these "vain imaginations." His true adventure
books were those of David Grayson. One of his intimate
friends has said, in regard to both fiction and poetry, that
"Mr. Wanamaker read to rest and amuse himself," but
that there were few works of imagination that he was really
attached to and remembered.

Wanamaker never had the time to become a bibliophile.
The pursuit was too engrossing. But he did dabble in old
books and curious bindings, as most men do who love books,
and there were extensive purchases from time to time of
Americana, especially relating to old Philadelphia. Among
world figures, Napoleon Bonaparte and Martin Luther were
favorites. The Luther collection, as complete as any in
America, was destroyed in the Lindenhurst fire. Wanamaker sometimes said that he wanted to write about Luther,
and that he was having the material collected for that purpose. He preserved a letter from a friend, written January
18, 1908, containing an extract from a Pittsburgh newspaper:

---

[1] He ordered large extracts from *Pollyanna* to be published in the *Book
News Monthly*. For a long time he mentioned this book in every possible
connection. He didn't like the heat, and wrote on the afternoon of June
25, 1913: "To fuss about the heat is futile. One had better play the Pollyanna game and be glad it isn't hotter." Getting news of the sales of the
last book of Gene Stratton Porter or Florence Barclay was as good sport
to him as following baseball scores was to some men.

Sometimes it requires a catastrophe to reveal a man's real inner life to the world. In a sense, this is true of John Wanamaker, the revealing light in his case having been the recent disastrous fire that destroyed the Wanamaker home at Jenkintown. The fact thus disclosed is that Mr. Wanamaker, in addition to his multifarious duties as merchant prince, public man, Sunday school superintendent and art collector, had planned becòming an author. In each man's soul is some cherished dream or purpose that he confides to none. Mr. Wanamaker's dream was to write a life of Martin Luther. To this end, he had gathered material from all over the world. Perhaps the greatest loss inflicted by the flames was not the palatial home, but this data, lovingly and laboriously collected through many years.

Of devotional books and Bible commentaries and lives of saints nothing needs to be said. They belonged to his religious life and marked neither development nor idiosyncrasies in his intellectual life. We cannot escape the conclusion that John Wanamaker's reading was largely utilitarian. He appreciated books for their educational value to himself and others, and, as he grew older, for pure recreation. In his business and his Sunday school he found the outlet for his spirit of romance and adventure. His æsthetic nature was satisfied in building and adorning his stores, his Bethany, and his homes. What he learned of psychology, of philosophy, and of government came from contacts with people and conditions.

CHAPTER XXII

THE MOMENTOUS DECADE: GROWTH OF THE BUSINESS

AT Oak Hall it had been the habit of the proprietor to make a tour of inspection every morning and every afternoon. Even when the business had grown to cover two acres in the six-story building he did not give up his rounds, and he always seemed to be able to find time to put on his hat and go over to the Chestnut Street store. In the first year of the Grand Depot he added Thirteenth and Market Street to the itinerary. But when the opening of the general store brought new responsibilities, and authority in the different departments was delegated to carefully picked men, all experts in their own lines, it was assumed that the chief would no longer feel the need of supervising in person the details of the business.

But day after day Wanamaker appeared as usual, morning and afternoon, at every counter, sometimes greeting the clerks and asking them how things were going, but more often just standing for a minute, and then passing on. It was realized that his ubiquity had still to be reckoned with. It was the way he got his exercise. It was the way he studied. It was the way he made his people feel, not that they were under the eye of the taskmaster, but of the kind and sympathetic leader, whose presence brought strength and inspiration.

"The finest fertilizer for the field is the foot of the farmer," he wrote one day, indulging with the joy of a child in making an alliterative sentence. None expressed more graphically his shrewd and homely philosophy of life.

None revealed more strikingly the reason of his success. He was not shut up in an office, directing the business as a theoretical problem. He was on the floor, in contact with clerks and customers and merchandise. He was accessible to everyone, eager to put things right when they were going wrong, and welcoming suggestions and ideas of others as heartily as he gave expression to his own. He wanted to create the feeling that Wanamaker's New Establishment was a co-operative undertaking, founded for mutual service. Then it would follow logically that expansion, improved mechanism, and greater efficiency were as much to the interest of customers and salespeople as to the interest of the merchant.

In the critical struggles of the first year he had not needed letters of friends to impress upon him the fact that the new responsibility he was assuming was one that involved the well-being of thousands. His success or failure meant the success or failure of the people who were working for him and, in some degree, of those who sold him goods. But, with the confidence and enthusiasm of a neophyte, he looked beyond himself and his store family to the buying public of Philadelphia, and identified the fortunes of his enterprise with the success or failure of the principles of merchandising he had long been announcing and of Philadelphia's hope of getting high standards of service in retail shopping.[1]

---

[1] In view of the criticism sometimes heard that Wanamaker ignored the pioneer work of others in general storekeeping in the United States, it is important for his biographer to emphasize the fact that Wanamaker repeatedly spoke of other merchants and gave them full credit for what they had done in the great development of dry-goods establishments. For instance, the first anniversary announcement of the "opening of the dry-goods section of the Grand Depot," published on March 12, 1878, stated: "Many persons have considered the enterprise an experiment, and many more express and manifest a warm interest in building up in Philadelphia an establishment the like of which New York has had for a long time." It was not long, however, before it dawned on Wanamaker that his store was unique in conception as well as in its rapid growth and in the size it attained within the first decade of its foundation.

We have said that the experiment of converting the Grand
Depot into a general store was pronounced an unqualified
success by Wanamaker after the first Christmas. The critical
period had been safely passed. Philadelphians took to "the
new kind of store." When he came to the first anniversary
Wanamaker found little difficulty in financing the renewing
of stocks and the opening of new departments. A gallery
was built along the Market Street end to hold the china and
glassware. From one counter hosiery developed into a department, and a new department was opened for small children's clothes and layettes. A thirty-four page catalogue
indicates that before the end of the year "the Wanamaker
Grand Depot" was carrying virtually all the lines listed in
Whiteley's London catalogue of the same year.

But Wanamaker realized that if he were going to make
his general store what he intended it to be, a group of specialty shops, each with a complete stock, success could be assured only by acquiring the eleven dwellings facing Chestnut Street on the plot from Thirteenth to Juniper Streets,
and extending back to Kelly Street. The idea was ambitious
and risky. It seems incredible that within a year of the time
when he did not know whether he was going to pull through
or not Wanamaker should have decided to make so radical
an increase in his floor space and his investment. But there
was no turning back. Business was rapidly developing westward on Chestnut Street, and merchants were already ne-
gotiating with property-owners on both sides of the street
for the conversion of ground floors into shops by purchase
of the buildings or by long leases. The proprietor of the
Grand Depot had to act quickly or he would see others reap-
ing where he had sown.

One by one the Chestnut Street houses were bought, and
although Kelly Street still remained, Wanamaker soon
owned all the land through to Chestnut Street. At the end

of the third year of "the new kind of store" a Philadelphian
wrote:

> This unexampled enlargement has made constant changes in the
> premises an absolute necessity, and there has hardly been a secular day
> since 1876 but what artisans and mechanics have been at work in some
> part of the place.
>
> It has been idly said that Mr. Wanamaker kept men making alterations
> for the sake of constantly presenting something new to the public, for the
> sake of something to talk about, for the sake of advertisement.

The completion of the purchase of the block on which the
present store stands was celebrated by a "grand illumination." On November 11, 1878, it was announced that the
store would be open that evening from 7:30 to 10 to show
what the Grand Depot had to offer for the Christmas season. Nothing would be sold. The people would be invited
simply to "look around." In the newspaper accounts of
this event we find Wanamaker first referred to as "the merchant prince." An exuberant reporter saw the event thus:

> The whole area, as viewed from the galleries and towers, was a sunlit
> sea of heads. The élite in fashion, the solidity and wealth, the youth
> and beauty of the city poured through the points of entrance to the Grand
> Depot in a steady stream of humanity that was at times resistless in its
> onward rush. Once in the crowd, nothing but patient following of your
> leader could get you out of it, except at the expense of great muscular
> exertion and collapsed breathing apparatus. What was the cause of the

GREAT OUTPOURING OF THE MASSES?

A simple announcement that displayed upon the hundreds of counters,
radiating from a common center, and throughout the monster establishment, were to be seen more of the productions of Europe than Phineas
Fogg saw in his marvellous "Journey Round the World in Eighty Days."

Lighted up by myriads of gas lights, colored by the glintings of
numerous reflectors, were to be seen—not the living animals of that wonderful trip, the tigers of the jungle, the denizens of the mountain slopes,
the winged beauties of the forest—none of these, but their skins were
arrayed in the fur department, gotten up in more tasteful form, to avert

the chilling winds, than even the Royal Bengalese ever saw, or the Sahibs who, on elephant back, invaded their lair in Farther India.   The cocoons of China and Japan, of Lyons, of Lombardy and Venice, had given up their silks, velvets, and satins, and in the manufactured form most dear to the feminine eye, the product was spread upon the counters.

There were columns more of this in the *Public Ledger*. The reporter seemed specially impressed with the fact that John Wanamaker's private office was heated by steam, that the chandeliers were powerful enough to enable one to see into dark corners, and

it would be possible for Adam and Eve, did they live now, in the days of the Grand Depot, to quietly slip inside its walls, become clad in modern costume, cap-a-pie, buy all their household utensils and adornments, provide for the amusement and dressing of their descendants, and prepare them for the tour of the world, whether they designed a sojourn in the arctic regions of eternal snow and ice, or a swing in a hammock under the luxuriant foliage of the tropics.

We have not quoted for the reader's delectation, or to illustrate the change that fifty years have made in "journalese" and copy-desk standards of newspapers. Philadelphia was not Squeedunkville with the *Public Ledger* for its daily mirror. We must remember that. It helps us to realize that in 1878 in a great American city Wanamaker's was genuinely "a new kind of store." The commonplaces of to-day were the sensations of our fathers. The lights and the collection of things for sale, coming from all over the world and lavishly displayed, justified superlatives in the news columns of the city's leading daily. The band that played that evening also had its headline in all the papers.

The newly-crowned merchant prince (Wanamaker is on record as having disliked this term) [1] was undoubtedly pleased with the success of his evening party to Philadel-

[1] In the private files we find a sketch of his life, prepared for an official publication, which Wanamaker carefully corrected in his own hand. He crossed out "prince" and wrote over it "pioneer."

phians, and the extravagant newspaper stories were good advertising. But he himself was dissatisfied with the "grand illumination." He noted dark corners that were not reached, and the fire hazard and stuffy atmosphere made him feel that the stunt was as dangerous and uncomfortable as it had been unsatisfactory in showing his goods. There was nothing to do but to keep open evenings until Christmas, as he had advertised. But his fertile brain had already begun to seek for a remedy. He was not long in finding it.

At the Centennial Exhibition the first machines for generating electric light were publicly shown, and they attracted the attention of Wanamaker. When they were taken to the Franklin Institute for investigation and experimentation, after the Centennial closed, the alert merchant followed closely the setting up of the machines and the experiments, at first discouraging, and thus gained his first practical knowledge of electricity. Difficulties were encountered in getting a single continuous light to burn over any certain period. Only one lamp at a time could be lighted, and it had the exasperating habit of going out at the most interesting moment of the experiment.

This did not deter Wanamaker from constructing a generating plant in the autumn of 1878. Before that he had experimental lights in the Market Street windows of his store, imported from Europe and fed by storage batteries. After the "great illumination" Wanamaker made up his mind that Thomas A. Edison held the key to the future of lighting. The Philadelphia merchant went to Menlo Park, and was surprised to find that it was a little station on the New York Division of the Pennsylvania Railroad by which express trains in those days—as now—sped past. He sought out the young inventor in his laboratory, which could hardly be dignified by that name in the early days. In his speech at the opening of the radio station in the Philadelphia store a few months before his death, Wanamaker said of this visit:

"I found him working in a kind of barn, over an electric bulb. His eagerness was like that of a madman. He refused to eat or sleep, being infatuated with the idea which he so soon thoroughly developed. I saw what was to make him the pride of the world, when he took the gold medal at the Paris Electrical Exposition."

Other conferences followed. It was the beginning not only of a life-long friendship between the two men,[1] but of a new era in the development of retail merchandising. The "electric bulb" contributed powerfully to make the fortune of great general retail merchants. Wanamaker led the way, and experimented with the new invention until the details of the installation of electricity in the Grand Depot were completed.

On December 26, 1878, Wanamaker's New Establishment was lighted by turning a few switches. The innovation made a greater sensation that the "grand illumination" of the month before. It was asserted that the mad John Wanamaker would end in burning his place up, and the Sunday newspapers (all his enemies, as he was theirs) declared that the city authorities ought to step in to protect the public from Wanamaker's folly. Many people were afraid to go into the store, and on the first afternoon crowds gathered outside to watch the Grand Depot blow up. Before many weeks had passed, however, the experiment was pronounced a success. Edison's incandescent lamp went on the market in 1879, and Wanamaker was the first to be able

[1] On August 10, 1922, Wanamaker said: "I spent an hour with Mr. Edison recently, and I believe his head is full of other ideas that he will bring to fruition for the benefit of mankind, as times goes on." See also vol. ii, chap. xxxiii.

to profit by this great invention, which largely removed both the fire risk and the uncertainty of electric lighting.[1]

Along with electric lighting Wanamaker had been studying ventilation, which he declared to be the *sine qua non* of basement salesrooms. Before the end of 1879 electricity had solved this problem for him, too, and a basement floor was started. The galleries also, thanks to electric lighting, could be extended. The selling space was doubled when the Christmas season of 1879 opened, and a year later Wanamaker advertised five acres under one roof. In 1881 the ground floor space alone was nearly three acres—"the largest space in the world devoted to retail selling on a single floor." The merchant's foresight in picking his location was universally recognized in 1881, when a newspaper stated:

> To enter the Depot at Chestnut Street and proceed straight through the main avenue to Market Street involves a walk of over 180 yards, and there are very few public avenues in the greatest cities where so many people will be encountered, and so much worth seeing will be met to attract the eye.
>
> On an ordinarily busy day there will be 2500 people an hour passing both ways under the clock at the entrance of the Arcade; and during a pressing season, as about Christmas time, it is within reasonable limits to say that a throng of forty thousand visitors surges through the main avenue daily.

By this time the Grand Depot had forty-six departments and over 2,000 employes. To solve the problem of quick

[1] Although it is claimed that Sir Joseph Swan put an incandescent light in the shop in front of his experimenting room, and kept it burning, before Edison discovered the incandescent lamp, there is no record, before the Grand Depot installation, of electric lighting in a building used by the public. Mr. D'Oyly Carte, in an address at the opening of the Savoy Theatre, London, on October 10, 1881, said: "I have been convinced that electric light in some form is the light of the future for use in theaters, not to go further. This is the first time that it has been attempted to light any public building entirely by electricity. What is being done is an experiment and may succeed or fail." The actor manager, of course, did not know of the successful installation of electricity in the Wanamaker store nearly three years before the Savoy adopted it.

sales a cashier's office was established in the center of the
main floor to which pneumatic tubes came from every counter. The first photograph taken after this innovation makes
the interior of the Grand Depot look bizzare and unsightly
to our twentieth-century eyes. We must remember that
novelties, however, are always attractive to those to whom
they are novelties. The pneumatic tubes were a drawing
card, and they remedied a condition that had become intolerable in large stores before the days of cash registers.

Philadelphia had not yet become accustomed to the great
convenience of electric lighting, good ventilation, and speedy
return of change, when Wanamaker advertised "steam heating throughout the building"—a far cry from three years
earlier, when a radiator in the proprietor's private office was
worthy of special newspaper comment. A vault was constructed, extending to the curbstone under the Market Street
sidewalk, for a steam engine and boiler to heat the building.
This improvement, following immediately upon the excava-
tion of the basement, was completed in a little over a year,
with no interruption to any part of the business. In 1882
the installation of elevators made possible upper floors, and
on the Market Street and Chestnut Street fronts began the
remodeling and expansion that never stopped until the new
building was finished in 1911. The physical changes in the
Grand Depot, and its extension to Chestnut Street, only kept
pace with the increase in the business. "The new kind of
store" was now supplying "every need of man, woman, and
child except food and fuel." There was food for shoppers,
however, as a modest light lunch room was opened, and a
candy counter. The sale of candy increased more rapidly
than that of any single article except books, and resulted in
the opening of a candy factory for making the higher grades
of sweets. On the day after Christmas, 1882, the Wanamaker advertisement announced that the business had once

more doubled in two years, and that there were 3,292 people employed in the Grand Depot.

This result had not been attained without risks and trials that went far beyond those of 1876 and 1877. In writing of the origin of Bethany we told how the eighteen-year-old superintendent had to stand before hoodlums, submitting to being pelted by snowballs and refuse. He won out because he could take punishment, in the sense in which that word is used in boxing. No man could have warded off all the blows. It was a case of standing up and continuing the fight. Wanamaker did not flinch. His faith in himself was magnificent. It won out for him. The business correspondence during 1882 confirms the statement made by George W. Childs in 1889, when he commented upon the appointment of John Wanamaker as Postmaster-General. Said Childs:

"About seven years ago he was badly pushed for money. He was solvent so long as he could keep his head up, but he had to do some lively hustling for cash. It became rumored about that Wanamaker was embarrassed, and that made his fight all the harder."

A similar statement would fit the situation a number of times in Wanamaker's business life. He was well on in years before he had got out of the woods financially. It is always so with men who are doing big things in business. Expansion is the road to success. But those who travel it find every step difficult and some steps painful. What weighs upon the personal owner of a great enterprise is a sense of responsibility to his associates and employees. He is conscious of the fact that if he goes under he carries thousands with him. In 1882 the general store had become an accepted fact in mercantile life and the great principles of which Wanamaker had been the doughty pioneer had come to stay, whether he failed or not. But upon how he thought

Phila Apl 3/03

My dear Mr Apsley

Yours of the 30th has had my best Consideration & I do not think with my heavy stocks I ought to Enter in to the speculation you propose. I think you ought also to be careful, as the future of this year is very uncertain

Yours truly
Jno Wanamaker

"IT WAS NOT BECAUSE HE WAS A BORN GAMBLER THAT WANAMAKER SURVIVED THE
FIFTH ANNIVERSARY OF HIS GENERAL STOREKEEPING."
(See page 223)

and acted, upon his daring and powers of endurance, rested the hopes of all who had cast in their fortunes with him. What burden is greater than this ? Whose shoulders carry it deserves all the reward that comes from success. The year 1882, a year of expansion for Wanamaker, was a year of depression for the city and the country at large. A boom era was drawing to a close, and the tide of prosperity which had carried forward men like Wanamaker menaced to leave them stranded as it receded.

It was not because he was a born gambler that Wanamaker survived the fifth anniversary of his general storekeeping and went forward steadily to greater things. He did not believe in what is called luck, and we do not find that his spirit of adventure betrayed him into a business policy that was unsound. He was not foolish or imprudent in his expansion of the Grand Depot. He made no rash decisions, and then waited to see how things broke for him, like the man who flips a coin in the air. His financial difficulties were due to the nature of the enterprise, which had to keep growing. Standing still or retrenching was more perilous than going ahead.

It is a curious and astonishing revelation to study and record from documents the life of this man. We are unable to find any evidence of the desire or intention to meet a financial crisis by what seems to an ordinary mortal the obvious expedient, a temporary pause, if not actual retrenchment, for the fear of throwing good money after bad. This was not Wanamaker's plan of action. Faced with demands for payments, he would order a few more buildings on Chestnut Street to be bought, and put his O. K. on blue prints of further construction. Then he would turn his attention to schemes for stimulating sales. He believed that if he could get the right kind of merchandise, display it well, and advertise it effectively, people would buy. The money would come in and the bills would be paid. The results invariably justified this belief.[1]

Wanamaker's chief anxiety, therefore, was not finding the money to meet the needs of his business which were rapidly increasing. Nor did he seem to fear any heavy falling off in the buying capacity of the people, due to bad times. He put all his thoughts on having goods to offer that would win and keep the confidence of the buying public in the Grand Depot, to making his store attractive and serviceable, and to presenting through the daily press accurate Wanamaker store news.

To win and keep the confidence of the public he impressed upon the buyers the necessity of keeping their stocks complete and up to the minute. If he heard that a customer had come to the Grand Depot, asked for an article they were supposed to carry, and was told that they were "out for the moment, but would have it in to-morrow," he wanted to know why to-morrow was not to-day. In one of the earliest recorded talks with buyers, in 1881, we find him declaring that a great store could never be built up upon the slogan, "Whatever you want we can get it for you." He pointed out that this method of purveying was that of the commission man and not of the retail merchant. He declared that the Grand Depot must be able to say with perfect assurance, "Whatever you want we have."

His second care was that the buyers should understand their obligation to make good what he said in advertising

---

[1] The tenacity of his conviction that if he sought to be a good merchant all other things would be added unto him is most strikingly put down when he answered the opinions of those who were inclined to think that the expansion of the business in New York would yield more satisfactory results if the store were moved to a new location. He reiterated the idea in the two famous sayings about the world wearing a path to the door of the man who invented a good mouse trap, and Mark Hopkins at the end of the log, by asserting, "If we strive to be good merchants we need not worry about the future of this business."

the Grand Depot, that it offered "the highest grade at the lowest price." But he refused to allow any buyer to offer low-grade goods simply to meet prices of other establishments. "No inferior goods at any price," he said. In regard to what are known as "seconds," he wanted it understood that articles so offered must come up to the general quality of the stocks. "Seconds" were not inferior goods, but simply the Wanamaker quality, damaged, shopworn, or containing some manufacturing defect or flaw which should always be pointed out to the customer.

To quantity and quality of stocks must be added style. This was Wanamaker's greatest struggle with his early buyers. He had around him some men who were excellent merchants when it came to gauging the quantities and varieties needed to meet the demand, and whose sterling honesty equaled his own. But they had little imagination or taste, and were disinclined to study styles. Wanamaker never felt that his great enterprise would fail for lack of money to carry it on or because of inefficient management. But as long as he lived he did worry over falling behind in the styles of his goods. He had a horror of any department becoming stereotyped, content to jog along handling what manufacturers and importers were offering. This easy road of merchandising it was not in him to follow. Point-blank he refused to follow it.

Here we have the secret of the hold he got upon the buying public of Philadelphia and the rapid growth of his prestige as a merchant throughout the country. It is interesting to discover from the records that the sales he originated, and which were immediately copied by other merchants, were not inspired by the desire or necessity of increasing the volume of business, but by the determination to keep stocks fresh and up to date. We have proof of this great fact in his notes of the period and in his talks to buyers.   For instance:

> Let me say that there is no room in the Grand Depot for old stocks. We are increasing our floor space this year, but not for that.   If one of your salesman sees an article around, unsold, until he gets tired of looking at it, how can you expect to find—ever—a satisfied purchaser for it? Mark down goods before they get out of style.   That is why we have our sales.   We must move the goods while they are still fresh and are still a good buy.   Don't think that being able eventually to sell without a loss is good merchandising.   I want to repeat that there is only one kind of good merchandising, and that is to sell to people only what they ought to have, not what they will take for a price.   The men who will keep this business flourishing are those who are thinking about what is going to be worn and what is going to be used.

But mere words and preachments, inspirational talks to buyers, scoldings and ravings, would not have made the Grand Depot a success.   Wanamaker created the machinery for enabling his buyers to carry out his ideals, and he stood behind them constantly, discussing their problems sympathetically, finding the remedy when things went wrong, and making it possible for them to apply the remedy.

This is how Wanamaker came to establish the first European buying organization for a purely retail American business.   In 1880 a resident buyer was sent to Paris, and opened an office at 22 Rue Richer.   It was the beginning of a system that was to cover the world in the tireless search for goods to offer for sale in Philadelphia.   Instead of taking from importers what they happened to have on hand, the Grand Depot announced that its buyers would go directly to the sources and bring back to Philadelphia what they found. Styles in men's clothing and furnishings originated in London; in women's wear in Paris.   The best china came from Limoges, the best gloves from Grenoble, the best woolens from Manchester, the best linens from Belfast, and the best furs from Leipzig. There, and to every other place where styles and tastes originated, Wanamaker sent people out at frequent intervals.[1]

Of what they saw and learned they wrote directly to him, and when they returned to Philadelphia he plied them with questions, and sometimes sent them off again on the next steamer.

In September, 1883, Wanamaker wrote:

No such pains were ever taken in gathering any stock of a former season. We couldn't do so well, because we didn't know how. This last year has been one of decided progress. Growth is manifest in almost all of our departments and this means that our managers and people have grown. It takes a long time to know just how to provide for such a trade as ours, and quite as long to select the right people to serve the customers.

The problems of stocks were threefold—taste, quality, and quantity.

By seeing that his buyers had first-hand knowledge of foreign markets and by giving them the opportunity and machinery for purchasing abroad, Wanamaker made a notable contribution to the elevation of taste in fashion and dress and house furnishings in and around Philadelphia and as far as the reputation and influence of his name carried. The Wanamaker stocks set new standards, and educated the customers so that "they are no longer content to take the leavings of the ladies of New York, but insist on having

---

[1] In 1883 Wanamaker explained his innovation as follows: "Wanamaker's merchants buy many more goods than specialty shopkeepers dream of. The more these men buy the better they buy. They don't slight New York. But they also cross the ferry to Europe. Small merchants have never thought of going to Europe. But Europe is where most of the finer goods come from. Wanamaker's merchants go right to Europe after them; and they have the first pick. They save the New York handling and pulling about. Money goes farther in Europe. The manufacturers over there are delighted to send their prettiest things straight to this ancient and honorable city. And so the best things in all Europe fairly flow into our establishment." We note that at that time Wanamaker called his buyers merchants, indicating his original conception of the general store. Each department head was running a specialty shop.

stocks supplied direct from the foreign markets," as Wana-maker put it.

To get the quality of merchandise he demanded in quantity sufficient to meet the ever-growing needs of the store was a source of constant anxiety, and continued to require the same kind of enterprise and daring that had marked the youthful merchant at Oak Hall.

The proprietor of the Grand Depot had no inclination to become a manufacturer. He was content with his profit as a retailer. But he did not hesitate to make what he could not get. The candy factory, for instance, originated in the determination to sell pure sweets at a reasonable price.[1]

When he discovered that mattress-makers were trying to put off on him adulterated stuffings, he promptly opened a bedding factory. Sometimes it happened that merchants in certain lines, who were hostile to the new competition of general stores, had enough influence to prevent manufacturers from selling to them. When this happened he made what he could not get. An early instance of this occurred on June 3, 1881, when the first advertisements of the new fad of Morris chairs stated:

> They were made in our own factory because the maker whom we had employed threw up his job under threat of a boycott if he worked for Wanamaker.

The effect of this mercantile policy upon customers was soon noticeable in the astounding growth of the store in the face of all opposition. That it was maintained is demonstrated by a study of the charge accounts in the Philadelphia

---

[1] It was after the restaurant had been started as a convenience to shoppers that Wanamaker became a candy merchant. His reluctance to sell candy was based on his belief that it was harmful. He had to be convinced that pure candy was not only innocuous, but actually beneficial, unless taken to excess. But when he finally decided to stock sweets, he could be sure of pure ingredients only by having everything made in his own kitchen.

store. Some one invented a joke that went the rounds of Philadelphia thirty years ago.

"Did you see in the paper this morning the long list of names of people who are not going to buy at Wanamaker's any longer?"

"Why, no."

"Well, look and you'll see it."

"I can't find it anywhere."

"Yes, you can."

"No, I can't."

"There"—pointing to the death notices.

The rather grewsome pleasantry is repeated here because it contains a truth that the jocularly minded had not realized. Many thousands, whose names first appeared on the ledgers of the Grand Depot in the late 'seventies and early 'eighties, not only Philadelphians, but people scattered in states within a day's journey of, or farther from, Philadelphia, remained there as long as they lived. The first purchases were experimental. But after that customers continued to trade with John Wanamaker, not because he was always the cheapest to deal with, but because they had confidence in what he sold.

It was this confidence in the merchant (which soon became the principal asset of his business) that led people gradually to abandon the use of the term Grand Depot. It was not officially dropped until 1885, but long before that a new name, Wanamaker's, had been given the store by those who bought there—an unconscious but powerful tribute to the personality of the man who called his "new establishment" by another name.

While he was contending for new standards of merchandise and succeeding in extending to all kinds of merchandise the canons of style and taste that had already achieved recognition in the field of men's clothing by virtue of the lower

Chestnut Street store, Wanamaker had also on his mind
the problem of making the Grand Depot attractive and serviceable. Because of its mushroom growth and the constant alterations, it was not possible to do much with the ex-
terior of the building. But inside new methods of lighting and ventilation, and the installation of steam heating
and elevators, created an atmosphere of well-being and
efficiency in shopping. As the store grew, the founder's
mind was concentrated upon studying how to change the departments around in such a way that they would become
more serviceable in themselves and co-operate with one
another. "Store-planning," Wanamaker once said, "has little to do with theory. Experience is our only teacher, but
as conditions change we are always learning something new.
No department is ever anywhere for keeps."

To make the store attractive, thick carpets were placed
in the aisles; an art gallery was added in 1881; the permanent place of music to draw people was recognized; and
"days" and "anniversary celebrations" became as fixed a part
of the store's policy as "sales." Children's Day was started
in November, 1880, an idea that may have come from
Bethany, and from it there naturally evolved in Wanamaker's brain entertainments, exhibitions, and contests for
children, which soon turned the minds of the younger generation of Philadelphia at stated intervals to Wanamaker's as they were turned in the winter to the Pure Food
Show and in the spring to Barnum's Circus.

All that Wanamaker learned about advertising in Oak
Hall did not make him think he had come to the end of the
lesson. He was not satisfied with his earlier advertising
achievements, and he was constantly trying new methods
and studying their results. Wanamaker believed implicitly
in the paradox that success is a man's greatest danger. He
used to tell his Bethany people that satisfaction in achieve-

ment was all right only if it did not mean contentment in achievement. How to make his advertising effective was always his concern; but he never gave it more thought than during the first years of the Grand Depot. The period from 1878 to 1880 is of intense interest in the study of Wanamaker advertising, and detailed reference to it will be made later. Among the notable innovations, feats of pioneering, were the first full-page mercantile advertisements in a newspaper, which appeared in 1879, in connection with General Grant's visit to Philadelphia:[1] and the creation in April, 1880, of the reportorial style of advertising which Wanamaker originated to meet the needs of presenting to the public the varied merchandise of a general store.

Wanamaker was always proud of the visit of the great hero of the Civil War, whom he admired with an intensity that seems strange to us of a later generation. He often referred to the fact that he made the uniforms for Grant to use on his triumphal tour of the world, seeming to link this with Oak Hall's having clothed one of the first regiments to leave Philadelphia during the initial year of his mercantile career. When Grant looked over the Grand Depot from the gallery, and realized how minute and extensive were its operations, he turned to Wanamaker and said, "All this is like an army, and you are its general."

Had Wanamaker's original idea for the Grand Depot been carried out, with the co-operation of other merchants, he would still have been the greatest retail clothing merchant in the United States, but in general storekeeping his position would have been hardly more than that of landlord or of *primus inter pares*. As it turned out, the oppor-

[1] Grant made his second visit to the Grand Depot, and ordered a uniform for his trip around the world. He had already been to the Grand Depot during the Centennial Exhibition in 1876, and it was on that occasion that he likened Wanamaker to a general leading an army. In 1877, shortly after the inauguration, President Hayes followed the precedent set by Grant, and visited Wanamaker's just as it was being transformed into a general store.

tunity and responsibility of a greater undertaking than he had dreamed of were thrust upon him, and in a few years he had seen a hazardous scheme become an unquestioned success and one of the great mercantile establishments of the world. Rich before, he had become richer; known before, he had become better known. But the business had grown so vast that he felt the need of an able partner to carry on with him while he was waiting for his sons, undergraduates at Princeton, to join him in the business.

The idea was by no means a new one, and he had had his man in grooming for six years. Robert Curtis Ogden, born in Philadelphia two years before Wanamaker, moved to New York in 1852, where he was first an employee and then a partner, succeeding his father, in the clothing firm of Devlin & Co. for twenty-five years. John Wanamaker had known him since 1861, when they first met in connection with Y. M. C. A. work.[1] Like Wanamaker and Marshall Field, Ogden was an ardent Presbyterian and Sunday-school worker, and had been interested in the evangelistic campaigns of Moody and Sankey. Before the Grand Depot opened Wanamaker proposed that he should join him. The affairs of Devlin & Co. were not prospering, but Ogden did not care to leave his Sunday school in Brooklyn. We find a letter written by Wanamaker to Ogden on January 10, 1876, in which the Philadelphia merchant says:

I should have greatly enjoyed the proposed association, and I believe it would have been to our mutual profit. The only comfort is that I have had a little finger in shaping the events that make your path easier and more hopeful.

Two years later Devlin & Co., through no fault of Ogden's, became involved in financial difficulties resulting from Tammany scandals. Remembering the earlier offer and

[1] Founder's Day address, 1906: "My old associate and much loved personal friend since 1861."

thinking that it might be possible to get Wanamaker's co-operation in launching a clothing business in New York on the lines of Oak Hall, Ogden went to Philadelphia to put the proposition to him. Ogden's biographer quotes from his diary of November 19, 1878, as follows:

> A long and pleasant talk with Wanamaker. He is not inclined to make a clothing venture in New York. The sum of our interview was that when I am ready to entertain a proposal to go to Philadelphia, he will look over the business and see what he can offer me. I come back hopeful and glad I have gone there. He could secure me a managing place in the American S. S. Union. That is not what I want.[1]

Wanamaker was delighted when Ogden agreed to join his organization on January 1, 1879. But he came, not to help at the Grand Depot in the new general-store venture, but to give to Oak Hall the time Wanamaker could no longer spare and the high ability and competence as a clothing merchant that Wanamaker knew he had.[2] After four years at Oak Hall Wanamaker invited Ogden to join him at the Grand Depot, putting before him the alluring prospect of association in the great business that had just turned the corner and was now firmly established. He told Ogden that if Oak Hall and the Chestnut Street store prospered for two years under the management of his brothers and their associates, he would turn the two businesses over to them and invite Ogden to join him in general storekeeping. To quote Wanamaker's own version, Ogden "came reluctantly

[1] See P. W. Wilson, *An Unofficial Statesman—Robert C. Ogden*, page 50.
[2] In his life of Ogden, P. W. Wilson says that the pending failure of Devlin meant that "when he had passed the fatal age of forty, Ogden was faced by the terrible handicap which burdens the man who, so far as the world can judge, has not made good. Ogden's victory, therefore, was of a special significance because it followed defeat and came late in life." It was a man who had seemingly failed whom Wanamaker invited to become his associate. But he was amply rewarded because "he had to face the competition of men whose keen brains quickly adopted his ideas and added to them their own. On Wanamaker's historic achievement in retail industry, Ogden brought to bear a broad and philosophic brain."

because he said he knew nothing of the dry-goods business. I told him that he knew almost as much as I did and that we could both learn. And we did."

On June 15, 1885, the three firms of John Wanamaker, John Wanamaker & Co., and Wanamaker & Brown were dissolved. John F. Hillman retired from the firm of John Wanamaker, at Thirteenth and Market Streets, and Robert C. Ogden and Thomas B. Wanamaker were admitted to partnership. Wanamaker & Brown became Wanamaker & Brown, Incorporated, with William H. Wanamaker as president, and John F. Hillman vice-president and treasurer. The lower Chestnut Street store, John Wanamaker & Co., became a limited partnership formed by Samuel M. Wanamaker, William H. Wanamaker, Isaac D. Shearer, and F. Marion Wanamaker, as general partners, and John Wanamaker as special partner.

Freed of the responsibility and care of the two clothing establishments, and supported by his old and trusted friend, Ogden, and his eldest son, who had recently graduated at Princeton, Wanamaker now had associates, financially interested in the business, whom he needed in order to cope with an expansion that called for more than he felt that he alone would be able to give. But we must remember that during the critical years from 1877 to 1883 John Wanamaker was alone at the Grand Depot, that he established the general store single-handed, and that he shared authority and responsibility with none when he was shaping his mercantile policies in the new venture. And it was around one man that the ever-increasing army of employees had grouped and were trained.[1]

---

[1] The partnership, too, was solely of profits, not of ownership. Robert C. Ogden and Thomas B. Wanamaker put no money into the business. It all continued to belong to John Wanamaker. Consequently, although there was technically a partnership and a firm, the friend and the son were more correctly associates. It was the same with the other son, Rodman, when he was taken into the firm in 1902. Wanamaker referred to Ogden and Thomas B.

In 1883, two years before the partnership, when Robert C. Ogden and Thomas B. Wanamaker came to Thirteenth and Market Streets, the last of the Chestnut Street buildings had been acquired, the basement and galleries had been completed, and the merchandise was spread over eight acres, under the care of 3,000 employees. The Mail Order Bureau was receiving and answering an average of a thousand letters daily, and buyers were going to Europe by the dozen.

A new step forward had been made in ventilation. In his *Philadelphia Store News* for September, 1883, Wanamaker said that he had been conducting "expensive and extensive experiments for over a year under the skillful hands of an English engineer of high repute. The motive power is a mammoth Corliss engine, made by Mr. Corliss in his works at Providence to our special order." The statement went on to describe the eight hundred outlets from miles of metal pipe, distributing fresh air evenly at counters, desks, offices, and departments. "One million cubic feet of fresh air enters the building every hour, and our temperature is ten to twelve degrees lower than on the street. It is calculated that the air in the house is changed every three hours."

In 1885 the last step was taken to make a solid block of the Grand Depot and its Chestnut Street extension. Kelly Street was removed from the city plan, as the title to all the land it served had passed into Wanamaker's hands, and was made into a transept with stained-glass windows bearing the portraits of Robert Morris and Stephen Girard at either end. The new system of ventilation and the elevators had made possible adding upper stories from Kelly Street to Market Street. These were joined over the new transept by bridges,

Wanamaker most frequently as "my associates." When they retired from the firm they retained no interest in the business and bequeathed none to their families. John Wanamaker was the sole owner.

and what was once Kelly Street was roofed over with glass.
The spirit of the place and the dreams of the future are
indicated by what Wanamaker wrote of the actual and the
ideal. After explaining that the establishment had "grown
as Topsy growed, 'cause she couldn't help it," he went on to
confess:

There is no virtue in the oddity of the place. No doubt, it would have
been better every way if, in the beginning, a great brick building had been
put up, towering into the air, full of cars going up and down, with great
windows, courts, skylights, with all the "modern improvements," carpeted
and upholstered from bottom to top, heated and ventilated evenly in
winter, fanned by the cooling breezes in summer, and with all the facilities for turning its vast and various merchandise into money.

But it wasn't done. A village of temporary shops has grown up instead;
shops on shops; shops on top of them; only some of the walls out between,
so that people and things can move about.

But people don't see the partitions. They see the great open spaces
filled with bustling business, and the organization by which it is all one;
and they wonder how Mr. Wanamaker can be so great a man as to understand it all, make it all, drive it all, and keep it from going to pieces.

Bless you; he doesn't do any such thing. He has a little army of
people under corporals, sergeants, captains, colonels, generals, and a whole
staff of aids. But we haven't time for military figures. The aids are
merchants themselves. Why, Mr. Wanamaker doesn't pick out the colors
and shades of next fall's kid gloves. He hands over the money to experts
to buy them with; and by and by he wants his money back again; and, if
it doesn't count right, he has a terrible look in his eye.

The tenth anniversary of "the new kind of store" was
the Centennial of the adoption of the Constitution, which
was celebrated by Philadelphia with great *éclat*. It was
Wanamaker's opportunity to contribute to the celebration
by an historical and educational exhibition of the changes
in manufacturing in America in a hundred years. On the
ground floor, at the Chestnut Street end, was reproduced
an old Philadelphian dry-goods shop of 1787, and along the
main aisle men and women in Revolutionary costumes spun

flax, wove silk, knitted stockings, and made shoes. On the second floor a cottage of a hundred years before, furnished with antiques, heralded the new era of taste in American house furnishings.

After these ten years of belief in offering the public the best that money could buy in the most attractive setting he could devise, Wanamaker was able to advertise that his retail store was the "largest in America." [1]

And two years later the British Warehouseman of May 15, 1889, said:

Mr. Wanamaker is looked upon by the citizens of Philadelphia as a power in the land. He is the owner of the largest retail establishment in the world, and there are few charitable or commercial movements in the Quaker City with which his name is not associated. He employs fifty heads of departments, who command the vast industrial army, numbering over 4,000 persons, that forms the working force. Whiteley's, of West-bourne Grove, Shoolbred's, the Glasgow Colosseum, Kendal Milnes', or the Paris Bon Marché would be lost in such a gigantic structure as that owned by Mr. Wanamaker.

At the time the Grand Depot was turned into a general store many able business men, who had studied carefully or who had themselves had experience in the development of a large retail business, believed that no truly great establishment could be built up without being underpinned by a wholesale business. A. T. Stewart and Co.'s position in New York had been attained by developing simultaneously the wholesale and retail fields in dry-goods; Marshall Field and his associates, Palmer and Leiter, were launching their retail business in Chicago after the great fire on the foundation of supplying dry-goods by wholesale to the merchants of the Middle West. The experience of John Wanamaker had been the same as that of A. T. Stewart and Marshall Field. He had built up the greatest retail clothing store in

[1] It covered 250 x 500 feet, and had a floor space of fourteen acres.

the country while he was enjoying the advantages of being under the same roof a wholesaler and manufacturer. But the experiment of "the new kind of store" had been carried through a decade to unrivaled success solely by retailing.

We have seen how Wanamaker undertook to supply himself with goods only when he could not get what he wanted in the market. But the momentous decade of his merchandising career had been paralleled by the marvelous rise of Marshall Field & Co. in Chicago. Field had partners, of course, where Wanamaker had none, and it was not until the early years of the twentieth century that Marshall Field's retail business equaled that of Wanamaker.[1] On the other hand, the Chicago firm was doing a tremendous volume of business in its wholesale department, and seemed to enjoy certain advantages from wholesaling and retailing together that Wanamaker did not have. The decade had been marked by the rise of other general stores in many American cities, including Philadelphia, and Wanamaker was beginning to have lively competition. These considerations, added to the change in his own position, due to giving up Oak Hall and the lower Chestnut Street store and taking in Ogden and Thomas B. Wanamaker as partners, led John Wanamaker to enter the wholesale dry-goods field.

In the early part of 1887 he purchased the wholesale business of Thomas J. Mustin & Co., and later in the same year that of Riegel, Scott & Co. To house his new wholesaling enterprise he put up a six-story brick building on an opposite

[1] In an advertisement in the thirtieth anniversary month, March 28, 1906, Wanamaker said: "Up to two years ago this one Philadelphia store held the banner of America for actual business done. When the late Marshall Field doubled the area of his new building in Chicago he stepped two or three millions ahead of us in sales." But the retail business in Philadelphia and New York was ahead of that of his Chicago rival. When Marshall Field died, in the settlement of the estate it was disclosed that the retail business for 1906 had been $26,500,000. In that same year John Wanamaker did $37,000,000 in his two stores, the Philadelphia store going a shade over $20,000,000.

corner of Thirteenth and Market Streets. But Wanamaker was never a man to do anything on a small scale. At the end of 1887 he purchased the largest wholesale dry-goods business in Philadelphia from Hood, Bonbright & Co. The newspapers announced:

The sum which Mr. Wanamaker is said to have paid for Hood, Bonbright & Co. is $1,600,000, and he continues that business in the building which had been built for the firm by the Girard Trust, at the southwest corner of Eleventh and Market Streets, paying therefor an annual rental of $67,000.

The wholesale dry-goods business of Hood, Bonbright & Co. was third in the United States. Wanamaker entered into the new venture heart and soul. He worked steadily, day and night, on the inventory of the stock. He declared at the time and afterward that he had never had such fun. It was a great adventure, consolidating the business of the three wholesale houses. His leadership had never been more vigorous and successful, and the virtually unlimited scope of his merchandising genius quickly made itself felt in this new field. He was soon doing a wholesale business of $20,000,000 a year.

On July 11, 1888, John Wanamaker was fifty years old. A life-time of achievement seemed to have been crowded into less than thirty years. But Wanamaker felt that he was only beginning—he was always only beginning. His joy was in adventure, and he faced the future with the same zest for doing things that had led him to open the doors of Oak Hall twenty-seven years earlier. Shortly before he died, he said, referring back to the first act of his mercantile career, sweeping out the store, "I have always had a broom in my hand." The broom was still there when he was fifty, and he looked about him to see where he could next use it.

CHAPTER XXIII

THE MOMENTOUS DECADE: GROWTH OF THE MAN

THERE is an Eastern proverb about "the ways of a man" not being clear to himself, much less to others, "until he has passed his two-score." The Arabs are not impressed with precocity, and they think that it is best for the man who achieves great things in his youth to die young lest his deeds be "confounded by the folly of later years." This certainly would have fitted John Wanamaker had the experiment of the Grand Depot and "the new kind of store" failed. If later generations were able to attach importance to pioneers who blazed the trail for a time and then got lost in the fog, we should realize how many notable feats were performed by those who never reached the end of the trail. John the Baptist is virtually the only forerunner whom the Church has canonized and whom the world has remembered. And he has not come down to us through history.

In writing the story of Wanamaker—and in reading it—one feels that there must have been other young merchants who had his vision, his fertile imagination, his ability to do great things in the world. But we do not know who they are, so we cannot give them the credit that is their due. In other cities than Philadelphia, and in Philadelphia itself, they were thinking as he thought and laying the foundations for great structures that they hoped would win for them a place in history. But they died or quit or failed on the threshold of accomplishment. That they are forgotten is one of the hard facts of life. Would not the significance of what John Wanamaker did at Oak Hall have escaped the attention of the next generation, had 1877 terminated the story? It is because of what came afterward that what went before is remembered and recorded.

The momentous decade in the Wanamaker business—the decade of its founder's forties—was also the momentous decade in the life of the man. It was then that he was "making good." It was then that he saw the principles of merchandising that he, as a clothing merchant, had heralded, applied to the whole field of retailing. It was then that men ceased to ridicule his advertising. They were busy copying it.

We once saw a youngster fixing his football. He was red in the face when the leather cover was taut. But he knew he had to hold on and keep blowing until fumbling fingers had tied the little rubber stem.

"Jehoshaphat!" he exclaimed, when it was all over. "I don't mind blowing 'em up, but that last part certainly is hard!"

Years later the boy was reminded of his experience with the football when he was tempted to relax before a successful business effort was solidly grounded. John Wanamaker in the 1880's was cited to him as an illustration of a man who had the sense to keep on straining every nerve after the leather on his ball was taut. Tying takes a long time and is an art in itself. And the currents and influences outside of business hours that give a man the power to hold on are many and varied. A successful career cannot be faithfully depicted simply by narrating the development of a business. How Wanamaker lived and grew outside of his store during the ten years before his fiftieth birthday, the training of his thinking powers, the education of his tastes, and the broadening of his horizon, all contributed to make it possible for him to put permanent foundations under what he had built and to go ahead with what was to follow.

Almost at the beginning of the decade a third bereavement came to Wanamaker. He had lost a son in infancy and a daughter at the age of five. On June 27, 1881, Elizabeth Deshong Wanamaker died. The place she held in her eldest son's life was very great. After his father's death, twenty years before, at the outset of the Oak Hall career, Wanamaker had brought his mother back to Philadelphia. She had her own home and was privileged to see her boy become wealthy and famous. She was a member of the Christ Reformed Church, in the neighborhood where she lived, but as long as her health lasted she went frequently to Bethany on Sunday afternoons, and was known and loved by all there.

Wanamaker wrote of her not long after her death: "Her smile was a gleam of heaven, and it never faded out of her face to her dying day." It was because of his mother's strong and constant influence upon him, which he felt with peculiar force during the trying days that followed the launching of the Grand Depot, that Wanamaker denied that he was a self-made man. He did not like the term. "How can a man boast that he is self-made," he asked, "when he owes everything to God and mother and wife?" His Bethany Mother's Day messages are full of tributes to Elizabeth Wanamaker, and he mentioned her frequently in the store editorials. We have before us a slip on which he put down some adjectives he wanted to use when writing of his mother. They are: "Cherished, treasured, adored, idolized, tenderly loved, sweet, precious, perfect Mother." And he had on his desk Lowell's lines under her photograph:

"She doeth little kindnesses
     Which most leave undone or despise;
   For naught that sets one's heart at ease,
   Or giveth happiness or peace,
     Is low esteemed in her eyes."

Mary Wanamaker felt that a country home was essential
to her husband's health.   She knew that she must get him
interested in a place accessible to his business that could be
easily reached at nights in the spring and autumn.   It seemed
the one way to give him change and recreation.   Rest she
knew he would not take, and when she suggested trips he
always answered that he had to keep his finger on the pulse
of the business.   She did not argue with him in regard to
this.   The enterprise was of a kind that required the constant presence of its promoter; and promoter he was—in
the best sense of that much-abused word.   There was no
way of prying him loose from Bethany on Sundays, and
Mrs. Wanamaker was sympathetic and eager to do her own
part in that great work.   Before the first trip to Europe
they had planned summers abroad, which would be partly
business and partly pleasure; but for that they had to wait
until the children were a little older.   Not a summer home
for a couple of months, then, but a place that could be lived
in at all seasons was the ideal when John and Mary Wanamaker were still in their twenties.

The pre-occupied Market Street merchant was not difficult for his wife to handle when she proposed a house in
the country.   He had always wanted to get back to the
country, and happy off hours were spent in exploring the
environs of Philadelphia.   In 1868, when Wanamaker was
thirty years old, he and his wife made the first purchase
at Chelten Hills, near Jenkintown, from Isaac Mather,
whose title went back to an original grant from William
Penn.   It was a house on the side of a hill, set in the midst

of great trees. Over the house they could not grow enthusiastic. But the site was what they had dreamed to find.

The diversion of a home in the country was as important
to Wanamaker's growth as travel. The Old York Road
goes through a country unrivaled for beauty and variety
around Philadelphia. Society, taking the step across from
Germantown and Chestnut Hill, moved out the main line
of the Pennsylvania to Bryn Mawr and beyond. The
suburbs served by the Reading never became fashionable.
But the Wanamakers saw no reason to make a change from
their early choice of a country residence.

For some years the Wanamaker home was unpretentious.
The death of Hattie cast a deep shadow over the earlier
period of country life; and the 1870's were years of uncertainty, of risks, of startling changes in Wanamaker's fortunes, of straining every nerve. But gradually the man who
was building up a great business in the city came to love his
country home and to find there the refreshment that he
needed. Chelten Hills was easy of access by train, and not
too far to drive into town. Mrs. Wanamaker and her husband were both fond of horses. The months in the country
were fine for the children; and entertaining was easier at
Chelten Hills than in town.

The Wanamakers waited only until "the new kind of
store" proved successful to build a country home in accordance with their needs and wishes. Additional acreage was
acquired, which made Lindenhurst one of the large estates
of the neighborhood. The original buildings were erected
between March and November, 1880. Many additions were
added up to the completion of the plans in 1884, and great
care was paid to the landscape gardening. The house stood
on high ground with an artificial lake below, in which the
house was mirrored. In 1882 a two-manual organ was
installed. In 1885 additional properties were bought to

The Original Cottage at "Lindenhurst"

house farm employees, and in 1887 four neighboring estates were acquired to enlarge the gardens. Within seven years the Wanamakers had an estate of one hundred acres, every detail in the creation of which had been supervised by themselves. It was at Lindenhurst that they found their recreation and companionship with each other and with their children. As in the case of everything else that he had to do with, the great merchant remained attached to his country home throughout his life.

Wanamaker in his forties had become heavy enough not to appear, as he had seemed earlier, taller than his slightly less than six feet. But although the face and body had filled out, he was not overweight, and he looked younger than his years. There was no streak of gray as yet in his brown hair of fine texture; his face had a good deal of color; and the appearance of youth was accentuated by the fact that he was always smooth shaven, not as usual a custom in those days as it is now. His forehead and gray-blue eyes tended to give him an aquiline look, especially as the lower part of the face seemed small by contrast. But he was better-looking than he had been in the 1870's because the face was fuller. He spoke quickly and in a low voice, and his eyes and face always lighted up when he spoke. The ever-present smile attracted people and held them. People sometimes wondered whether he was impulsive or deliberate, because his nervous way of talking conflicted with the good low pitch of his voice. But none had any doubt as to his kindliness. He never had to make an effort to seem interested in all people and all things with which he came in contact.

As his store and Sunday school had grown to enormous proportions, and as he began to be interested in a multiplicity of things that would seem to make life complicated, his intimates wondered whether it would be possible for him to retain his memory of people, his temperament of enthusiasm for everything, and his accessibility. But he did. To describe him Terence could fairly be quoted: "*Nihil humani alienum puto.*" He went through the days as Tolstoi declared a man should live—with a lively personal interest in every human being whose life touched his, if only in passing and fleetingly.[1] Success and a multitude of cares made no difference in that characteristic of the boy and the young man which transcended everything else about him—the interest in men and things that led him to keep pouring himself out at all times.

Wanamaker in his forties had learned that a man does not have to hold anything back, that he need have no fear of spending himself. He had discovered that living is like drawing water from a well—one can keep letting down his bucket and always pull it up full. The spirit of the man was shown in the way he walked, with a springy step, up on his toes all the time. And he had the habit—also significant—of taking the arm of the one with whom he walked.

Lindenhurst—as far removed from business as if it were another world—brought out the irrepressible playfulness of the man in the earlier days. He would join in games with the children and their friends, run around just like a youngster, and be ready for horseplay and rough house. When he was playing he was happy himself, and he made every one around him happy. Thus he avoided the danger which threatens every man approaching middle life. Cares and responsibilities weigh on him more than he realizes, and he yields to the temptation of being too serious, of holding his natural instincts too much in check, of postponing playtime that he used to give and that he could still give to loved

---

[1] The Russian novelist's diary records: "The most powerful weapon for the conquest of real happiness in life is to emit from oneself, like a spider, without any restraints, a whole lot of love and to catch into it whomever one encounters—a child, a woman, an octogenarian, a policeman."

ones until a little later, making the plea to himself that he must strain every nerve to get ahead with his work. A little later never comes. The children grow up. What has been allowed to lapse cannot be revived.

It was one of the greatest joys of his life that Wanamaker was able to give his boys the opportunities for education that had been denied him. As sons of a prominent Presbyterian layman they naturally went to Princeton, where Thomas graduated in 1883 and Rodman in 1886. The father and mother took a great interest in the boys at college, and enjoyed having their friends at Lindenhurst. During this period they had two sets of children; for the girls were so much younger than the boys.

In the autumn of 1886 Rodman married Fernanda Henry at St. Mark's, Philadelphia. On April 27 of the next year Thomas married Mary Lowber Welsh at Holy Trinity. It was the year following this that Mrs. Wanamaker went abroad with her daughters. After their return, in the autumn of 1889, the older one, Minnie, made her début, first in Philadelphia and then in Washington. In October, 1889, President and Mrs. Harrison spent their first week-end at Lindenhurst, on the occasion of the launching of the *Philadelphia* at Cramp's shipyard. The débutante daughter had been chosen to christen the cruiser.

Lindenhurst was a spring and autumn home rather than a summer place. Philadelphians are fortunate in having the Atlantic coast near by, with fast train service to make possible commuting. Wanamaker was never keen about long stretches at the sea. But his wife and children loved the shore. A cottage was bought at Cape May Point—at the very tip of New Jersey—with broad porches looking out upon the Atlantic toward the breakwater at the entrance of the Delaware River. Here, as at Lindenhurst, they kept open house. The guests were mostly those with whom

Wanamaker had contact in his religious work. He was once asked why a merchant and a man of the world should spend so much of his time with ministers. "Well, I always have," he answered, "and I guess the reason is that I like them."

His wife once laughingly said that her first entertaining on a large scale as a young housewife, with small children and a modest equipment, was for evangelists and parsons, and that it became a habit to have them around. The national reputation of Bethany Sunday School attracted eminent churchmen, and they always accepted eagerly the invitation of Wanamaker to speak in Bethany Church or Sunday School and to go afterward to Lindenhurst or Cape May. Until he entered national political life Wanamaker's social relations did not include men whose interests outside of business were not largely devoted to church. He made no business friends for the sake of business. The increasing ramifications of his business brought him into bank and railroad directorates. But, although he joined clubs, he did not frequent them; and he rarely dined with business associates —outside his own store family—except on formal occasions.

As in the 1870's, he went beyond the horizon of home and church only on trips abroad, and not much then. We find him in London at the end of June, 1880, as a delegate from the Pennsylvania Sunday School Association to the International Convention to celebrate the Raikes centenary. He was in Europe again in 1881 and 1885. In 1887 he attended the annual meeting of the Y. M. C. A. in London in April, and spent the summer abroad. The correspondence of this year is meager. But there are letters indicating that he was interested in starting a branch of the Y. M. C. A. in Zurich; and he was among the guests of Robert Garrett at a dinner at Homburg given in honor of James G. Blaine. Interviewed by the New York newspapers on his return in September, he contrasted the progressive spirit of America with European conservatism in a statement that showed him to be still imbued with the American tourist's conception of the Old World. His letters to Bethany friends of the same period revealed a similar narrowness, which was soon to disappear. In June, 1888, his wife and daughters sailed for a year abroad. He joined them in France for Christmas of that year, accompanied by his sons.

On one of the trips of the 1880's, when electric lights were still a novelty, one night in the dining salon there were flashes, followed by darkness, and then more flashes. Passengers began to think that the ship was on fire, and panic was developing when Wanamaker and his wife took charge of the situation in superb fashion. Wanamaker rose to his feet, secured the attention of the alarmed people, and told of his own experiences with electricity, explaining just what was happening. The incident made a deep impression on all who were on board. It was reported by the captain, and Wanamaker received a letter from the French line, complimenting Mrs. Wanamaker and him and thanking them for their presence of mind.

The reading of biography teaches us that all men grow most slowly where their pride is affected. They can stand anything else, sorrow and disappointment and passing through the deep waters financially, and stand the gaff valiantly and gloriously, where a little hurt to their pride makes children of them. It is a mistake to believe that men of high position, much in the public eye and in the press, are impervious to, or grow callous in the presence of, criticism and gossip and misstatements. We find this interesting illustration in the files of 1885. In July of that year Wanamaker wrote to George W. Childs, proprietor of the *Public Ledger:*

Your biography in the *N. Y. World* yesterday referred to a failing man who owed his prosperity to your taking 40,000 trade dollars on a/c of a $60,000 account, and people are saying that I am the person. I felt chagrined and hurt and I regret to say that after a night's reflection I do not feel any better.

I am sure that you would not willingly place me in such a position as the newspaper article does, and I did not know that your office was nervous about my account, and considered that running my advertisement, amounting in the course of years to several hundreds of thousands of dollars, was a kind of a favor done to me. The article intimates that the trade dollars payment was a kind of compromise of a debt. I cannot tell you how much I feel all this. I had taken a large quantity of trade dollars from poor people, and thought if I could get the newspapers to take them I would have their alliance in supporting the bill before the Senate to redeem them. I supposed you took them to hold. I'd rather you would return them to me than make a loss. Let me pay my accounts weekly in gold rather than be published as your debtor or charity patient.

Childs promptly responded:

The article alluded to could not have given you more pain and mortification than it did me, and I was sorely tried to know what could be done in the matter. No one living has a higher or juster appreciation of you, and what you have done, than myself, and I do assure you that the publication in question was not of my seeking, nor could I have possibly thought that such an unjust and inconsiderate statement could find its way into print.

One consolation—such things are read and forgotten, and even now, you could hardly find any one who remembers having read it. If there is anything I can do in the future to make amends for such a terrible annoyance, I shall not fail to do it. I feel deeply grieved over the whole matter, but it will not be an unmixed evil as far as you are concerned.

This letter, of course, closed the incident. The warm friendship between the two men remained unbroken, and three years later Wanamaker tried to have Childs nominated for the Presidency of the United States. We could cite other instances of deep hurt. Wanamaker did not get angry over malicious statements concerning his business and himself, but he grieved intensely. He used to say, "I am cut to the quick," and it was true. Only after he had been four years in Washington and had gone through bitter political campaigns in Pennsylvania, did he acquire equanimity in the face of affronts. But even then, schooled as he was, he used to get hurt—and he suffered.

On November 11, 1884 the employees of the three Wanamaker establishments gave a dinner to their chief at the old Hotel Bellevue. He responded to the toast:

> There is a history in all men's lives,
> Fig'ring the nature of the time deceased,
> The which observed, a man may prophesy,
> With a near aim, of the main chance of things
> As yet not come to life.

Full of Lindenhurst at the time, Wanamaker told his store people of how the trees and shrubs had fared. The only successful planting was when good stock had been rooted in good soil and was constantly tended. Nothing just grew of itself. All had to be spaded and fertilized and watered. He could not do it himself—he could not even hope to see that it was done. He had to trust to gardeners who were interested in seeing that what was planted thrived through care. It had been the same way with the business. All that had been done he realized was due to the loyalty and industry of those who worked with him. The only prophecy of the future he would venture to make was that the business would continue to grow because of that loyalty and industry. As for himself, he was simply the coworker—of little account or consequence without other people's hands and hearts. He raised a laugh by telling them how an autograph concern had sent him a lot of letters of famous men. Among them he found one that he had written. It was priced—"30 cents."

This modesty, one of his most striking characteristics, which was the test of his growth, was demonstrated in 1887, when the newspapers of Philadelphia wanted to give him a fiftieth birthday dinner at the Union League. To the committee he wrote:

> With very great gratitude for the honor of your most generous proposition, permit me to say that I should not feel it to be right at this time to accept it, since I am yet on the scaffolding of an incompleted building in the sphere of my proper life work. I do not feel that I have yet attained to that which is in any large degree commensurate with the truest purposes and plans of my life.

CHAPTER XXIV

IN NATIONAL POLITICS: THE CAMPAIGN OF 1888

AT THE beginning of 1898, ten years after the memorable Harrison campaign, a man who had evidently recently discussed national politics with John Wanamaker, wrote to him from Denver:

> You seemed to me when I talked with you singularly open to the truth, and free from prejudice, save one utterance, which I thought was not the most mature product of your mind. You said, "I could never be anything but a Republican."
>
> In the abstract, the statement may be correct; but in the concrete, it is incorrect. You are not a partisan Republican. You are not, cannot be, a political partisan. Seeing this was what caused me to say to you, "Your mind is more comprehensive than that of Harrison." I saw this at once. Harrison is a real partisan and sectarian. You could not be either, try as you might, and though you might endeavor to think you were.

The correspondent was writing, of course, after Wanamaker's sensational fight against the Quay machine in Pennsylvania. Wanamaker had proven that he was instinctively incapable of partisanship or sectarianism at every stage of his life. Strong and fearless individualism was a dominant characteristic. He was never bound by precedents in business. John Chambers, implacable foe of the goose-step in religion, was his spiritual father. In business and religion Wanamaker always led. He never followed. It was not in him to be what the Pennsylvania Dutch element contemptuously called a *ja brudder*. But in politics, despite the bitter conflicts with state and municipal bosses, he somehow remained a "regular" Republican. He would not be read out of the party, and he worked loyally with party leaders in every national campaign from 1888 to 1920. He seemed to have a contempt for mugwumpery. Shortly before the election of 1916, he wrote at Saratoga Springs, "My first presidential vote was given for the first presidential candidate of the Republican party." Through thick and thin, from Lincoln to Harding, he stuck by the party.

In 1888 he was called an opportunist, and the reproach was repeated many times after that. In view of the absence of opportunism from his record in every other phase of his career, however, this explanation of his stalwart Republicanism does not satisfy. The Denver correspondent said that his fidelity to the party at times when his avowed principles would have dictated a break with the organization was due to prejudice. Does this not come nearer to the truth?

A high protective tariff as opposed to free trade or tariff for revenue only was the great economic plank of the Republican party. His support of protection—at that time, at least—hardly represented a conviction, and it certainly did not coincide with the interests of a retail merchant whose great forte had for many years been importing. Wanamaker was an enthusiastic advocate of government regulation of the liquor traffic, and very many of his best friends were distressed by his close affiliation with a party that refused to pay attention to the liquor issue. His utterances at Bethany could be construed as an indorsement of aggressive anti-saloon politics, and three months after he became Postmaster-General he was still telling his Bethany people to "vote prohibition"! [1]

Wanamaker's Republicanism was grounded in a senti-

[1] But this did not mean voting for the candidates of the Prohibition Party. He wanted Bethany people to support local option in the State and to advocate legislation for educational propaganda against alcohol in the public schools. See Volume ii, chap. xxi.

mental attachment he had formed for the new party in the days of bitter passion that preceded the Civil War. Like most Northerners of his generation, it was "the party of Lincoln," the party that had saved the United States from disruption; and independent thinking and broad-mindedness did not avail to free him from the notion that deserting the Republican party meant disloyalty to the principles for which Lincoln and hundreds of thousands of the Grand Army of the Republic had given their lives. He refused to admit that a new generation brought new problems which radically transformed party policies. The name Republican evoked a flood of precious memories, and whatever might be the great issues of any particular presidential campaign, loyal men born north of the Mason and Dixon line ought naturally to be Republicans. Innovations and changes in business were to be welcomed, and the outward form of church organization was not a matter of vital importance. But the nation was always to be saved through the Republican party!

In 1888 the Republicans had hardly recovered from the crushing and unexpected blow of Blaine's defeat. It was generally admitted that Cleveland had been elected because of the gratuitous insult offered to the Catholics of New York by an overzealous clerical friend of Blaine's. But slips like that of Burchard's do not turn an election except where the contest is close. Cleveland had piled up heavy votes in normally Republican states, and his conduct as President had won him the confidence of forward-looking people of all parties. Blaine was still the great Republican leader, whose personality stirred the imagination. But his prestige was not what it had been, and most of the party leaders realized that it would be foolish to attempt to run him again.

John Wanamaker was just beginning to come into national

prominence. He joined with other Philadelphians in suggesting George W. Childs, publisher and editor of the *Public Ledger*, as the strongest candidate available. Everybody knew Childs, and there was no doubt about his views on public questions. He had long been a constructive and forceful influence in national politics, and he was admirably equipped to oppose Cleveland on the tariff issue. At the Republican convention, however, which Wanamaker attended as a delegate, the backers of Childs found what all backers of candidates from Pennsylvania have found in national conventions, that hailing from the most Republican of states was a fatal handicap. The Presidential nomination is not a reward for past performances, but rather a bait to tempt the voters of an uncertain state. Coming from Pennsylvania eliminated Childs. Wanamaker's own name was mentioned—not for the last time—as a strong candidate to win business men. A boom for Wanamaker was launched at Chicago, and the delegates were circularized with Wanamaker literature. The Philadelphia merchant promptly disavowed the efforts being made on his behalf, denouncing the boom as "ridiculous and outrageous." He did not have to do that. Even had he been as strong a figure nationally as Childs—and he was not—his Pennsylvania origin would have caused him to be discarded before the candidates were voted on.

It was after he returned from the Chicago Convention that Wanamaker first attracted national attention in politics. He was expected to announce his intention of supporting Harrison, being perfectly satisfied with the candidate. All leading Republicans were rallying around the Indiana lawyer who had been defeated in his own state for re-election to the Senate the year before. It was not playing the game to doubt the wisdom of the choice. But Wanamaker was frank enough to declare that Harrison's prospects of election were not good, unless the party woke up, and he gave his reasons. Cleveland, he said, had made a big mistake in the radical downward revision of the tariff, but his administration was strongly entrenched, his beautiful young wife had a remarkable hold on the affections of the people, and the outworn methods of campaigning, which party leaders seemed disposed not to change, would fail to elect Harrison.

Senator Quay was National Chairman. He did not relish Wanamaker's outspoken criticism of Pennsylvania politics, and he feared what afterward happened, that Wanamaker might become the leader of the reform element within the state. But both he and Cameron, the other Pennsylvania Senator, recognized the necessity of putting the campaign on a business basis, and they knew that if Wanamaker could be brought into camp and given work to do, the campaign might be conducted more vigorously. They were alarmed at the apathy of the Republicans, and they knew that what Wanamaker had said was true.

Quay already had Wanamaker's name on the list of Pennsylvania presidential electors, which was a perfunctory honor. He suddenly decided to ask Wanamaker's aid in the campaign, and telegraphed him for an interview. Wanamaker's first impulse was to put him off or even to answer that he could not see him, but he did not want to seem lacking in courtesy or in interest in the party's success. Quay came, and urged him to take an active part in electing Harrison. Wanamaker consented, provided the National Committee would agree to the creation of an advisory board made up of business men, with its own treasurer, and given unrestricted power in raising and deciding upon the expenditure of funds. The board should be large and representative, covering the whole country, but its efficiency would depend upon having a small executive committee with full power to act. Quay was not greatly pleased with the stipulations. But he was out to win, and he realized that Wanamaker's suggestion was the practicable plan for getting a campaign fund and arousing interest and enthusiasm, without which the chances of victory were slim. The Cleveland administration was, as Wanamaker had said, well intrenched, and the confidence among business men in Cleveland made the Republican leaders very anxious.

John Wanamaker and Thomas Dolan called a meeting of ten men in Philadelphia, each of whom subscribed $10,000. With this sum as a nucleus, and the tariff issue as the argument, manufacturers were approached, and additional contributions were collected. The Democratic press and campaign speakers charged that Republican business men under the leadership of John Wanamaker, chairman of the finance committee, were attempting to defeat the will of the people in order that they might advance their own interests. Exaggerated figures were given, and after the election it was charged that Wanamaker had sent $400,000 to Quay to buy the districts in Long Island whose vote carried New York for Harrison and decided the election.

In our day the money raised by the Wanamaker committee does not seem excessive. But it was the largest sum used in a presidential campaign up to that time, and the fact that every other Republican except the head of the ticket was defeated in New York looked suspicious. Platt and Elkins were accused of having made a deal with the Democrats to thrown down Cleveland in exchange for state and municipal control. But Quay was generally given credit for the election of Harrison. His political movements in the New York situation had been skillful. If there was any collusion between state leaders of the two parties, Quay at least had to make good on the opportunity offered him!

The financial backing of the Advisory Board, however, was an essential factor in enabling Quay and Platt to handle a seemingly hopeless situation. There is no more evidence than in any other election, however, that the money was wrongly used, and we must remember that the expenditures were under the control of the finance committee. Wanamaker denied both the size of the fund and its last-minute effectiveness. In an interview he said:

"We did not need $400,000, and we did not raise it. But we raised more than $200,000. My contribution was $10,000. We raised the money so quickly that the Democrats never knew anything about it. They had their spies out, supposing that we were going to do something, but before they knew what it was, we had them beaten. They were not beaten in November, nor in October, but long before that."

When the charges of the wrong use of money and the unfairness of a huge campaign fund in 1888 were repeated in after years, Wanamaker reiterated his denial of the misuse of funds, pointing to the unblemished reputation of the men who were not politicians that he had gathered around him, and justified the collection of the fund. He expressed the belief that it was right to ask business men in various parts of the country to provide "the sinews of war" for a campaign on the ground that it is better "to insure good times than to have to start to build them up again." Large sums can be spent legitimately in an educational campaign to persuade and convince the voters of the soundness and advantage to the country of one party policy or set of policies over another.

Wanamaker's defense of the large campaign fund was hard to answer. With vigor and shrewdness he called attention to the great size of our country, the impossibility of the personality of the candidates being any longer known to all the new generation of voters growing up without traditional American background, and the need of thousands of campaign speakers and the printing and distribution of tons of literature to reach all the people, which imposed upon National Committees the necessity, which had not before existed, of raising very large sums for expenses.

When National Chairman Quay went to congratulate President-elect Harrison, after "the verdict of the people" had been rendered, he found Harrison overwhelmed by the good news and disposed in true Presbyterian fashion (for he was a pious man) to believe that Providence had been on the Republican side. "Providence," he said in his cold and solemn fashion, grasping Quay's hand, "has given us the victory." Quay listened politely to this explanation of how New York had been wrested from the Democracy, and made no comment. But afterward he expressed to the veteran journalist, Colonel A. K. McClure, his opinion that Harrison was "a political tenderfoot." "Think of the man!" Quay exclaimed. "He ought to know that Providence hadn't a damn thing to do with it!"

But Wanamaker had, and none knew this better than Quay. He saw the letter written by General Clarkson, Vice-Chairman of the National Committee, on November 13:

The name of John Wanamaker, who never failed us in purpose or trust, and whom the public was always willing to believe and the people always willing to follow, was the sufficient tower of saving strength to us—and by grace of its help we won.

Clarkson went on to pay tribute to Wanamaker's sagacity, courtesy, energy, and modesty—enumerating these virtues by name. Quay knew that the Clarkson letter was a gentle way of calling attention to the fact that the country and the party expected the National Committee to give Wanamaker a substantial reward, and he wondered whether some means could not be found of putting his fellow Pennsylvanian in

London or Paris. It was Quay's own initiative that had brought Wanamaker to the fore in the campaign. The Harrison victory placed Quay in a position of power and prestige in the Republican party. But it had not been accomplished without giving power and prestige to another man whom the next decade was going to reveal as Quay's bitterest and most dangerous political foe.

CHAPTER XXV

THE APPOINTMENT TO HARRISON'S CABINET

THAT Blaine, outstanding figure in the Republican party, would be Secretary of State was not questioned. There was precedent for giving a disappointed leader the office next after the Presidency. But for two months after the election no word came from Indianapolis regarding Cabinet appointments. The country was deeply interested, because Harrison himself had not been the choice of the bosses, and they wondered just how independent he could and would prove himself to be. It was rumored—and the rumors multiplied with the delay—that party leaders had handed him a slate, and that General Harrison had balked. Many newspapers, while admiring his independence, warned the President-elect that upon careful Cabinet selections depended the success of the new administration.

The situation was unique. It was the Republican party's first return to power after a Democratic administration. The election of Cleveland in 1884 had terminated the succession of victories unbroken through a quarter of a century. The older generation of Republican statesmen was dying out. Upon General Harrison and his advisers was imposed the task of building up again the party machinery with newcomers. It was certain that the Cabinet would have to include men who had brought about the restoration of the party, but in the eligible list were some who were unpopular in the country and whom Harrison himself did not want because

(Copyright, 1889, Notman Photo Co., Boston)

PRESIDENT HARRISON'S CABINET

Reading from left to right: Noble, Wanamaker, Rusk, Miller, Proctor, Windom, Tracy, Blaine, the President

of their open hostility to civil service reform. It was a question, too, in view of the criticism of the way the election had been handled, whether it would be wise for Harrison to put the seal of approval upon methods that had been challenged (and of which he claimed to have no knowledge) by including in his official family men who were directly responsible for the victory.

Pennsylvania, as usual, had contributed the largest vote in the Republican column, and Cameron as well as Quay had done yeoman work for Harrison. Harrison may have been sincere in attributing his election to Providence. But he knew that the principal factors, humanly speaking, had been his National Chairman and National Advisory Chairman. When Quay found that Wanamaker could not be dumped on a foreign shore, but would have to be invited to Washington, he inspired newspaper comment on the wisdom of having a business man at the head of the navy. Our navy needed to be thoroughly reorganized. This was an item in the talk about the necessity of "a business administration." A business administration is always promised when one party succeeds the other, but not when it succeeds itself.

Who among those whom Harrison should reward was more of a business man than John Wanamaker? Not as a politician, but as a business man and a religious leader, was he nationally known. Like Harrison, Wanamaker was a Presbyterian elder, and he could be relied upon to help the President in keeping politics as clean as possible at Washington.

Because the Pennsylvania Senators were afraid that Wanamaker would not be "reasonable" on the patronage question in the Postmaster-Generalship, the position he was best fitted for, his name was put on the tentative slate as Secretary of the Navy. Vice-Chairman Clarkson, of Iowa, who was popular with all the party leaders and who was as good a politician as he was a business man, was cast for Postmaster-General. It seemed unwise, however, to include in the Cabinet two men who had had so much to do with the actual machinery of the campaign. Harrison did not know Wanamaker. Clarkson was a personal friend, and the President-elect wanted him, in case one of the two had to be eliminated. Much as they distrusted Wanamaker, Harrison's political advisers felt that he could not be left out. Clarkson was dropped.

On January 19, 1889, when the newspapers were still gossiping, a letter marked "confidential" was brought by hand to Wanamaker at his Philadelphia office. It read:

INDIANAPOLIS,
January 17, 1889.

MY DEAR SIR:—

We did not have the pleasure of meeting during the campaign, and I have had it in contemplation for some time to ask you to visit me here. Will it not be convenient for you to come at some early day? You are at liberty to name any time that is most convenient to you, as I shall always be at home.

Very sincerely yours,

BENJ. HARRISON.

The letter was in the President-elect's own handwriting. He misspelled Wanamaker's name both on the envelope and inside. Its meaning was evident. Had not its recipient been aware of Harrison's cold and undemonstrative nature, he might have considered the letter restrained and ungracious. There had not been lacking the kind of friends to tell him that General Harrison had wanted to offer the Postmaster-Generalship to Clarkson, and that in deciding upon Wanamaker he had capitulated to arguments of party leaders and resigned himself to circumstances. Wanamaker must have coveted national recognition from his party very much to have answered, as he did, that he would make the visit to Indianapolis immediately.

For the first time since the pioneer days of the 'fifties John Wanamaker returned to Indiana. It was at the request of a President-elect to receive one of the highest honors in the land. Wanamaker wanted the Cabinet post. But he did not intend to accept it as a reward for services rendered in the campaign.

Harrison and Wanamaker took to one another immediately. It was a sudden discovery of affinity. Each was unlike what the other had expected. Harrison was not as stiff and unbending as Wanamaker had thought he would find him. Wanamaker was far from being the ambitious business man ready to accept office as a *quid pro quo*. The President-elect was already weary to death of the importunity and self-seeking of many whom he had thought were friends for friendship's sake. Here was a stranger—but one to whom he was under very great obligation—stating in the very first minutes of the interview that Clarkson had done notable work in the campaign and would be an ideal selection. Clarkson came from Iowa, a state that should have recognition; and he would fill the post creditably. Moreover, Wanamaker had heard that Harrison's heart was set on Clarkson, and Wanamaker was perfectly willing to step aside. At the same time, he did not disguise the fact that he would accept the Postmaster-Generalship, if Clarkson refused it, and that he felt that he could render service to the President, the party, and the nation in that position. He made it plain that he would not have accepted the navy portfolio, had it been offered him, and that he would not now accept the navy in any readjustment.[1]

Harrison was taken aback for a moment. This was not the Wanamaker he thought he would see. Then he said that the decision had been made. Keen reader of men, Wanamaker realized that Harrison set great store by Clarkson, and he noticed the use of the definite article rather than the possessive pronoun. Harrison had answered, "The decision has been made," not, "My decision has been made." He insisted on the spot that the President-elect telegraph and offer the post to Clarkson.

Clarkson's answer was to inquire whether Wanamaker would take the Postmaster-Generalship if he did not. Having ascertained that Wanamaker was willing, the Iowan matched the Pennsylvanian's generous spirit. He not only refused the direct offer of the post, but added that Wanamaker was needed in the Cabinet; and he volunteered to serve under Wanamaker as First Assistant for a year, so that the administration would have the benefit of his political experience.

Both for Harrison and Wanamaker the Indianapolis visit was a stroke of good fortune. It was manifest that Harrison had decided to offer the Philadelphia merchant a place in his official family with considerable reluctance. The personal meeting with Wanamaker opened Harrison's eyes. Clarkson's gesture, following closely upon his discovery of what Wanamaker was really like, confirmed the impression made upon him by the first meeting, that Wanamaker was a man to tie to. Harrison had every reason to trust Clarkson's political judgment, and after this exceedingly personal

[1] Powerful reasons against the appointment of a Pennsylvania business man at the head of the Navy Department had already been submitted to Harrison, with Wanamaker's approval. Harrison had been told that it would be impossible for Wanamaker to have a Cabinet post in which he would have to award very large contracts to Pennsylvania steel mills.

test, Harrison believed that Clarkson regarded Wanamaker as a precious political asset. From this time on Harrison was unmoved by the assaults of politicians and the sharp criticism of newspapers. He now knew that the things said about Wanamaker were untrue. Respect quickly ripened into affection, and the Postmaster-General whom he had selected from a sense of obligation became his friend for life.

In our age neither policies nor personalities in national politics affect us deeply. We do not hate unduly, nor is our enthusiasm aroused to fever heat. Most Americans are only mildly Republican or Democrat. It may be that we have become indifferent to party politics or that our country is now too large and life too complicated for any one policy or issue to affect us vitally. Certainly we do not become agitated over the alleged shortcomings of men in official life, as our fathers did. It is difficult, therefore, for us to realize the intensity and persistency of the storm of abuse that had to be weathered by those who accepted political office a generation ago. Almost everybody knew and cared who were in the Cabinet, the Senate, and the House, and the interest was great in state and municipal politics. Nowadays few Americans could give the names of the President's Cabinet, much less tell anything about the vices or virtues of the incumbents. This indifference may be bad for the country. But it makes much more comfortable the lot of those who hold high office.

Wanamaker was not the type of man that generally entered politics forty years ago. Philadelphia had become accustomed to his fertility in ideas, and knew from long experience that the ideas which he himself clung to and backed were likely to prove sound, even epoch-making. The country at large, however, and the new friends in politics, did not know that the Postmaster-General was more like

Edison than Barnum. The reforms he instituted and the startling innovations he advocated upset equally small and large fry. Immediately he became the principal target of abuse and ridicule in the Harrison administration.

The very fact of his selection for a Cabinet post was roundly criticized. Outside of his home town only the name of Wanamaker was known, and, except in church circles, it meant simply a shop.[1] How was a shopkeeper fitted for a Cabinet post? The story was spread that Wanamaker had no real interest in Republican politics, and that he had purchased the Cabinet post by paying $40,000 to the national campaign fund. It was a business transaction. The nation was to be the sufferer. Another story was that Wanamaker's part in the campaign to elect Harrison had been that of the salesman. Was he not a merchant? Did he not translate everything into terms of buying and selling? What more natural than that he should have been given the job of selling the Cabinet and diplomatic posts? And he had bought one for himself!

These stories, once in circulation, did not cease to be repeated long after the Harrison administration passed into history. Senator Platt, for instance, left a statement, to be published after his death, in which he said that Elliott F. Shepard asked Senator Brice, chairman of the Democratic National Committee, if he had heard that "an attempt had been made to sell a position in President Harrison's Cabinet." Senator Brice replied: "It was reported to us at Democratic headquarters that a gentleman of prominence, who was active in raising campaign funds for the Republican Committee, approached the manager of the land-grant rail-

[1] "Until John Wanamaker went into Harrison's Cabinet he was one of the most widely advertised men in the country, but advertised impersonally as a business. Outside of his native city, when Wanamaker's store was spoken of, it was only vaguely understood that there must be such a person. With his entrance into political life he became an important national figure."—New York *Herald*, September 29, 1896.

roads with a proposition that if they would contribute a large sum of money President Harrison would allow them to select the Secretary of the Interior, who would look after the government's interests in their roads." Asked whether he knew that the story was true, Senator Brice said that he was only telling what he heard and that Wanamaker was the man mentioned. Platt's statement said that Shepard remarked: "It could not have been Mr. Wanamaker. I always supposed it was Mr. Platt." At the time the posthumous Platt papers were published, M. J. Dwyer, editor of a Washington newspaper, declared that Wanamaker told him just before the end of his term as Postmaster-General that he had given $40,000 to the Harrison campaign fund on condition that he be appointed Postmaster-General.

On March 10, 1910, when these stories were given to the press, John Wanamaker said to reporters at the Hotel Plaza: "There isn't a word of truth in either statement. That is all I have to say." And yet in the Bull Moose campaign of 1912 a prominent supporter of Roosevelt gave wide circulation to "the tyranny of the machine" of the Harrison administration, which Roosevelt "defied and exposed." The Bull Moose letter said:

In a free talk with congenial spirits, President Harrison once said: "When I came into power I found that the party managers had taken it all to themselves. I could not name my own Cabinet. They had sold out every place to pay the election expenses." This statement had point, because the New York papers had just headlined as a fact that "the U. S. Post Office had been sold to a business man for $50,000." History confirms the fact.

Not a shred of evidence was ever produced to substantiate the charges. If anything of the kind had occurred, Senator Quay would have known it, and he would certainly have produced the evidence when he was fighting for his life against Wanamaker a few years later. There is no doubt that promises were made, many of them, and it is probable that certain diplomatic posts were, as they had been before and since, offered in return for campaign contributions. There could have been nothing of this kind in connection with Cabinet positions, however, for Wanamaker was not consulted in making up the slate, and, although he wanted a Cabinet place, there is evidence that he did not consider General Harrison in any way obligated to give him one.[1]

Condemnation of the inclusion of Wanamaker in the Harrison Cabinet was not confined to Democratic newspapers and to ill-natured radical journals, whose editors were only too ready to impugn the motives of wealthy men. *Harper's Weekly*, for instance, said editorially, just after the inauguration of Harrison:

Wanamaker is in no sense a leader of the party, and before the late election he had been unknown in political life. We have stated frankly the reasons why his appointment must be deeply regretted. They are not affected by the fact that he is undoubtedly a man of great executive ability and of kindly and generous impulses. It was not for these reasons that he was appointed. We have no grounds for supposing that he sought the appointment. But it is none the less to be deplored.

The accusation that he had bought a place in the Cabinet and had been forced upon Harrison did not bother Wanamaker once he had met Harrison and they had discovered the mutual attraction. It was untrue, and Wanamaker never worried over things that were manufactured out of

[1] Numbers of letters, containing offers of aid in pushing Wanamaker to the front, were received by him during and after the campaign. We select an amusing exchange of letters. A ne'er-do-well, who had once been a friend of Wanamaker's, but who had drifted off into "bumming his way" instead of working for a living, wrote: "My dear John: I know what you are after. I think you may win it, and though there is no love lost between us, I will help you in a way you do not dream of, to reach your goal; but if I give you my services there must be some honorable arrangement between us whereby I get full value for services rendered." The response was to the point: "My dear William: If you know what I am after you know more than I do, and I do not see how you could help me."

the whole cloth. But the jibes and sneers and ridicule of the newspapers hurt him deeply. He had always regretted his scanty education, and, up to the time he became Post-master-General, he was not sure how he would fit into the wider field of service that had called him away from store and Sunday school. His social contacts were largely in religious circles. Perhaps there was something in the cartoon that represented him in the Post Office Department standing with a measuring tape over one arm and calling, "Cash!" He resented malicious attacks upon his integrity and high-mindedness as a business man. After nearly thirty years of business life in Philadelphia *sans peur et sans reproche*, during which he had triumphed over the slanders of his enemies and had won the confidence of Philadelphia, it was hard to have to be maligned by the opposition press all over the United States. His business reputation and conduct were his most precious possessions. Had he realized how he was going to be lied about, it is doubtful whether he would have been willing to pay the price of high place in the Government.

The New York *World* led the attack. It was Pulitzer's first experience with the loss of election, and he got it into his head that Wanamaker was responsible for Cleveland's defeat. He put his brightest young men on Wanamaker's business trail, bidding them unearth and dish up every fact that might be twisted into a story that would discredit the new Postmaster-General. Day after day the *World* tried to disseminate poison gas about Wanamaker. Custom House returns and reports were gone over with a fine-tooth comb. Not finding anything against the Wanamaker Store, Pulitzer's reporter on that special trail brought in the figures of repayments for overcharges or wrong charges made to Wanamaker's since the election. This was a natural routine transaction. But it was made to appear that Wanamaker had used his political influence to get refunds and rebates from the Treasury Department. Wanamaker & Brown, with which he was no longer connected, had sent out their usual circular letter to postmasters in smaller towns offering them commissions on business obtained. Wanamaker was accused of using the machinery of the Post Office Department to help along his business.[1]

To show the length to which Pulitzer was willing to go, there can be cited a letter of a column and a half from the *World's* Berlin correspondent, in which it was stated that Mr. Wanamaker was employing sweatshop workers in Berlin who, for miserable wages, "too little even to live upon," made garments that are sent to the City of Brotherly Love to sell at good prices. This, declared the *World*, was the kind of man that had become Postmaster-General. The only foundation for the story was that the Wanamaker firm, like other large American stores, had bought in the Berlin market German-made cloaks that were probably of sweatshop origin. The *American Economist* took up the cudgels for Wanamaker, and answered the *World* as follows:

> Suppose a cloak made in Berlin could be imported and duty paid for $13, while the same cloak would cost to make here $15, and Mr. Wanamaker should choose not to import Berlin-made cloaks at $13, but should pay $15, to have them made in Philadelphia or New York. Would not his competitors have their cloaks imported at $13 and consequently sell them at $2 less than Mr. Wanamaker? Would American consumers pay $2 more for a cloak simply because it had been made here? If not, the experiment would simply tend to eliminate Mr. Wanamaker from the list of successful merchants. Berlin-made cloaks must doubtless sell in Phila-

---

[1] The clothing firm of Wanamaker & Brown, Philadelphia, is another of those gigantic concerns for which the United States has long been famous. This house, following up the practice of previous years, issued recently a circular to postmasters inviting them to become sales agents. A storm of indignation arose from the Democratic and Mugwamp press, accusing Mr. Wanamaker of endeavoring to use in his trade the employees of the Federal service, of which he is the head. With singular zeal and unanimity, however, the newspapers of Philadelphia rallied round their fellow-citizen.— *British Warehouseman*, May 15, 1889.

delphia at the same prices at which American coats of like style, quality, and repute sell. Mr. Wanamaker, like all other merchants, must adapt his prices to the demand.

Newspaper abuse had to be ignored or it would have sapped his energy. There was so much of it that he could not correct misstatements. It was unnecessary for him to deny in Philadelphia the lack of safety of his building, the slavery of his employees, unfair competition with small shop-keepers, cheating the customs, avoiding taxation, and sharp business practices. And elsewhere the criticism could not harm his business. But sometimes he was provoked to respond, especially when letters came from church people stating that his hypocrisy was casting a reflection upon the church. To one correspondent he wrote a vigorous letter in which he offered: "If the statements you refer to are found to be facts after an investigation by an impartial committee, I will contribute $10,000 to any ten charities that the mayor of your city may designate."

That the misrepresentation and violent abuse continued unabated throughout the four years in Washington and afterward was largely due to the enemies Wanamaker made in the performance of his public duties. The Louisiana state lottery, and other smaller lotteries were not suppressed without backfire. The express companies and the telegraph companies left no stone unturned to discredit the man who wanted to terminate their monopolies. His success in public office was in itself a fact that could not be forgiven by those who feared him in business life. And from this time on to the end of his life he was made to realize that the new personal form of extensive advertising which was a great factor in his business success was a kind of boomerang. No matter what he did as a citizen and a churchman the petty-minded and jealous were going to see in every activity the merchant, thinking of his wares. This truth was neatly and forcibly

expressed in verses written by a clever New York news-
paperman:

"My name is John; I run a great big store
And I make money; which is not surprising,
When you reflect that each year I do more
    Of advertising.

"I advertise in papers great and small
And everybody knows I'm enterprising;
But then, whate'er I do, they, one and all,
    Say: 'Advertising!'

"When I was born, if they could have foreseen
The heights to which I have of late been rising,
The comment on my crying would have been:
    'He's advertising.'

"I started once a mammoth Sunday School—
My duty to my neighbors recognizing—
But every day some narrow-minded fool
    Said: 'Advertising!'

"If, as a business man, I take a hand
In a municipal reform uprising,
The others in it are a faithful band;
    I'm 'advertising.'

"I bought a famous picture recently,
My best artistic judgment exercising,
And now all jealous Gotham says of me:
    'He's advertising.'

"I've given my employees co-operation,
They will do better work for realizing
A share of profits; but full half the nation
    Says: 'Advertising!'

"I worked for Harrison in '88;
  Now in his Cabinet I sit, advising;
  Whene'er I'm mentioned in affairs of state,
      I'm 'advertising.'

"No doubt 'twill be the same thing when I die.
  They'll say I did it for the eulogizing—
  Which is not grudged to others dead; but I
      'Am advertising!' "

CHAPTER XXVI

POSTMASTER-GENERAL: DISAPPOINTMENTS

AS IN his early days at Oak Hall and when he launched the Grand Depot, John Wanamaker, upon undertaking the management of the greatest business department of the American government, had to suffer criticism and wait for the triumphant vindication of the law of "handsome is as handsome does." In his fifties he was as much stimulated and spurred on by opposition as he had been in his twenties and thirties. When he discovered that the big interests which he was opposing as a public duty were subsidizing attacks against him and were spreading absurd legends of Wanamaker the man and merchant, he was more determined than ever to "put across" ideas which he brought with him to Washington, and others which came to him in the first few months of his new position.

The day he went to Washington to report for duty after his confirmation by the Senate, Wanamaker met on the train the former postmaster of Philadelphia, General Bingham, who had been elected to Congress. Bingham was enthusiastic about the great things that were to be done in the Post Office Department, and Wanamaker was delighted to find a member of Congress who was thinking along the same lines as himself. Wanamaker never needed any influence from the outside to make and keep him optimistic and enthusiastic. But a Congressman so thoroughly alive to things that ought to be done to improve the postal service and widen its usefulness was a pleasant discovery. The two men parted with a hearty handclasp. "We shall work together," announced

Wanamaker, "for all these things." "By all means!" answered Bingham. But when Wanamaker faced the House committee, and made his plea for authority and funds to carry out the particular schemes that had been discussed, Bingham had nothing to say. He seemed to have lost his enthusiasm. Later he became a backslider, and voted against Wanamaker's proposals in committee and on the floor of the House. The interests whose monopolies were threatened by the extension of the Post Office Department's activities had intimidated General Bingham along with his less informed colleagues. Bingham had yielded to political pressure. He could not stand the gaff of supporting what he had told Wanamaker a few months before were excellent goals for the new Postmaster-General to set for himself.

Wanamaker was cut from different cloth. The more he was attacked and opposed the better he fought. After the manner of all men, he disliked criticism and condemnation. But bullying and threats were incentives to action, not deter-rents. To secure immunity and have peace he would not give up or compromise. It was not in him to take the easy path. In a fight he schooled himself to accept blows phil-osophically. His reward came when the public woke up to the fact that his assailants in the press were inspired by the Louisiana Lottery gang, Senator Platt of the American Express Company, and Jay Gould of the Western Union Tele-graph Company. He began to be loved for the enemies he had made, and whatever lack of faith some had in his ideas and plans, none failed to pay tribute to his fearlessness as well as his efficiency. Harrison's misgivings about some of the Wanamaker proposals were profound, and they were shared by Morton, Blaine, and Elkins. The very bitter-ness and intensity of the opposition aroused, however, kept them from adding to the Postmaster-General's difficulties by adverse comment. In the midst of the storm raised over rural free delivery, postal savings, parcels post, and government telegraphs and telephones, Secretary of War Elkins expressed the feeling of the Cabinet in one terse sentence. He said with his inimitable chuckle, the best in Washington until Taft came along, "It isn't only the Lord that loves a fighter."

The rural free-delivery service in 1925 carried the mail to thirty million Americans over routes that would encircle the globe eighty times. The cost to the Department was $90,000,000. This achievement in a country of "magnificent distances," as Wanamaker called it when he first brought the problem of rural free delivery before Congress, is the result of one of the earliest of the Postmaster-General's recommendations to Congress. On October 1, 1890, the Fifty-first Congress passed a joint resolution, authorizing Wanamaker to test in small towns and villages the practicability and expense of extending the free delivery system to offices of the third and fourth class and to regions outside the free-delivery radius of the larger offices. Wanamaker had contended that the postal system belonged to all the people and should serve all. He had declared that no person should be penalized for living in the country, and with his true pioneer instinct he was ready to make the experiment on a small scale in the firm belief that it would prove feasible for the Post Office Department to deliver mail to those to whom it was addressed, no matter where they lived. Because it should be done, he argued, it could be done. At any rate, the burden of proof was on the government. When a person put a stamp on a letter and dropped it in the mail box, had he not paid for its delivery?

Using the authority granted by Congress, but seriously handicapped by the absurdly small appropriation of $10,000, Wanamaker began rural free delivery in a number of small communities varying in population from three hundred to three thousand. Describing these experiments, his personal secretary, Marshall Cushing, wrote:

Between Feb. 1 and Sept. 3, 1891, the forty-six experimental offices aggregated 285 months of free delivery service, at a total cost of carriers of $4,320.69, and a net profit to be credited to the free delivery service of $850.50. An entire year, aggregating 552 months for these forty-six offices, would have resulted, according to the above proportion, in a net earning of $3,812.54. With an appropriation of $200,000 for the next fiscal year the net earnings, on the same basis, would have reached $76,250.80; and with an appropriation of $500,000, the net earnings would have been by the same figures, $190,627, and with an appropriation of a million dollars, $381,254. Of course the implication is that the service would be put on in communities of areas and densities of population similar to those already experimented with. But it is evident that it could be put on in regions more and more sparsely settled.[1]

But it did not work out that way! Wanamaker was limited by definite appropriations. In business one can use a surplus to develop a new department, or transfer what is earned in one department to make up a temporary deficit in another. Money is invested quickly and liberally in the hope of coming out even and later making a profit. The government official's hands are tied when he is conducting a business operation. Interests that could use political pressure thought that rural free delivery would do them harm. Neither the argument of service nor of feasibility as a business proposition moved them. If Wanamaker had had a free hand he would certainly have gone ahead and have extended the service. He would have demonstrated that rural free delivery was practicable. But it looked like a scheme to help along the parcels-post propaganda. Was not this the reason that some of the stanchest Administration papers condemned the idea as extravagant and declared that it would bankrupt the country? The Postmaster-General was not going to be given a chance to prove that it would not.

[1] *The Story of Our Post Office*, p. 1001.

A Republican newspaper of Brooklyn, which had done yeoman service in electing Harrison, for example, said editorially with fine scorn that the Postmaster-General ought to ask the government next to present every farmer with a free telephone and a free telegraph instrument.

The ugly side of politics and public life—questioning men's motives—came to the front when it was hinted that Wanamaker was planning to go extensively into the mail-order business, to the detriment of the country store, and that his advocacy of rural free delivery was to prepare the way for a nefarious scheme of crushing country stores as he had done independent shopkeepers in Philadelphia. Going to town for mail was the farmer's diversion and the store-keeper's opportunity. Harrison's Postmaster-General, to put money in his own pocket, would strike at the root of village economy and society. What a hypocrite! What a menace! This same sort of abuse was heaped upon Wanamaker when he advocated the parcels post. Combined with rural free delivery, it would easily be seen how the postal system was going to become an adjunct of mail-order houses and city department stores. Wanamaker professed the desire to serve the farmer. In reality he was serving the city interests of himself and other soulless monopolists.

All this hurt, and hurt deeply. But a man cannot take high public office and expect not to be hurt. It did not deter Wanamaker from going ahead. Slander and misinterpretation of motives served to increase his enthusiasm. In 1891, in his report on the postal service, he referred to the incipient demand for rural delivery and the recommendation he had made for the extension of rural deliveries. All that was needed was an appropriation. He said:

I could not commend anything to the attention of Congress with more confidence than this proposed addition to the postal facilities, first, because it is so easy, and, second, because it is so far reaching, and, third, because it seems to me so patriotic.[1]

Throughout 1891 the Postmaster-General worked with the National Grange, the Patrons of Husbandry, the National Farmers' Congress, and State Farmers' Alliances, and got them solidly behind his idea. Numerous petitions were sent to Congress. On January 5, 1892, Representative O'Donnell, of Michigan, introduced "A Bill to Extend the Free Delivery System of Mails to Rural Communities." This bill, over which Wanamaker had worked hard, provided for the R. F. D. system along exactly the lines that it functions to-day. It was the vision and the charter of rural free delivery. But Congress was unwilling to sanction the six-million dollar appropriation the bill carried. Even an amendment appropriating the sum of $100,000 to be used in "experimental free delivery in the country as distinct from cities and towns" was rejected when the Post Office Appropriation Bill was before the House at the end of May. A month before Wanamaker retired Congress consented to spend $10,000 for this purpose! His successors under Cleveland, Bissell and Wilson, refused this appropriation, even when it was doubled in 1895, on the ground that nothing could be done of value with so little money.

One of the striking by-products of Wanamaker's agitation for rural free delivery was the better-roads movement. In the early 'nineties there were no automobiles. But bicycling was becoming a nation-wide sport, and the popular sentiment was beginning to demand that main roads at least

[1] When rural free delivery had become an accomplished fact, Wanamaker said, at a dinner to Postmaster-General Meyer, in Philadelphia, October 26, 1907:

"The P. O. Department of the future, I believe, will have more to do with the election of our presidents and Congress than all the national, state and city committees. The big majority of President Roosevelt was brought about by R. F. D. The country people reading and thinking in the silence of their own homes made up their minds what was the right thing to do."

be better kept. When Wanamaker was told that one of the chief obstacles to his rural-free-delivery idea would be the impassable roads and that millions of Americans lived where it was difficult for vehicles to reach—impossible if rural carriers were on bicycles—he answered: "I am glad to know this. R. F. D., like bicycling, will make for better roads, and that is a crying need. A nation's strength and progress are bound up with the improvement of communications, and it is the duty of the whole community, for social and patriotic reasons, to work hard on the roads." Almost as an afterthought, he added, "If there are millions, as you say, to whom it will be difficult for rural carriers to get mail, how do the children of those millions get to school? Better roads mean a better America." [1]

More complete failure than in rural delivery met the efforts of the great postal pioneer to give the American people the benefits of parcels post. When he had the honor of putting into the mail bag the first package mailed from Philadelphia at the inauguration of the parcels post service on January 1, 1913, Wanamaker said:

"I have been on the Parcels Post turnpike since 1889, when I made an earnest and urgent argument for it in my first annual report. The possibilities of the postal system to encourage people to go to sparsely settled sections of the country, to compel construction of roads for mail deliveries, and to contribute to the contentment and prosperity of the nation by mail services are beyond arithmetical calculation."

In 1890, 1891, and 1892 the Postmaster-General's annual report continued to plead for parcels post, adding to cumulative argument a mass of detailed statistics about the

[1] Many years later Wanamaker stated that his early interest in Henry Ford's cheap automobile was largely influenced by the effect it was going to have upon road-building. He foresaw what was going to happen when millions all over the country wanted to use the new means of transportation. See vol. ii, chap. vii.

benefits and the financial practicability of this form of service. But Congress could not be carried along the path of this innovation even so far as the authorization—without adequate appropriation!—accorded the Postmaster-General to experiment with rural free delivery. Asked once why this was, Wanamaker gave an answer that has gone down in history.

"Mr. Wanamaker, why can you not inaugurate parcels post?"

"There are five insurmountable obstacles: first, there is the American Express Company; second, the United States Express Company; third, the Adams Express Company; fourth, the Wells-Fargo Express Company; fifth, the Southern Express Company." [1]

It was characteristic of Wanamaker that he should keep on fighting for parcels post until the fight was won. His testimony and his arguments in Washington in 1911 and 1912 contributed to the victory. On January 20, 1913, Fourth Assistant Postmaster General Graw wrote to him:

We are all aware of what your position was when presenting your views to the Committee, and your painstaking efforts are clearly apparent. We have all the reports, and perhaps nobody has studied them more carefully than myself. At the present time we had far less against us, the forces you name cutting less figure, or at least their influence was less potent. The final outcome cannot but be gratifying to you, as it is to us, and discloses the fact that you were only temporarily defeated and that

[1] On the eve of the long-delayed adoption of parcels post, Wanamaker, according to stenographic notes in the private files, said to S. S. McClure in his private office on February 9, 1912:

"These great corporations have absolute control through the representation they have in the ownership of stocks—express companies, which are owned by the railroads through the officers having that stock—they are the people that are back of the express companies and are opposing the parcels post. They own the stock of the express companies."

your efforts finally bore fruit. In other words, that the work done by you was the forerunner of what was to come. The triumph is as much yours as ours, and we are glad to join you in the rejoicing.

We have seen how the Postmaster-General crossed the ocean to observe how his infant sea post-offices were working. In Europe on that trip he spent his time studying government operations of parcels post and other innovations that he was urging upon Congress in the annual reports to the President and the hearings before committees. Some of his statistics he gathered through the consular service. He also sent competent subordinates to study European postal systems on the spot. His delegates to the Universal Postal Union were instructed to gather all the data they could.

In the same painstaking fashion, with the co-operation of the Treasury Department, he gathered the facts upon which to base a plea for the establishment of a postal savings system. He was convinced that at least $400,000,000 was hoarded in the United States—unbanked, idle, and of no use as a tool of commerce and a medium of exchange. He contended that the result of the establishment of postal savings would be the placing of the bulk of that great sum in active use. While most native-born Americans of old American stock trusted banks, the foreign-born, who were increasing amazingly in number and earning capacity, did not. They would trust only the government, and so long as the government offered no facilities for savings they would continue to hoard their money in the old stocking and under the mattress until they had enough to send home to Europe to be banked in government institutions there. This contention he thought he proved by marshaling imposing figures on the money-order business done with the countries from which most of our immigrants came. Making due allowance for money sent abroad to support relatives or buy property over there, he asserted that a large portion of the money that went out of the country could be kept and put into circulation over here.

The plan for postal savings was simple. It involved only a little extra bookkeeping. The expense would be virtually nothing. It would not mean government competition with banks for deposits. Wanamaker suggested that post offices receive amounts on deposit up to $250, and allow the same yearly rate of interest of 3 per cent, that the post offices themselves received from the banks for balances. The money would go to the banks all the same. But the small depositor would have a government guaranty. This guaranty he felt would be sufficient to induce the ignorant and overcautious to give up their hoardings and to keep money here rather than send it to Europe. As for the low rate of interest, those who hoarded were getting no interest at all. They would certainly prefer 2 per cent from Uncle Sam, whom they could trust, to 3 per cent from banks, which they evidently did not trust!

"Another evidence of Wanamaker's freakish judgment," said his enemies. The postal-savings scheme was roundly denounced by newspapers and banking interests. As in the case of parcels post and of government management of telegraphs and telephones, it was looked upon as an alarming and subversive move towards government encroachment in the field of private enterprise.

Shortly after the retirement of the Harrison Cabinet came the panic of 1893. Wanamaker expressed the opinion that the panic probably would not have occurred had the hoarded wealth of the country been in circulation; and he added that it would have been in circulation if there were a postal-savings system available to people who did not trust banks. What could possibly be more safe than postal savings, since everybody knew that the law could make the post office a preferred creditor, protected by the bank surplus and the double liability of the stockholders?

Few gave any attention whatever—much less serious attention—to Wanamaker's contention. But during the panic of 1907, when he himself was among the most embarrassed of America's great business men, he returned to the charge. He said:

"I believe there wouldn't be any money panic as there is to-day all over this country if we had postal savings instead of Milwaukee banks and real estate trust companies. I believe there is a great amount of money not in circulation. I said that when I was in Washington and since. The money is hid away in old stockings, in chimneys. I believe $500,-000,000 more would be in circulation if we had postal savings banks. The banking interests have always been able to stop that as interfering with their interests."

The panic of 1907 led to a popular demand that a postal-savings system be inaugurated, and this became one of the achievements of the Taft administration. In June, 1910, Congress passed a law establishing postal savings along the lines of Wanamaker's earlier recommendation. First-class post offices began to receive savings deposits at 2 per cent in 1911, and the system was extended to post offices of the second and third classes. It has worked out surprisingly well in all the large manufacturing and mining centers where the foreign-born element predominates, demonstrating that Wanamaker was right in believing that a government guaranty would bring out hoardings and partially prevent sending money abroad. Whether the sums thus put into circulation are sufficient to prevent a money panic is problematical. The passage of the Federal Reserve Act, two years after the inauguration of postal savings, made forever impossible a satisfactory test of the validity of Wanamaker's belief.

Postmaster-General Work said in his official tribute to the memory of Wanamaker:

John Wanamaker was one of the first crusaders for the establishment of postal savings. So ambitious was he to prove its blessings to the wage-earning classes of the country that he travelled about, speaking before business organizations and financial associations, in an effort to break down all opposition to postal savings. John Wanamaker thus stamped his name indelibly on the postal history of the United States.

The suggestion that raised the bitterest opposition of all was Wanamaker's advocacy of government ownership of telegraphs and telephones. The telephone industry was still in its infancy. When he declared that it was bound to become a factor of greater importance than the telegraph as an indispensable means of communication in business and personal affairs, the new Postmaster-General was called an erratic visionary. He recommended that the government take over the telegraph lines and that the telephone companies be bought out by the government before a new monopoly was established.

The argument was simplicity itself. Telegraphic and telephonic communications were as natural and legitimate a function of the Post Office Department as distributing mail. With its vast equipment and increasing army of employees the Post Office could handle telegraphs and telephones more economically than private companies could ever hope to give service. An incalculable benefit to the people would result through bringing telegraph and telephone rates down to cost. Moreover, all the people had the right to demand telegraph and telephone facilities. Private companies could never be expected to give service except at a profit. In sparsely settled regions, when the vastness of the country was considered, a telegraph and telephone system could be operated only by the Post Office Department, which already had the buildings and the employees. All forms of communications could thus be extended to all the people. As proof of his contention the Postmaster-General cited the example of the British Empire and European countries, where the government was exercising these additional functions through their postal administration. They could give much cheaper rates, quicker service, and, most important of all, far wider service. Wanamaker said, in his annual report for 1890:

It is sometimes maintained that telegraphic service can be performed more cheaply by private hands. If this objection is good, it holds against all kinds of government work. Public revenue ought to be collected by private hands. The laws ought to be administered by contracting parties. A banking firm ought to manage the Treasury, and the postal business should be handled by a syndicate. The question is, what is the best and safest for the public interest, as well as what can the general public afford to use?

The next year he returned to the charge—more specifically because of the ridicule and denunciation which his suggestion had met. His statement was frank and explicit, and, backed by a wealth of statistics, drawn principally from Great Britain, the best country to cite as an example, he stated, because "British institutions and the political and economic concepts of the people are like our own." He submitted to the President arguments and figures prefaced by these words:

The first telegraph was operated by the Post Office Department, and it was an evil hour for the people, when against the protest of the Postmaster-General, it was surrendered. I want to see the two great servants of the people, the Post Office and the telegraph, reunited, and the telephone brought in to enhance the value of the combination. Public interests, private needs, and the popular will call for these agencies to perfect the great postal system of this country. The longer their employment is delayed, the greater the aggravation and injustice to the people and the costlier it will be to secure them. Sixty-four million of people are taxing themselves to-day to the amount of $7,000,000 annually to maintain the

Post-office plant, and are denied the right to vitalize this magnificent machinery with the mightest force which science has given to render that machinery most effective. The electric current belongs to the people by right, and is bound to become their servant, not of a class nor of one-sixty-fourth part of the population, as at present.

This second report created a sensation, and it was indicative of the weakness of the case against government ownership that the newspapers condemning the report carefully refrained from quoting Wanamaker's facts and arguments. People did not know that the first experimental telegraph, constructed from Baltimore to Washington by Morse, was paid for by congressional appropriation, and was sold to private interests after having been run for several years by the Post Office Department. Only Americans who have traveled realize the cheapness of telegrams in England and on the Continent, and the quicker and wider delivery service. The American public had never before been informed that only a million of the sixty million Americans used the telegraph, while nearly four millions of the thirty-five millions of Englishmen used it.

Wanamaker's critics had no answer to his argument that, while the government follows the settler with mail and would do so with the telegraph lines, the telegraph under private ownership "goes where it can find a paying business only." They were silent when he published figures showing 95 per cent of the world's telegraph lines outside of the United States were government owned and managed, generally as an integral form of the postal system. Few newspapers dared to print the statement of Wanamaker in his fourth annual report, issued December 5, 1892, that two companies in the telegraph business were producing gross revenues nearly one-third as large as the entire postal revenues, his warning that these were becoming more valuable monopolies every year, and his prophecy that in time a great telephone trust would impose upon a public that was forced to use its service rates that were all the traffic would bear.

It was lack of knowledge of the facts that militated against the Postmaster-General's receiving the popular support that he confidently expected to have in his campaign for taking over the telegraph and the telephone. He knew that the Western Union and the Postal Telegraph companies constituted a monopoly, exacting huge profits. But the people did not know it, and as it touched very few of them, comparatively speaking, they were not vitally interested. The telephone was a thing of the future; and did not Wanamaker himself say that only one person in sixty had the habit of using the telegraph? Only in dire emergencies did most people give the telegraph a thought. Wanamaker was right when he said in his 1890 report:

That man must be willfully blind who does not see the vast and rising tide of public sentiment against monopoly. Here is a purpose of the people, and no man or set of men can turn it aside. In one form or another the public imperatively demands cheaper telegraphy, and the Post Office Department can supply at less cost than any corporation, unless the latter has rent, light and fuel free, and carriers and clerks without pay.

But where he went wrong was in assuming that the people knew that the telegraph companies were a monopoly, or, if told, would be agitated about it. In connection with the Louisiana Lottery's evasion of the law John Wanamaker pilloried and threatened to expose the express companies. This just happened to fall in with his advocacy of and their opposition to parcels post. Similarly, although it was not necessarily done with that intention, his conflict with the telegraph companies over their charges for government messages was interpreted to be a clever maneuver to smoke out of the telegraph companies a public confession of just how great were their profits. That would open the eyes of the public!

The Post Office Department, under contract, was paying exorbitant rates to the Western Union. Wanamaker sought to have the rates reduced. He had several interviews with Jay Gould, who was not unfavorable to compromise. Probably Gould saw that if there was a fight, his adroit adversary would compel the Western Union to give figures of the actual cost of service. But some of Gould's associates, notably Green, maintained that Wanamaker must be fought to a finish. The way they went about it was not to meet argument with argument, but to vilify Wanamaker and to strike at his business in Philadelphia. Banks were induced to call his loans and refuse him credit. An effort was made to corner his commercial paper and force him into bankruptcy. Manufacturers doing business with him were threatened with curtailment of credits if they sold him goods.

Had he been a newcomer in big business or had he been caught off guard in the amount of his paper upon the market, the Gould interests might have seriously embarrassed him. But it is doubtful if with all their power they could have ruined Wanamaker, for bankers and business men in Philadelphia rallied around him and formed a pool to advance him millions of dollars. Some of these friends had to fight for their lives afterward because of this beautiful exhibition of loyalty to their fellow-townsman. In fact, the Gould interests vindictively pursued for years some who had thus offended. Wanamaker did not have to call upon the pool, but he never forgot those who stood by him in the hour of need. It was a stirring testimony of confidence that heartened him in the struggle.

Encouragement was lacking in the Cabinet and among most of his friends, who thought his judgment wrong in this question. But the Postmaster-General had introduced a bill for co-operation between the Post Office and the telegraph companies. It established what were to be known as "postal telegrams," which the postal service would collect, deliver to sending offices of the telegraph companies, and distribute at the other end. These deferred telegrams were to be transmitted at a greatly reduced rate—twenty words for fifteen cents up to three hundred miles, twenty-five cents in a second zone, and fifty cents in a third zone. Aside from two cents on each message for letter postage, the telegraph companies were to be allowed all the revenue from postal telegrams. The bill forbade priority of dispatches, except for government business. To encourage the opening of additional telegraph offices in regions not served by the existing systems, postmasters were authorized to become also employees of the telegraph companies and to have in their offices operators paid by the companies. Wanamaker pointed out that a large part of the transmission could be done at night on idle wires.

Although there seemed to be immediate profit in it for them, the telegraph companies fought the bill, and it was defeated. No valid argument was advanced against it. By his three-zone scheme Wanamaker had provided against the objection of disparity of distances. The lobby of the telegraph interests was too strong. The telegraph companies were afraid of postal telegrams just as the express companies were afraid of rural free delivery. They looked upon it as an opening wedge for the realization of Wanamaker's complete idea, and they did not intend to allow him to get his foot in the door.

Like many other original ideas that did not come into their own until many years had passed, the Wanamaker scheme of deferred telegrams, dispatched at night, is now a commonplace. In the United States, of course, deferred messages, called night letters, are a feature of a business still in private hands. In England and France the letter-gram idea was adopted in 1913.[1] It is universally used by cable and wireless companies.

Corporations dealing in public-service utilities have always cleverly managed to keep public opinion favorably disposed towards private ownership. Electric lighting and water systems, railroads, telegraphs, and telephones, they assert, are so important to the common weal that the commonwealth must not be allowed to interfere with the great service they are rendering the people. Who suggests, as Wanamaker did, government ownership, has sinned against the principle of solidarity of interests of the propertied classes! He has shown also a lack of common sense! Argument, figures, proof from the example of other governments, democracies like our own, avail nothing. When Wanamaker asked why, if the Post Office handled letters promptly and efficiently, it should not do the same with telegrams—as all other countries did—he was frowned upon for having committed the unforgivable sin.

Risk of social ostracism did not dismay him. He never failed to put in a word for government ownership of all means of communication, although astounding increase in the value of telegraph and telephone franchises and properties made the proposition more difficult to realize in successive years. In 1907 at the Meyer dinner in Philadelphia, in 1911 at a luncheon in his honor given by the merchants of New York, and on New-Year's day of 1913, when he mailed the first package by parcels post, Wanamaker reiterated his recommendation that the government take over

---

[1] A British correspondent wrote to Wanamaker on April 4, 1913: "This is the fruition of your deferred-telegraph service suggestion, having for its basis the collection at point of origin and delivery at destination through the mails. It has taken Great Britain twenty-two years to come to your idea."

the telegraph and telephone systems. At the Jubilee luncheon in November, 1911, he said:

"I am clearly of the opinion that the Government owes it to the business interests and the family life of the nation to take possession of all the telegraph companies. The people have a right to a perfected service that only the government can give, to the use of wires without the delays that special interests now secure at times, and to the lower rates now necessary and possible."

On January 14, 1912, Postmaster-General Hitchcock announced that he would recommend to Congress the acquisition by the government of the telegraph lines. He pointed out that in fifty of the leading countries in the world, including Great Britain, France, Germany, Austria-Hungary, Italy, Russia, and Japan, government-controlled telegraphs had long been in profitable operation, most of them in connection with the postal service, as his predecessor Wanamaker had planned for the United States, and that the systems were conferring enormous benefits in prompt and cheap service upon a population of not fewer than 950,000,000. The suggestion not only met with violent protests from the great financial interests, but brought forth a severe rebuke from the White House. It was officially explained that Hitchcock had spoken without the authority of the President and that his suggestion would be ignored. Harrison was at least more kindly to his Postmaster-General than Taft showed himself to be. But there is generally a panic at the White House when a Cabinet officer has the temerity to put the common weal above private interests.

Both in the organization of the department and in the insoluble problem—at least it has always proved insoluble—of equitable rates for the various classes of mail matter Wanamaker battled against great and disheartening odds, as

his successors ever since have done.[1]   Many of the laws
under which the department was doing business were framed
in conditions that were totally different.   One dated from
1792 and many others had been passed before railroads
came into being.   But for all their manifest absurdity, whenever they had touched some established interest or traditional political prerogative, Wanamaker found that Congress believed in the Medes and Persians.

In his 1892 report, after three years' experience and study
of rates, Wanamaker said that book and newspaper mail
was being carried at the loss of six cents a pound, while the
letter rate paid twice over the cost of handling first-class
matter.   Being a business man, he naturally suggested lower-
ing rates on letters and raising rates on printed matter.   On
the bulky pieces, of size and weight sufficient to make a
noticeable mileage difference in cost, it seemed to him that
none could dispute the reasonableness of the zoning system.
He saw the postal deficit increasing, although he knew how
it could be kept down.

Another hornets' nest!   Publishers in Maine were flooding the United States with cheap magazines, hardly more
than advertising mediums, and series of digests of "the
world's classics" and other books, which were entered as
second-class mail matter.   One Augusta house was sending
tons of mail weekly all over the United States from this

---

[1] In the private files we have found evidences not only of Wanamaker's
continued interest as long as he lived in remedying the abuse of second-class
matter, but also of enmities incurred by this agitation.   A fellow Philadelphian, who felt that making periodicals pay their way would cripple his business, heartily disliked Wanamaker for his zoning idea.   It was an open
secret that Wanamaker helped by figures and advice every Congressman who
tackled the problem of equalizing postal rates.   We have found a report
prepared for Wanamaker by one of his employees, dated June 26, 1905, which
contains the volume of foreign mail service during five years, analyzed
to show cost, income, profit and loss; figures of second-class rates in
foreign countries; and an estimate of the cost to our Post Office Department
of carrying second-class matter internally.

remote corner of the country. When Wanamaker used the Maine publishers as an illustration of how private business was being virtually subsidized by the Post Office Department and how under cost printed matter rates were partly responsible for the deficit, these men were strong enough to get the Secretary of State to put a word of caution into Wanamaker's ear.

"The Congressional base of supplies expects the department to be self-sustaining," said Wanamaker to the President, "but there is no disposition to pass the necessary legislation." And he was deeply stirred by the injustice of compelling the Post Office Department to perform at great expense services for the other departments without being allowed to estimate the value of these, and charge them off against the deficit. The franking privilege was the abuse he had most in mind.

While he remained keen and enthusiastic and a splendid fighter to the very end of his term—and ever afterward—for the victory of his great innovations, he was pretty nearly ready to give up the hope he had entertained of transforming the department into an efficient business organization. There is something pathetic about the statement in his last annual report:

There was nothing to be done this past year except to trudge along the old roads, for Congress at its last session passed no bill affecting the postal service in any substantial way.

And four years later, in 1897, he said to an interviewer that while he did not like to criticize the Post Office and postal matters since he had gone out, he could say that the machine was not rightly organized and managed as it should be. He put his finger on the source of the evil and indicated its hopeless character:

"The real boss of the department is Congress at the other

end of the city on the hill.   Congress makes the laws which
govern the department, and the Postmaster-General is dependent upon Congress for everything he gets.   There are
scores of ways in which the business might be bettered, if
the Postmaster-General had only the power to act.   He has
not the power, however, and our postal system will never be
what it should be under our present system of government."

CHAPTER XXVII

POSTMASTER-GENERAL: SUCCESSES

THE nomination that General Harrison feared might prove a liability became one of the most precious assets of his administration. It was as General Clarkson had prophesied. Wanamaker demonstrated that he had excellent political sense and tact. He was easy of access, and was able to meet and put in a good frame of mind men whom the administration needed to conciliate. His affability made up for the President's reserve. He was a reformer without offending the bosses; and a party man without discouraging too greatly the reformers. He made blunders with Congress and the newspapers, as every inexperienced man in Washington does; but he was able to retrieve himself quickly and sometimes got an advantage out of having made a wrong start.

Though Wanamaker shared the President's ideals and supported him vigorously in his efforts to make the administration efficient and less political, he was practical in crises in which Harrison tended to remain stubbornly theoretical. At heart Wanamaker was as rigid a Puritan as Benjamin Harrison and Levi P. Morton. But thirty years of pioneering in business and church, with ups and downs, had taught him that while an individual could order his own life as he would and live without compromise, any form of group betterment was a slow process. Men in power had to recognize existing conditions. Recognition did not imply condoning and approving. Wanamaker had learned by bitter experience when to go ahead and when to slow down. Full steam up all the time in the process of revolutionizing the political system was unwise. The risk of shipwreck was very great. Wanamaker had reached the degree of maturity where he knew how to distinguish between courage and recklessness, between vision and delusion. He possessed to a remarkable degree "the tact of the possible," which the precocious young Cavour had declared in his youthful diary to be the most essential quality of the "useful statesman."

During the first few months of the administration, when Wanamaker was under fire more than any other member of Harrison's official family, he was able to prevent his chief from making the irreparable blunder of accepting the drastic program of civil service reformers, most persuasive of whom was young Theodore Roosevelt, who had not yet come to "the tact of the possible." Wanamaker's check upon Harrison won him the dislike of Roosevelt, whose resentment betrayed itself in unkind personal reflections upon the Postmaster-General. And yet it was Wanamaker's moderation and common sense that did much to put the Republican party once more upon solid foundations that later made possible Roosevelt's elevation to the Presidency.

The 1884 election had made serious inroads upon the old Republican leadership, especially in New York, New Jersey, Ohio, and Harrison's own state of Indiana. Connecticut and Vermont were feeling the strain, and nascent Republican influence in West Virginia, Kentucky, and Tennessee had suffered a setback. The most pressing practical problem confronting General Harrison was to reform—in both senses of the word—the party machinery without demoralizing or destroying it. At first Harrison did not comprehend the danger of a too sudden and too sweeping extension of the merit system in appointments. He had entered upon the Presidency with a zeal for abolishing the spoils sys-

tem that made the White House favorable ground for civil
service seed-sowing of the Theodore Roosevelts.

Much to the joy of party leaders, the new Postmaster-
General insisted that the President give full weight to Congressional claims for patronage. It is true that the Post
Office Department had many more appointments than any
other branch of government service, and that Wanamaker's
opportunity to discuss the civil-service problem with the
President was unique. But none the less he seemed to have
the clearest vision in this matter of all the administration
advisers, and he was admirably seconded by Clarkson.
Wanamaker's standards of efficiency forbade the selection
of incapable men. He was adamant on this point, and was
not disposed to accept blindly the first or even the second
choice of Senators and Congressmen in every instance. He
reviewed the qualifications of applicants as conscientiously as
if they were to enter his own business, and he did a great
deal to increase the working of the merit system in promotions. But he thought that the incoming Republican administration should not go to the extreme of ignoring the claims
of those who had always considered themselves the legitimate dispensers of patronage, and that the party advantage
of having jobs to hand out should not be sacrificed at one
fell swoop. He was genial and patient and tactful, and
frequently persuaded those who came to him to put first
on their lists men whom he was willing to have get the
places. Although there were times when Harrison felt that
Wanamaker and Clarkson were too "practical" in their political conceptions, he did not question the sincerity and honesty
of these two advisers. Neither had personal political ambitions. That had been demonstrated at Indianapolis.

Harrison's political experience was greater than Wanamaker's. He had the education and the cultural background
that Wanamaker lacked. A keen mind and legal training

enabled him to build up a powerful brief for his point of view. In these circumstances it was difficult for Wanamaker to take issue with a man who had so decided an advantage over him in talking things through and in forming judgments. The state of mind of the President, too, had to be reckoned with. If he had made compromises with his conscience in achieving the Presidency—mounting rung by rung the political ladder—he always intended to act with the purest idealism when he arrived at the goal. Wanamaker, with little political background and having nothing to atone for, could not understand the President's impatience with facts and disinclination to trim his sails even a little bit. Wanamaker looked at the patronage question as one demanding the use of common sense. Provided the privilege was not abused, there was nothing distasteful to him in the idea of the spoils belonging to the victor. The interests of the public did not necessarily have to suffer by taking into account preferences of politicians in making appointments. Why not, then, seeing that another battle was ahead four years hence, conform within reasonable limits to a system that enabled the party to distribute rewards to henchmen, to strengthen the prestige of legislators, and to keep alive loyalty and enthusiasm?

Little has been recorded concerning the patronage policy of Benjamin Harrison. All we know is that those who were expecting a sweeping extension in civil service reform were disappointed, and attributed to Wanamaker, because of his post, decisive influence in discouraging Harrison from doing what they believed Harrison wanted to do and would do. The enemies of Wanamaker declared that for all his fair words he was a politician. Many of his friends were surprised that he did not take the attitude toward the patronage question that he adopted towards virtually every other problem of service and efficiency for increasing the usefulness of the department. Had Wanamaker known his Browning, he might have told them:

> The common problem, yours, mine, every one's,
> Is not to fancy what were fair in life,
> Provided it could be, but, finding first
> What may be, then find how to make it fair
> Up to our means.

Because the Post Office Department had grown steadily, keeping pace with the development of the country, and because it was the only branch of the Federal government that penetrated to the smallest hamlet in every state and territory of the Union, its policy in regard to patronage was the first to attract nationwide attention. It affected local politics everywhere, and was of utmost importance from the purely party standpoint. Local political machines drew strength from patronage, and it was inadmissible that civil service in the lowest rank of postmasterships should be built upon the foundation of an organization created by a party that had been in power for only a brief period—and for the first time in a quarter-century. Wanamaker believed that promotion through merit should be initiated first of all among the minor employees in the larger post offices. He recommended a beginning in this direction, and during his term he succeeded progressively in extending the scope of promotions through civil service examinations.[1] If he offended civil service enthusiasts it was because he felt that the old system of appointments should be changed gradually.

The year 1889 was the centenary of the United States. But the Postmaster-General had been a member of the Cabinet only sixty years. Washington thought the office

---

[1] On July 1, 1891, a Board of Promotions began to function. It was created "to improve the civil service within the departmental service by examinations and promotions and equalization of salaries in every post office of fifty or more."

was not important enough to be represented in the Cabinet, and succeeding Presidents continued to regard the Post-master-Generalship as a routine administrative function of secondary importance. When the Postmaster-General was given a Cabinet place in 1829 it was largely because of the department's importance in rewarding party workers. It was a long time before public opinion realized the vital importance to the nation of the rôle of the Postmaster-General. Referring to this curious fact, which can hardly be said to have changed until Wanamaker assumed the office, an eminent historian has said:

Yet there is now no other department of government in which the people take so large an interest as that over which the Postmaster-General presides. The number of men who care whether the Indians get their blankets and their rations on the frontier, whether one company or two are stationed at Fort Dodge, whether there is a fleet of gunboats in the Mediterranean Sea, is extremely small. But the sun never sets without millions upon millions of our citizens intrusting to the mails letters and postal cards, money orders and packages, in the safe and speedy delivery of which they are deeply concerned.[1]

John Wanamaker's work as Postmaster-General, criticized and belittled as it was at the time, has come to be regarded as the most brilliant and lasting achievement of the Harrison administration. It is a demonstration of what a business man can accomplish in a government post, provided he employs in the service of the public the same talents and energy that he has used in building up his personal fortune. The Wanamaker Store grew out of the ideas of a young man, applied to conditions of his time in a spirit of boldness and persistence. The greatest of these ideas was that of giving service to the customer, and it was made practicable by Wanamaker's ability to inspire those who worked for him with his own spirit and zeal.

[1] McMaster, xxi, p. 58.

His success as Postmaster-General was due to the fact that he was in Washington the same John Wanamaker he had always been in Philadelphia. Only now his customers were all the people of the United States, of every region, of every class. How could the mail service be improved? What new advantages could the Post Office Department give to the people? From March 4, 1889, to March 4, 1893, these were the questions constantly in his mind; and he managed to get them into the minds of more than one hundred and fifty thousand employees. Service to John Wanamaker meant not merely doing the best that could be done with things as they were, but in thinking of additional things to do. New ideas! Always new ideas![1]

He brought to the Post Office Department the guiding principles of his store management, that employees should have adequate pay and proper hours, and that they should be one big family, working for as well as with one another and imbued with the spirit of family loyalty. The Philadelphia merchant put into operation in Washington the ideas of the relations between executive head and subordinates that had made the Wanamaker business and the Bethany Sunday School organizations notable for loyalty and zeal. Continuous personal contact with those working

[1] In December, 1890, every postmaster received a copy of the Annual Report, with the following letter:

"The Postmaster-General has caused to be sent to you a copy of his annual report for this year. He directs me to ask you if you will kindly study it and write him, as fully and frankly as possible, what you think can properly be said, either against the recommendations contained in it or in support of them. He desires to gather the best practical postal opinion obtainable from all quarters of the country as to the best means of improving the postal service in every branch and detail. The Postmaster-General would therefore be much indebted for an early reply to this request."

In annual reports he said he got a great deal from studying letters of complaint and criticism, and newspaper comment. This was applying a method that he had used from the beginning of his business. For example, he wrote to a man in Denver: "Anyone who aids in improving the postal service by pointing out defects, or by making suggestions, performs an act of good citizenship and is a friend of good government and especially of the Post Office Department."

with him was essential to Wanamaker. It was not in him to direct impersonally a machine, and he was not dismayed by the multitude of postal employees of whom he had become the chief. Immediately he began to make the postmasters and subordinates in obscure villages as well as in large cities feel that they had direct contact with the Postmaster-General. With his infinite capacity for detail and his enjoyment of human contacts he carried this part of the vast work he had undertaken through to the end of his four years with vim and zest. So deep an impression did he make upon post office people that they kept coming to see him and writing to him as long as he lived. It was the thing to do for any man who had served under Wanamaker to make his private office the first objective in a visit to Philadelphia or New York. Generally there was time only for a handshake and a word of greeting. But it was given in a way to make the recipient feel that he was the only person John Wanamaker was thinking about. He could put that same magnetic touch into his correspondence. When he left office he signed over sixty-nine thousand letters of appreciation to every postmaster on the register in the service of the government.

He used to summon the more important postmasters to Washington for conferences, where he would go over the problems and difficulties of the department, and ask their opinion. Wherever he traveled during those four years he called on the postmasters, and in the cities he went through the post office buildings greeting and shaking hands with the men at their work. He changed the *esprit de corps* of the entire service by directing county postmasters to travel and come into personal contact with the employees under them. Whenever a carrier or a railway clerk was killed or performed some special act of heroism or merit he sent letters of condolence or congratulation. The reason for this he explained some years later in these beautiful words:

> Business is not a matter of machinery; it is not a great granite building; it is not iron and steel and rock; it is the human force that is in it. It is the man. What we are after, I am sure, is to see that every man becomes a better man and has a greater sense of responsibility and a larger vision of things that ought to be done.

Wanamaker's ideal for the Post Office Department was set forth in his first annual report:

> The people simply want the system administered with such efficiency and economy that it shall offer them more and more accommodations and tax them less and less. The only method I suggest by which all their desires may be gratified is not merely to talk about the application of business principles to the department; it is really to apply them.

None knew better than John Wanamaker, from his own business experience, how property values were increasing in the larger centers of population and how rapidly their growth made existing facilities hopelessly inadequate. He did not have to be persuaded by local chambers of commerce and Congressmen of the advisability of looking ahead and getting title to land. The government was paying enormous sums for rentals all over the country. Every expiring lease had to be renewed at higher figures. Additional quarters had to be provided. He was not afraid of being accused of favoring "pork barrel" legislation where it was clearly demonstrated that acquiring land and putting up buildings was a sound business proposition. As in the question of patronage, listening to local politicians did not necessarily mean betraying the interests of the public. Frequently what was advocated for party interest and for the prestige of the Congressman was at the same time a good investment for the government.

Before the Committee of Appropriations and in his reports the Postmaster-General championed, on the ground of economy, the policy of building post offices in proportion to the business done. At one time he demonstrated that for $21,000,000 the department could house properly every post office doing considerable business, in centers where buildings were not already owned, at a saving of $750,000 per annum over interest on the investment. There were few instances in which the Federal government had made a mistake in erecting its own buildings. He contended that the Post Office Department should combine with the Department of Justice and the Treasury Department in adopting a comprehensive policy of substituting government-owned buildings for leased premises for post offices, Federal courts, and custom houses. This could be done on a business basis, independently of any local political question. The administration should not be afraid of asking Congress for increasing appropriations each year to meet the needs.

Wanamaker's first innovation in Washington was to assume that Uncle Sam ran the government as a business, with business hours. As in his store, he appeared at his office in the Post Office Building before eight o'clock, to the astonishment of the colored doorkeeper and the dismay of everyone around the department. The captain was on the bridge before the ship started out for the day's cruise. For four years he kept this up—an unheard-of thing in Washington. He expected department heads and clerks to be on the job on time and to stay until the end of the day. On the other hand, he stopped Sunday work, and one of his first investigations was the salary scale, which he determined should be revised upward until every employee received adequate compensation.

Shortly after he became Postmaster-General, he said to the *Philadelphia Record* correspondent:

"I want to keep the mail bag open to the latest possible

minute, then get it to its destination in the shortest possible time, and then get each separate piece of mail to the person for whom it is meant in the quickest possible way."

Wanamaker felt that the principle of increasing sales through giving satisfactory service, upon which he had built up his great business, could be applied to the Post Office Department. The better the mail served the people, the more the mails would be used, and the increase of revenue would meet the expense of efficient service. One of his subordinates brought to him the idea of the postcard as we now have it. He saw its merit, and introduced it. Another suggested chutes in hotels and letter boxes in clubs. Wanamaker put them in. He initiated the idea of house letter boxes for depositing and taking up mail, which was a convenience to individuals and speeded up wonderfully the work of carriers, making deliveries more expeditious, and increasing the revenue of the department. He extended the railway post offices to street cars, beginning the experiment in St. Louis, where mail was sorted in transit and handed out at substations or directly to carriers on an eighteen-mile route.

One of his most successful ideas for speeding up the service in cities was that of pneumatic tubes, which he had seen successfully working in Europe. The Berlin Post Office, for example, with the most extensive pneumatic system in the world, had published figures to prove that tube dispatch paid its way. Wanamaker had long been using pneumatic tubes in his store. Why not in post offices of the big cities? "Rapid mail service, in our large cities," he declared, "is as important to business as good blood circulation to the body." He went before Congress with elaborate statistics, argued that city people were paying so much for the volume of business they created that they had a right to quicker service, and pointed out that there was an actual profit in running city post offices. This, he contended, justified pneumatic tubes. Anyway, they would pay for themselves; they would help business; and they would remove from the streets wagons that were encumbering traffic. There would be less and quicker handling. He wanted to see New York and Brooklyn connected by tubes, and an adequate system, such as European cities enjoyed, in operation in Chicago before the World's Fair opened.

But he was able to get only an appropriation of $10,000 for experimenting. This he used in 1892 to connect the main Post Office in Philadelphia with its nearest substation. Not much progress had been made when he retired, but he had the satisfaction of seeing pneumatic tubes grow from his small beginning to fifty-seven thousand miles of double lines in twenty years, in New York, Philadelphia, Boston, Chicago, and St. Louis. The New York tubes handled a million letters a day, and, with the rapid shift in the elongated business district, saved the special delivery service from breaking down altogether.

Like all importers, Wanamaker had long suffered the annoyance of delays of varying length in getting his foreign mail. The degree of congestion at the New York Post Office and the time of day steamers docked frequently made a difference of a day or two in the delivery of European mails. The obvious remedy was to have the mail sorted on ocean steamers just as on railroads, so that it could be forwarded immediately to distributing points upon the arrival of the steamers. The difficulty lay in securing the co-operation of foreign countries. During the second year of his term Wanamaker was successful in making an agreement with the German government and getting an appropriation from Congress to cover the costs of opening sea post offices on eight steamers of the North German Lloyd and four of the Hamburg American Line.

On the day before Christmas, 1890, a tri-weekly service was inaugurated with Germany. Each government furnished a postal clerk. Mails were sorted in transit, and from two to fourteen hours were saved in the New York Post Office alone. The saving in time was more considerable for other points. In his annual report for 1891, after having made the trip across the ocean himself to follow daily and check up on the work of the sorting clerk, the Postmaster-General said:

> The sea post offices have proved a distinct success, and incoming foreign mail is now dispatched throughout the country anywhere from two hours to a week quicker than it used to be. I recommend the employment of a steam tug in New York Harbor to make this service more efficacious.

Increase in immigration, tourist travel, and commercial exchanges brought about a rapid growth in the volume and frequency of postal communications with Europe. Wanamaker's experiment soon demonstrated its value in speeding mails and in relieving the New York Post Office from a heavy burden. Other European governments fell in line as it came to be realized that sea post offices were indispensable and also no more costly than handling the mails after their arrival. Now mail is sorted on the high seas as a matter of course, and before passengers disembark it is generally on its way to the railroads, ticketed to all distributing points in the United States and Canada. Wanamaker's modest little steam tug, which Congress allowed him after much debate, has become a fleet of postal boats in half a dozen Atlantic and Pacific ports, either government owned or operated by railroads on contract.

Had the airplane been invented in Wanamaker's day, there is no doubt that its use for carrying mail would have been promptly advocated in the Postmaster-General's annual reports. As it was, he did suggest the use of balloons, which traveled fast, if uncertainly. Anything to speed up the service. More than eighteen years after his retirement, Wanamaker was rejoicing in the first dispatch of air mail from Washington to Mineola on September 1, 1911. He wrote that day:

Why weren't the Wrights a little earlier with their flying machines? Then I would have had the credit of this innovation, provided always Congress would have listened to me. It generally didn't.[1]

We see that Wanamaker's endless, wearisome discussions with congressional committees and the necessity of wasting his energies in lobbying for the most reasonable and natural demands were still remembered and rankled. For a man who had spent his money in his business as he pleased for thirty years and was going to do it for another thirty years, the financial experiences of the Postmaster-Generalship were a severe and irksome discipline. Congressmen were not like bankers or business men. They could not be convinced by plain figures. "If they would only see as far as the ends of their noses," Wanamaker once exclaimed, "I should feel encouraged. But they don't see at all!" Every executive dependent upon Congress for fixing his budget, and working from year to year on appropriations or grants, which are never increased even to meet proved needs without a struggle, finds this fact the most serious handicap and killjoy he has to face.

With larger discretion in arranging the details of his budget, with authority to curtail here and expand there, with the power to experiment freely as he had always done, Wanamaker felt that he could have accomplished much more than he did and especially that he could have made

[1] As in other postal matters, interest in air mail did not die out. Wanamaker was over eighty when a definite air route policy was adopted by the department. Numerous papers in Drawer 103 of his private files show that he followed closely the vicissitudes of the air mail service from 1918 up to the last year of his life.

the department as it was far more efficient. What hurt him most was his inability to remedy injustices in the distribution of work, due to lack of authority to readjust appropriations to meet changed conditions. This was revealed in a frank speech in Cleveland in 1891. Wanamaker was with the Presidential party. Following his custom he slipped over to the post office. To the assembled employees he said:

"The postal service is not a set of public buildings and a book of regulations, but it is the brains and hearts of 150,-000 men, and its goodness is measured by the intelligence and devotion of the silent, steady, every day workers such as you, who stand at your office cases and tread the streets from door to door with your heavy burdens of mail. I beg you not to think that the Department at Washington is a heartless machine of old wheels belted with red tape.

"The long hours come from twenty men being loaded with the work that fairly calls for twenty-five men. The five men short are because of a short appropriation. If the Department could be trusted with sufficient money to remedy this overburdened system, there would be no dissatisfaction with the hours."

The theory that the government divided its functions into departments for efficiency's sake and to insure the most convenient distribution of labor was an earnest conviction of Wanamaker's. He fought the tendency to consider the departments as units, each interested solely in itself and going its own way. In creating his great mercantile establishment with its variety of departments he had already realized that here was a dangerous tendency that had constantly to be combated. The Post Office was a business, yes, but also a service. The people owned it. Its machinery and its powers should always be at the disposal of the government for any purpose that would contribute to the well-being of the people. It was this broad conception of

the functions of the department that made John Wanamaker a great constructive force in the Harrison administration.

With all his soul and brain he used the vast machinery of
his department to aid the Department of Justice in enforcing
laws passed for the moral welfare of the people and in the
suppression of every kind of crime; to aid the Treasury
Department in preventing smuggling; to aid the Interior
Department in its encouragement of backward and undevel-
oped regions by increasing transportation facilities and better
roads; and to aid the Navy Department by making possible
the building of fast ships that could at any time be converted
into cruisers.

His ideas did not always work out. Some of his proposals
were rejected outright, and others were adopted only
experimentally and half-heartedly. But even in his disappointments, such as rural free delivery, postal savings,
parcels post, and government ownership of telegraphs and
telephones, he did not have to admit failure except in the
matter of telegraphs and telephones. He lived to see his
other pet schemes adopted as he had conceived them.

But he was privileged himself to suppress lotteries; to be
godfather to the American merchant marine, revived by
subsidies from his department; to sign the memorable convention of the Universal Postal Union in 1891; and to
establish a Postal Museum at Washington.

The change in public opinion on the lottery question followed the same course as earlier in regard to slavery and
later in regard to alcohol. At the beginning of our national
life none dreamed of viewing lotteries as immoral and
therefore outside the law. On the contrary, they were generally run by the state. The American Congress of 1776
instituted a national lottery. It was a favorite method of
raising money for public purposes. But gradually sentiment

was created against lotteries. Church people began to believe that they were ruinous to morals and detrimental to the well-being of the people. Legalized gambling of this character was declared to be a blot upon nineteenth-century civilization. When the moral obliquity of gambling was preached the discovery of its social and economic harm was easy. The propaganda against lotteries was strong in all English-speaking countries. The last notable lottery in England was suppressed in 1860. But long after that many of the American states had legislated against lotteries just as they had pronounced against slavery. When John Wanamaker became Postmaster-General, lotteries were legal only in Louisiana, where the Louisiana State Lottery Company held a twenty-five year monopoly under a charter granted in 1868. The anomaly existed of one state in the Union benefiting, because it had the use of the mails, from an institution illegal in all the other states, and continuing with impunity its nation-wide operations. That Louisiana would renew the charter in 1893 was hardly to be doubted, because the Latin character of its population made it see no wrong in lotteries and because a large sum would accrue yearly to the state treasury from the renewal.

Under these circumstances Congress acted. On September 19, 1890, a bill was passed, directing the Postmaster-General to forbid the use of the mails to lotteries and making it a crime to attempt to use the mails for the lottery business. No order was more welcome to Harrison's Postmaster-General. Wanamaker was not only convinced that lotteries, in common with all forms of gambling, were a sin, but also that they were a social and economic evil.

The Louisiana State Lottery put up a bitter fight, and tested the constitutionality of the Act in the Supreme Court. Pending the decision, the Louisiana legislature voted to extend the lottery charter in return for an annual payment to the state of $1,250,000. In view of the action of the Federal government, however, the Governor of Louisiana courageously vetoed the bill. But the charter did not expire until 1894. Pending the verdict of the Supreme Court, the lottery officials thought they could ignore or evade the law. Wanamaker proved himself a vigilant and vigorous fighter. Disregarding bitter personal attacks and threats, he went into the Federal district courts and secured fifty-six convictions in the first nine months of the Act's operations. After the Supreme Court declared the anti-lottery law constitutional, the board of directors of the Louisiana Lottery issued a notice prohibiting employees from putting lottery matter in the mail. They turned to the express companies. Wanamaker then appealed to the Department of Justice, and instituted prosecutions against the Southern Express Company. Realizing that it was beaten, and abandoning hope of a profitable business in the United States even if a new legislature and Governor renewed its charter, the Louisiana Lottery Company transferred its offices to Honduras.

But while the law had been aimed principally at the one remaining state lottery, its provisions included all lotteries. Wanamaker interpreted this to cover foreign lotteries as well, including operations and lottery bonds of foreign governments. That this was a necessary interpretation of the law was universally recognized, because otherwise it would have been easy to continue the lottery evil from Latin-American countries, notably Mexico. In 1891, for example, the Juarez Lottery was compelled to plead guilty to 550 separate indictments in the United States Court at El Paso. After paying heavy fines, its president wrote to Wanamaker:

I beg to assure you that hereafter, in good faith, the Gran Loteria Juarez will strictly comply with all the laws of the United States with reference to the use of the United States mails.

By this was meant, however, only giving up the practice of bringing lottery circulars across the frontier and dropping them, judiciously scattered, in the United States mail. The Mexican and other foreign lotteries thought that the International Postal Convention would require the United States to receive and distribute all mail matter coming from foreign countries. But they had reckoned without their host. Wanamaker was too smart for them. He got the Secretary of the Treasury to rule that lottery tickets, circulars, and advertisements were liable to customs duty as printed matter. Article XI of the Convention forbade mailing articles liable to customs duty unless clearly stamped for customs examination. The lottery companies were between the devil and the deep sea. If they did not so stamp their mail matter Wanamaker promptly confiscated it. If they did, the addressees had to go to the post office to claim the lottery tickets, and when these were opened they were confiscated as illegal. A test case was lost. Since Wanamaker's day no large lottery operations have been possible on American soil.

What constituted a lottery operation was, of course, not always clear, and the companies against whom the law was aimed tried to embarrass the Postmaster-General by raising the cry of discrimination. Here, again, Wanamaker showed "the tact of the possible." He refused to allow the issue to be befogged. Public opinion was with him in the enforcement of the law against the lottery companies, and he had the good sense to avoid persecution of, and annoyance to, innocent local and individual cases of schemes of chance. He announced in his 1891 annual report that he had "no intention of making the law odious."

In his report for 1891 Wanamaker said that the revenue from foreign postage showed a surplus of over a million dollars, which he suggested ought to be turned into mail subsidies. These subsidies were justified, he argued, to secure regular and quicker service, to make new and direct commercial exchanges with countries not now reached, to develop new and enlarge old markets, to help build up a powerful naval reserve, and to establish a training school for American seamen.

This pronouncement in favor of government aid in reviving the American merchant marine met with more immediate and generous response than most of Wanamaker's ideas. Congress passed an act to encourage the foreign trade of American steamship lines using vessels of American build, owned and officered by American citizens, and having a fixed proportion of American crew. The vessels were to be constructed under the supervision of naval officers, so that they would be adapted for conversion into armed cruisers. The government reserved the right at any time to buy the vessels thus subsidized and add them to the navy. According to tonnage and speed, there were four classes of subsidy from four dollars to two-thirds of a dollar per mile traveled on each outward voyage. This form of mail subsidy had already been adopted by European governments, notably France, Great Britain, and Germany.

The new mail service under the American flag went into operation in 1892 on lines from Galveston and New York to the West Indies, Central America, and South America; from San Francisco to Panama and Hong Kong; and from New York to Southampton and Antwerp. In order to accelerate the extension of the American flag in the transatlantic passenger service, Wanamaker succeeded in getting Congress to consent to the naturalization of two liners, the *City of Paris* and the *City of New York*. In the last month of his term, he had the joy of seeing these vessels, fitted with sea post offices, begin to carry the American flag.

The mail subsidies act of 1891 may have been a bit premature. The American people were not prepared for ship subsidies on an extensive scale because they had not yet come to realize the vital rôle of foreign trade in our commercial life. Manufacturers and bankers were not yet keenly interested in foreign markets. Having lost the habit of the sea, because all the energy of the nation had been invested for thirty years in the internal development of their own vast land, Americans had to be born again as a seafaring race. And the American merchant marine encountered insurmountable obstacles in competition through the fantastic and unequal conditions imposed by our laws upon the operation of ships of American registry. Wanamaker had to wait only seven years to have the naval utility of his plan demonstrated in the Spanish-American War. But until the World War taught its lesson mail subsidies led to the building of only two American transatlantic liners![1]

The achievement remains none the less a crown of glory for the Philadelphia merchant who knew how to look into the future and point the way. He never ceased to be an enthusiastic advocate of an American merchant marine, and he often lamented the national lack of vision. Mail subsidies, he often said, were a means to an end, and he protested against charging them up to the Post Office Department, thus causing a deficit that could not rightly be counted as working expenses in postal operations. He believed that the State, Navy, War, and Commerce Departments received

[1] Its contract with Postmaster-General Wanamaker encouraged the Pacific Mail Steamship Company to invest $10,000,000 in building new ships. But the order given to Cramps' Shipyard for the *St. Louis* and *St. Paul* immediately after the subsidy bill passed was the beginning and the end of the American line's enthusiasm for American-built ships. Mail subsidies were not sufficient to overcome the additional expense of running transatlantic liners under the American flag.

more direct benefit from encouraging the building and oper-
ating of American ships than the Post Office Department.

It was a source of pride to Wanamaker that the memorable Universal Postal Union Convention, establishing recip-
rocal exchange of mail matter, was signed during his Postmaster-Generalship.   More than fifty powers agreed in
this treaty to accept from one another mail at uniform rates
of postage.   In announcing the conclusion of the arrangement Wanamaker pointed out the transcendent importance
of the Universal Postal Union as an agency in the promotion
of international peace and good will and as a means for
facilitating commercial exchanges.   "It brings the world
together," he said, "as nothing else has ever done before in
all history."

A corollary of world-wide postal intercourse was the
establishment in 1891, the year of the treaty, of a Postal
Museum at Washington.   Here were gathered records and
relics of the history of the American postal service.   The
first mail pouches, uniforms, saddles, and insignia of dispatch riders, the first special coaches on star routes, the
means of carrying mail on the first railways, photographs,
maps, charts, and graphs, illustrated the development of
postal communications in the United States.   But as Wanamaker's object was also to get before the people the universal character of postal service and to educate and stimulate them by showing what was being done in other countries, he collected every kind of postal device to trace the
efficiency and evolution of postal service.   The exhibits in
the museum showed how mail was being carried in primitive
and backward countries, where difficulties we hardly
dreamed of had to be overcome and conditions with which
we were unfamiliar had to be met.   In contrast to these,
and to point to our place in the scale, the methods employed
in advanced European countries were set forth by actual

models of postal devices we had yet to adopt but which were in common use in Germany, Austria-Hungary, and the British Empire. This museum, Wanamaker said at its inauguration, was to drive home the great lesson that "the footprint of the mail carrier is the signpost of civilization."

CHAPTER XXVIII

POSTMASTER-GENERAL: GROWTH OF THE MAN

WHEN a man has passed his fiftieth milestone he is supposed to be entering upon his prime. With most men this is true. The decade from fifty to sixty gives the ideal combination of health—and consequent vigor and will —with the advantages of experience and training. In the first half-century the best that is in a man is spent in acquiring his foundation and background. Wanamaker had had an early start. When Harrison became President, he was far ahead of men of his age, because he was already well on the way to success at the time that virtually all his worthwhile contemporaries were being mustered out of the army. The Civil War had taken from them golden years that had to be made up.

In deciding to leave his business and devote all his time to public service before he reached his fifty-first birthday Wanamaker showed that he had a true sense of values and that he intended to practice what most apostles and examples of success limit themselves to preaching. He could not have known that the amazing longevity of his mental and physical faculties were going to make the four years in Harrison's Cabinet simply a picturesque halfway stage in his career. But it was none the less an astounding and courageous move for a man who had always been the soul of his business to drop completely out of it. This was what accepting Harrison's offer meant. He did not give up Bethany. That could be run on Sundays. But he did sacrifice abruptly his own peculiarly ubiquitous rôle in the management of his great store. Of course he had confidence in the ability of his associate, Robert C. Ogden; his two sons were still in the twenties, only a few years out of college. And he may have felt that he should give them an opportunity of learning how to assume responsibility without being constantly dominated by a father still young, strongly individualistic, and far too prolific in ideas of his own to be a good teacher for his boys. But, considering how the business had grown around and been inspired by his masterful personality, the greatness of the price he had made up his mind to pay for his Cabinet position cannot be overestimated.

What were the influences that led a man of his age, with a constantly growing business that fascinated him and that still demanded the best that was in him to give it up and engage in the activities and minutiæ of the Postmaster-Generalship?

In none of his voluminous writings did Wanamaker attempt to indulge in self-analysis. Three years before he went to Washington, he had answered the request for a sketch of his life by a telegram that has become a classic, "Thinking, trying, toiling, and trusting in God is all my biography." On the desk that he had left in Philadelphia the place of honor had long been given to the daily thought of Appeles, *"Nulla dies sine linea."* He was too good a Calvinist to believe in chance or accident, and he used to say that if a man looked too far ahead he would certainly stand still. At widely separated intervals in his life we find him telling his Bethany scholars, "Don't imagine you can look beyond until you have climbed the hill." He set great store on vision, and was prone to give more serious attention than most busy men to the wildest ideas of his own and others. But the man of action asserted itself in

MRS. JOHN WANAMAKER
(Taken about 1895)

him so strongly that dreams meant decisions or they were forgotten. He made a clear distinction between thinking and dillydallying.

Having the simple-mindedness of the man among a million, it would be absurd to attribute to Wanamaker too deliberate and complex weighing of the pros and contras when he made up his mind to accept Harrison's offer. Of course he felt that he could safely leave his business. But having reached this conclusion, the deciding factors in his becoming Postmaster-General were probably unconscious, with the exception of a single one.

No doubt the honor itself appealed to him. It is pleasant to have national recognition. No doubt the prospect of four years of Washington life as a Cabinet member was an attractive prospect for a man with a wife who enjoyed being hostess and with daughters in their teens. Who does not wish the women of his family to enjoy the fruits and prestige accruing from his success? Mrs. Wanamaker was spending a year abroad with Minnie and Lillie. After their return, he would be able to give them a home in an atmosphere where social prestige did not depend upon a large income and a name in business, but upon the father's position as one of the highest officials in the nation.

The thought of other fields to conquer was a splendid stimulant to a man of Wanamaker's caliber. His restless spirit was in danger of becoming impatient and unhappy if his talents and energies had to continue to be directed in a business whose striking success had for the moment eliminated the type of problem that was meat and drink to John Wanamaker. He had got beyond the point where the title of merchant prince gave him satisfaction. At the age of fifty it is natural for a man to want, even though he does not know it, the opportunity to do something different, something that has a wider influence, and something that

will win for him a greater reputation than he ever had
before.

The one motive that he recognized and admitted, however, was the call to public service. As a young man he
had been denied the privilege of fighting in the Civil War.
He had always given unstintingly of his time and strength
to public activities in Philadelphia. The exigencies of his
growing business had up to this point prevented him from
accepting public office. Within recent years he had felt
obliged to decline candidacy for Congress and for the mayoralty of Philadelphia. He felt that his experience and his
business ability could render service to the nation in one
particular Cabinet post. That is why he told Harrison in
Indianapolis that he had made up his mind to refuse the
navy.[1] It proves that his dominant motive was not getting
for himself and his family the prestige attendant upon a
place in the Cabinet. The only reputation Wanamaker
cared for was that of achievement. As Postmaster-General
he felt that he could do big things.

The challenge to his pioneering instinct was irresistible.
He went into the Post-Office Department with the same
eagerness for adventure that had led him to start Bethany
and Oak Hall. He had long been convinced that improving
communication facilities was one of the most important
functions of government. The mail service, like the railways, was an artery upon whose proper functioning depended the health of the nation. The postal problem in
a country as yet sparsely settled presented difficulties that
could not but attract him. So much had to be done! He

---

[1] Henry L. Stoddard, who seems to have been an unofficial go-between in
the negotiations preceding the announcement of Harrison's Cabinet, states that
Wanamaker told him to tell Harrison that it would not be wise for a Pennsylvania man to take the navy portfolio because steel for the armaments came
from the mills of that state. If Wanamaker were Secretary of the Navy, he
would be embarrassed in his activities and open to attack from the opposition
in the press and in the Congress.

knew that the rapid growth of cities, the great changes in the Middle West since the Civil War, and the phenomenal development of the Pacific coast states had not yet received proper attention at Washington. When he took office, there were only 102 first-class post offices, and star mail routes were lacking in some and inadequate in almost every part of the country. His ideal for the Post Office was the same as for the Wanamaker business. The postal system belonged to the people; and he often said, "The public has the right to get from their property all the privileges that their ownership entitled them to." We have seen what this belief led him to advocate and to do.

The new President's wife was not in the best of health. It was expected, as *Harper's Weekly* put it, that Wanamaker would "have one of the large and open houses of the Cabinet and be one of the entertainers of the administration. Indeed, it is probable that the social burdens of the coming few years will be borne by the Vice-President, Mr. Blaine, and Mr. Wanamaker." Here was the great chance for the talents of Mrs. Wanamaker, assisted by her young daughters, to have full sway. The Wanamaker girls, still in their teens, were at an ideal age to enjoy the younger social life of the capital; and their presence in the home contributed materially to the pleasure and social success of their parents. So the well-known house at 1731 I Street, which had been famous for half a century as the home of the elder Cameron and the elder Frelinghuysen, was purchased from the outgoing Secretary of the Navy. William C. Whitney had lavishly redecorated it and had added a ballroom, which appealed to Wanamaker as the ideal place for exhibiting the pictures he had been collecting. The contemporary descriptions of the Wanamaker ballroom, with Rosa Bonheur's "Return from the Horse Fair" and Bou-

guereau's well-clothed beauties in juxtaposition to the Mun-
káczy religious pictures against a background of Whitney
gilt and tints and enhanced by Wanamaker bric-à-brac, make
us smile at the taste of our fathers. In these descriptions
one finds no trace of Philistine malice. The generation of
1890 was still under the spell of the Victorian age.

But there was malice, and plenty of it, to greet the
announcement that the Wanamakers were not going to serve
wine at their dinners. Here was an innovation in the social
domain as "freakish" (we use the adjective frequently employed) as the Postmaster-General's telegraph and telephone theories in his official policy! However, it was soon
discovered that alcohol was not essential to hospitality and
good cheer. The Harrisons and the Mortons approved of
the Wanamaker stand on this question, and it gave heart to
the temperance advocates. In fact, press comment of the
day indicated a surprising growth in temperance sentiment
throughout the country. It was the same with Wanamaker's determination to have Sunday observed as a day
of rest in his department as well as in his home. Here,
too, the President and the Vice-President were in agreement
with him. The social world in Washington, made up so
largely of those whose ideas and habits were fashioned by
continental European standards, was a bit at a loss to accommodate itself to total abstainers and Sabbatarians. But it
did so, admirably and whole-heartedly; and it cannot be
said that Mr. and Mrs. Wanamaker suffered inconvenience
or annoyance, or were subjected to ridicule, because of their
rigid adherence to what they thought was right. On the
contrary, the stand they took won them universal respect.
The abuse heaped upon Wanamaker, and the stories that
were circulated about him, were provoked by political opponents of the administration, by disappointed civil service

enthusiasts, and, as we have seen, by the business interests whose monopolies his policies threatened.

At the beginning of his life in Washington, Wanamaker was bothered by office-seekers more than most Cabinet members, not only because his department had more offices to fill (even then there were more than 57,000 fourth-class postmasters), but also because of the stand he took in the application of civil service measures. We have already spoken of the value of his advice of moderation to President Harrison, and of how this caused him to be disliked by young Roosevelt. It is necessary to add that Roosevelt was one of the most active centers of anti-Wanamaker feeling. The strongly independent personalities of the two men, each determined to have his way, were bound to clash.

Roosevelt was appointed to the Civil Service Commission two months after Harrison took office, and he had been led to believe that the President was willing to go much farther than he proved to be along the path of a drastic and sweeping extension of civil service. It is easy to see how Roosevelt, who never did learn how to become reserved in his expressions of opinions of men, was betrayed into rather violent denunciation of the Postmaster-General. Roosevelt might have come to see what Wanamaker was driving at in his advocacy of making haste slowly had it not been for the presence of General George D. Johnston on the Commission. Johnston was an old Confederate general whom Wanamaker had met at a Sunday-school convention. He urged him upon Harrison as Democratic appointee. In the Commission, Johnston and Roosevelt were oil and water, and never agreed on anything, with the result that the fact of Johnston became in Roosevelt's mind a personal grievance against Wanamaker. In view of the later relations between the great merchant and the great President, this story of their first contact through four years that must have seemed very long to Roosevelt is not without interest.[1]

Appointments soon became history, and the Harrison administration could settle down to the business of governing the country. Recently Elihu Root quoted a verse from the office-seekers' hymn of 1889:

> The baby rules the White House,
> Levi runs the bar,
> Wanny runs the Sunday school,
> And dammit here we are!

Mr. Root explained that the baby was President Harrison's grandson, Benjamin Harrison McKee, around whom centered the public's interest in the White House, now that Mrs. Cleveland and her baby had gone. Levi P. Morton, the Vice-President, owned the Shoreham Hotel, where liquor was sold, although Morton was as much of a Puritan as Harrison and Wanamaker. Bethany Sunday School had leaped into national fame from the fact that the Postmaster-General was willing to leave his store, but made the trip back to Philadelphia every week-end to carry on his usual Sunday duties.

Had Wanamaker quit Bethany as he quit his business, he might not have gone back to it with the same mental attitude. Insensibly, four years away would have changed him. He would certainly have gone into similar work in Washington, but would have met different conditions and brand-new ideas. Might not his relations with the church,

---

[1] A man who had high official position in the Harrison administration, and who was later given a diplomatic post by Roosevelt, told the biographer recently that Wanamaker's principal grievance against Roosevelt came in the summer and autumn of 1892. Wanamaker seemed to refuse to believe that Roosevelt had gone West for his health, and thought that, having received office at the hands of Harrison, the young New Yorker should be on hand to speak in the presidential campaign. To Wanamaker, who made no allowances for physical incapacity, Roosevelt's action looked like disloyalty to the chief at a time when all his friends should have rallied round him.

his methods of directing the Sunday school and expounding the lesson, have been modified—in what ways one knows not—in a new church atmosphere where he was not building upon foundations laid in his youth and added to year after year, and where he would meet as equals pastor and co-workers with whom there were no common traditions? As it was, in his religious activities, the years in the Harrison Cabinet meant only an opportunity to show in a beautiful and striking manner his devotion to the work he had begun as a boy. It was a pledge for the future to all his Bethany associates.

Nor was there any change in his habits of work. In the leisurely atmosphere of Washington, where nothing happens before ten o'clock, the old dog could not be taught new tricks, as he used to put it humorously. Wineless dinners and workless Sundays and lack of respect for the transcendent authority of Tom Platt and Jay Gould did not really astound Washington as much as the knowledge that the new Postmaster-General left his house every morning promptly at 8:15, and was at his desk at 8:30. Milkmen said they had never before seen the department carriage, drawn by two small sorrel horses, but now they saw it every day. Other people had to take their word for it, all except Dan, the colored doorkeeper, who had served under thirteen Postmaster-Generals, and who now had to buy an alarm clock.

Before the stream of general visitors arrived, he had attended to his personal correspondence, had worked on special reports and problems, and had had a conference with his assistants. His afternoon hours extended until six. He never left earlier. "Why the astonishment?" he said, when newspapers and friends began to talk about his long hours and what they called his remarkable attention to his work. "I always ran my business that way, and is not this supposed to be a business job?" When some postmasters at a conference commended him for the difficult example he set, he answered:

"Gentlemen, you want to run your post offices as if there were another fellow across the street competing with you, and you were trying to get all the business."

"How do you get through so much?" asked one of his earliest interviewers.

"By never doing the same thing twice," Wanamaker replied.

He might have added that the secret lay also in the ability to get rid of visitors quickly without offending them. Nothing stood him in better stead in Washington than this art, which experience as head of a great business, coupled with care not to offend and a kindly spirit, had taught him. And no trait of his was more widely talked about and envied. And yet, at the beginning, there were those who misunderstood, and who remarked that Wanamaker made them uncomfortable by his obsequiousness.

For example, a New Yorker, who had no other claim to consideration than inherited money and an aristocratic name, reported to a group at his club with great gusto his impressions of a call on the new Postmaster-General. "It was positively painful," he declared, "to have a Cabinet officer treat me with so much deference. It was just as if I had come to buy a suit of clothes from him."

A young lawyer, who was destined to become President, asked, "How long were you in his office?"

The clubman grew red and stammered, and was finally compelled to acknowledge that he had been accorded three minutes. The laugh was on him. From the call he had taken away exactly the impression he had made up his mind to get, without realizing that Wanamaker had no time for him.

PHOTOGRAPH OF A WOODCUT WHICH APPEARED IN FRANK LESLIE'S ILLUSTRATED NEWSPAPER, APRIL 13TH, 1889, SHOWING MR. WANAMAKER ADDRESSING THE BETHANY BIBLE UNION, PHILADELPHIA

Wanamaker's ability to shake hands genially and push the visitor gently towards the door while beaming on him, was greatly admired by other men in high office who had their own hosts of visitors. One associate, when he later became Governor of his state, thought he could imitate Wanamaker. He tried the combined handshake and push on an old political supporter. But the man said; "It's all right, Governor, if you want me to go, but I won't be thrown out." In telling the story, the discomfited Governor declared: "It was the first and last time I tried the Wanamaker handshake. He can do it, but I don't believe anybody else in the world has the subtle genius necessary to perform it successfully."

Since others beside the New York snob remarked it—and some of them men of parts—it is probable that when Wanamaker first became Postmaster-General his geniality may have had something of the welcoming shopkeeper in it. What is more natural than that a man who had lived thirty years in retail business—and close to the business all the time —should bear the stamp of it? It may be just seeing what we are looking for, but we do think we can spot the preacher, the lawyer, the doctor, and the college professor. To boot, Wanamaker was a Philadelphian, and though his influence upon merchandising and advertising had already become international, and he could fairly be called an outstanding American, he had won his place in the world by sticking pretty closely to two streets in one city. The world had worn a path to his door, but up to 1889 he had remained a Philadelphian, with all the provincialism of those whose waking hours are mostly spent between the Delaware and the Schuylkill.

It was, therefore, a thoroughly transforming experience for a man of Wanamaker's background to be transplanted for four years at the heyday of a business career that was none the less narrowing because of its unique success. The

Philadelphia merchant found himself placed at the head of the nation's greatest business, with 150,000 men under him, working in every state and territory of the Union down to the smallest hamlets. He sat around a table with the group picked by the President to aid him in governing the country. Could he be the same man, after his advice had been asked and listened to in matters affecting the destiny of the nation? Like Horatio, he learned of things not dreamed of before. In knowledge, in vision, in confidence in himself, in the realization of his unusual talents and powers, he grew by leaps and bounds.

An inkling of what the close association with Benjamin Harrison meant in the life of John Wanamaker was given in an interview with S. S. McClure, who tried to get Wanamaker to write an autobiography in 1912. Wanamaker told McClure:

"I often regret I did not use my opportunity during the four years I spent in Washington to put down my impressions of Blaine and Harrison. Harrison still speaks to me. You see I have his portrait—it was made for me from life—on the wall over there, where I can always see it. What do you suppose he says to me? He says one thing every day. Now look at him. You remember him so well with that cold judicial appearance and his rather white skin. What do you suppose he is saying? 'Wanamaker, are you sure of your ground?' That's what he says to me every day.

"It is an abiding inspiration to have lived those years with him in the Cabinet. The questions we discussed! He said such wonderful things at the time of the Chilean trouble. Our soldiers had been shot and we were on the point of sending ships to Chile. A drunken fracas had started it. I remember in the discussion with the lawyers about the table, he said, with his fine sense of right, 'I am afraid we will be caught by concealments.' Just that sentence, 'Caught by concealments!'

"In discussing a man for a certain place, where there were a number of candidates—McKinley was one of them—speaking of this particular man, Harrison said, 'He is a bundle of spites.' Things like that run out of him all the time. Dear me, if I had only made a note of them!"

As far as the influence upon Wanamaker went, he did not need to make a note of them. Just the contact with Harrison, and others like Harrison, official and social contact, put Wanamaker into a new and larger world. He had eyes to see and ears to hear. Years later, at a convention of lawyers, Wanamaker stated that the intimate association with Harrison and other statesmen, who enjoyed the foundation of a severe and broad legal training, had been an inestimable blessing to him, a business man.[1] He confessed that his own lack of any other education than that of "hard knocks" and "doing things" had been brought home to him with peculiar force. In his experience with thousands of subordinates, very many of whom had enjoyed educational opportunities denied to him, he had perhaps comforted himself too much with the thought of the vast difference between acquiring knowledge and having had access to knowledge. After his years at Washington the value of a mind trained by study meant more to him—far more—than it had before. There was new significance in the text he had so often expounded, "Unless ye become as little children, ye shall not enter the Kingdom of Heaven." To be sure of his ground, in everything that he tackled, he had decided that it was necessary for him to become a child again, and to study with more care than he had ever done before a host of things outside his business.

[1] In a humorous aside, however, he stated that he did not "see why our legislators had to be ninety per cent lawyers."

We shall see how this discovery, of supreme importance to every man in middle life, not only enabled Wanamaker to keep the place he had won as the greatest merchant of his day throughout another thirty years, but also led him to achievement after achievement in other fields when most of his contemporaries were resting on their laurels.

As a boy there was the winter in Indiana, and at twenty the trip of thirty-five hundred miles in the Middle West. That was about all Wanamaker knew of his own country when he became Postmaster-General. During his first two years in the Cabinet he traveled very little. His knowledge of the postal field was limited to correspondence and the study of maps and figures. On April 14, 1891, he accompanied President Harrison on a five weeks' tour from coast to coast. The itinerary was privately printed by Wanamaker for the convenience of the President and his party, and we find from this that they went through Virginia, Georgia, Tennessee, Arkansas, Texas, New Mexico, and Arizona, to Los Angeles and San Francisco. Ten days were spent in California. Then the special train carried them to Oregon and Washington, Idaho, Colorado, Nebraska, Missouri, Illinois, Indiana, Ohio, and Pennsylvania. The total distance covered was over nine thousand miles.

Everywhere there were ovations, and wherever he could do so, the Postmaster-General slipped away to visit post offices. Wanamaker's first speech, following the President, was to an assembly of ten thousand at Atlanta. At San Francisco he made a notable address to the postal employees. His maiden effort at a full-length political speech was in Portland, Oregon, on May 5. His success led to calls for John Wanamaker at Seattle on the following day, and here he again proved, to his own surprise, that he could make a great crowd laugh and cheer him when he spoke on the issues of the day. He had not before realized that thirty-three years as superintendent of Bethany Sunday School

(*Photo. by Taber*)

IN SAN FRANCISCO IN 1891

qualified him for the rough-and-tumble of political speech-making.

This tour was Wanamaker's introduction as a public man to people of all parts of the country. Local newspaper comment indicates how strong an impression his personality made. The President delighted in featuring his Postmaster-General wherever the opportunity offered, and the affectionate regard the two men had for each other was noticeable. It confirmed what had been reported in the press from the very first day of his administration, that if Harrison had not wanted Wanamaker in his official family, as Wanamaker's enemies contended, he was showing it in a curious way.

The Sunday before he left Indianapolis to be inaugurated as President of the United States, Benjamin Harrison passed the plate, as he had long been in the habit of doing, in the First Presbyterian Church. The Sunday after he ceased to be President he was back in Indianapolis, passing the plate in the First Presbyterian Church. That was the kind of a man he was. It was a type that Wanamaker understood and could get along with famously. The very day before she left home to become the First Lady of the Land, Mrs. Harrison was seen, with a basket on her arm, doing her usual buying in the Indianapolis central market. That was the kind of woman she was. It was a type that Mrs. Wanamaker understood and could get along with famously.

At the beginning of the first summer of the administration, in June, 1889, the President and Mrs. Harrison, with Baby McKee, were guests in the large but unpretentious Wanamaker cottage at Cape May Point, where few rich people and no families in official life summered. Harrison liked it so well that he took a cottage there, and made it the summer capital. In the spring of 1890 Mrs. Wanamaker accompanied Mrs. Harrison on a trip to Florida. The President visited Bethany Sunday School, and he and his wife were guests at Lindenhurst when they visited or passed through Philadelphia. This presidential intimacy caused Mrs. Wanamaker, as well as her husband, and their country and summer homes, to become nationally known.

Over the closing days of the administration were cast the shadows of death and political disappointment.

Harrison was never popular with Republican leaders, big and little. He was too unbending, too consciously a man of high moral standards. Among his most determined opponents were the Pennsylvania Senators. Quay did not want four years more of what he called in an unguarded moment "Sunday-school politics." Cameron, weary of politics, anyhow, felt that between the Harrison-Wanamaker point of view and the civil service agitation, the lot of a Senator had become unenviable. Blaine, stricken with the malady that soon caused his death, had left the Cabinet, and many politicians, despite his condition, were urging him to contest Harrison's renomination. When Depew would not run, he was induced to bring pressure to bear upon Blaine.

It was here that Harrison learned the fine quality of the Wanamaker loyalty. Loyalty was an inherited trait in Wanamaker, and he gave it to his sons. In his long life he never threw anybody over. His attachment to friends was proverbial. He would rather be called foolish or erratic, he would rather stand in his own way, he would rather cause himself no end of inconvenience or annoyance, than seem to be lacking in support of those with whom he had worked. "If your memory isn't particularly good," he once said, "forget what you have done for others, and concentrate on training yourself to remember everything that anyone has done for you."

Wanamaker's loyalty kept him from getting out of the Cabinet when some others did. Loyalty and fighting spirit made him a factor in the President's renomination. The ensuing campaign, however, ended in bitter disappointment.

The Republicans were fairly well united, and put up a good fight. But the country was not satisfied with the McKinley tariff, and business men were not as sure of the Republican party's stand on sound money as they were of Cleveland's. Cleveland's star was again in the ascendant. He was by no means the speaker that Harrison was, and what he said did not go as well either on the platform or in the newspapers. But on the offensive Cleveland was not the same ineffectual candidate against Harrison that he had been when on the defensive four years earlier. The Republicans were outgeneraled in aggressive campaign tactics. In Indiana, for instance, an army of tin peddlers turned the farmers' wives against the McKinley tariff, and Harrison lost his own state.

Mrs. Harrison's failing health and last illness were a serious handicap to the vigorous prosecution of the campaign. Harrison was an unrivaled master of audiences. But he could not go far from Washington, and during critical weeks of the campaign he was at his wife's bedside. Mrs. Harrison died before the election. In this bereavement, as in the convention and during the campaign, Harrison leaned heavily upon Wanamaker. The years they had lived together, with their joys and sorrows, kept the two men fast friends. With his other associates, whom, like the President, he was destined to outlive, Wanamaker did not lose touch. These associations were ever after an influence in his life. When he was visiting President Taft in 1912, the old Cabinet room brought back a flood of memories. He jotted down on a scrap of paper:

As I sit here my eye wanders to the empty seats where in my time sat President Harrison, James G. Blaine, William Windom, General Proctor, Governor Foster, Senator Elkins, and General Rusk, seven of my old comrades, moved out and on to another world. How good the Heavenly Father is to let me stay and work along.

CHAPTER XXIX

PENNSYLVANIA POLITICS: GETTING IN

WHEN Walter Savage Landor said, "We are what winds and fountains make us," he put into one brief sentence the whole of biography. The winds blow from the outside, and they determine the form and direction of our activities. But the winds act only upon vital forces that come from within. The fountains must always be thought of in describing the winds.

The fountains of John Wanamaker's life had become accustomed to agreeable winds from afar, and had learned to respond to them. It was John Wanamaker of Oak Hall, of the Grand Depot, and of Bethany, who had lived in Washington from 1889 to 1893. He had no thought of giving up old activities for new. But however large a part they might still have to play in his life, the Wanamaker store and Bethany would never again be able to fill it. His restless genius could now not be fully satisfied, as it had in the past, by making the store and Bethany grow, and by continuing to do his bit, when opportunity offered, in municipal affairs. Philadelphia alone was too small for his business ideas and efforts. He had more time and inclination for politics than Philadelphia could satisfy. In the future, as we shall see, Bethany had to mean more to him than praising God at Twenty-second and Bainbridge Streets. So it was with his other religious interests also. He was beginning to think of the Sunday school, the Y. M. C. A., and the Presbyterian Church as world organizations, to whose national and international aspects he must give himself.

338

Before the Cabinet years Wanamaker's political education had been confined to Philadelphia. Now he knew a lot about Pennsylvania and national politics. To knowledge were added prestige and liking for the game. Many men have taken public office, as Wanamaker undoubtedly did, moved principally by a sense of obligation. After actual experience in politics, however, duty alone would not induce a man to keep seeking public office. It is too discouraging, too uncertain, a career in the United States. The visions of the idealist, the fervor of the crusader, may still remain; but experience has tempered them. Small men think of the pay roll and their reputation. Big men, if they have been defeated, seek vindication; and when they win they hope to win again, because the taste of power has acted on them like any other intoxicant. No man who had ever been President, no matter how high-minded he was, could bring himself to say, "I'd rather be right than President."

In Pennsylvania politics, fighting the Quay machine with a vim that astonished even himself, John Wanamaker was a force for good. His stirring campaigns were fearlessly and honorably fought, and that they were only partially successful and did not put him in the Senate or in the Governor's chair does not detract either from their glory or from their significance. But we must not fail to emphasize the fact that Quay's formidable opponent was eager to remain a political factor and believed for some years that he was destined to have a political career. He desisted from his efforts only when he saw that the door was definitely shut in his face.

As the years in Pennsylvania politics form a distinct episode, and were, unlike any other event in Wanamaker's life, without aftermath or lasting influence, the story can best be told apart. We must go back a few years, and then ahead as far as 1898, leaving the founding of the New York store in 1896 to a later chapter.

It was logical that the man who represented Pennsylvania in the Cabinet should feel that he had a responsibility for the activities of his party in his native state. At the beginning of the Harrison administration, in the off-year election of 1889, when voting was light, the Republicans carried Pennsylvania by the comfortable majority of 60,000. Quay felt that he owned the state, and the following year he ignored the popular gubernatorial candidacy of Hastings, who had done great work in the Johnstown flood. He forced the nomination of State Senator Delamater, banker and Standard Oil magnate. Not wanting to be read out of the party, Hastings bowed to the boss's will, and announced his support of Delamater. But his followers threatened open revolt, and it was soon realized that the Democratic candidate had a chance of election.

Wanamaker, as a Pennsylvanian, understood the righteousness of the indignation, and he shared it. But with nation-wide public opinion so evenly divided between the parties he saw how damaging to Harrison's chances in 1892 would be the election of a Democrat in Pennsylvania, the rock-ribbed Republican state. When called upon to put the party's national interests ahead of internal quarrels between bosses and reformers in the state, he not only came out for Delamater, but got the Secretary of State to make a speech in behalf of the Republican candidate in the Philadelphia Academy of Music. Wanamaker, presiding, told how on the journey from Washington he noticed Blaine singing when he crossed the Pennsylvania line. He asked, "What do you think Mr. Blaine was singing?" intending to go right on and answer the question himself by saying that the Pennsylvania-born statesman was humming to himself, "Auld Lang Syne." A boy in the gallery was too quick for him, and yelled out, "Annie Roonie," a popular song of the time. This convulsed everybody, and some hecklers started up:

> "She's my Annie,
> I'm her Jo;
> She's my sweetheart,
> I'm her beau."

Wanamaker stood the gaff well, and managed to recover the audience. But he never forgot that experience. He had learned what not to do before a large gathering that did not hold him in respect and awe, as his Bethany scholars did. The lesson stood him in good stead in his later campaigning; and never again did he ask a rhetorical question unless he was ready to go right on without pause for effect or breath.

Administration intervention did not save Delamater. Pennsylvania was carried by the Democratic candidate, whose clever manager, William F. Harrity, won thereby the Democratic National Chairmanship, and guided Cleveland to victory in 1892. The false position in which he had been placed, and the loss of prestige to the party in state and nation resulting from Quay's reckless contempt for public opinion in Pennsylvania, made Wanamaker furious. But he restrained himself, through loyalty to Harrison and the party. In his mind and in the minds of thousands of other influential Republicans were sown the seeds of rebellion against the Pennsylvania bosses. It was clearly seen that men like Quay would continue to rule, deciding upon policies and candidates under the influence of their own selfish interests, unless the party machinery was wrested from them. Otherwise refusal to support machine-chosen candidates meant simply throwing elections to the Democrats.

Quay's tyranny, exercised at a delicate moment when Wanamaker's hands were tied and he did not feel himself free to protest, made many who had trusted Wanamaker begin to assume that he had been corrupted by the official fleshpots at Washington. Had he not himself often repeated with emphatic approval to his Bethany scholars that "a man is known by the company he keeps"? The embarrassment to which a man is subjected in his business when he accepts a high official position has been illustrated by the attempt of the Gould interests to strike at the Postmaster-General through the credit of the Wanamaker store. Loving a fight, Wanamaker rather enjoyed that! But the embarrassment of having his name mixed up with politicians and their mixing private financial interests with politics cut him to the quick. Dimly did he then begin to understand the price of public office.

Devoted friends of John Wanamaker, who made no allowances for national party interests and for the loyalty of the Postmaster-General to a chief whom the bosses were planning to desert, wondered why and how long the man whom they knew to be upright and fearless was going to endure having his name associated with the names of politicians and convicts.

The first rumors that Wanamaker might try to be elected to the Senate from Pennsylvania were circulated while he was in the midst of his Cabinet career. When newspapers began to say that he had senatorial ambitions, the Postmaster-General gave out the following statement:

I have no ambition to be other than a good Postmaster-General. It is not reasonable for me to suppose that I can make myself great in the rôle of statesmanship. My whole training has been that of a business man, and while I might perhaps hope to make myself a great merchant, I could hardly expect to succeed more than ordinarily well in an untried field. I accepted the Postmaster-Generalship with a desire to do what good I could for the country, and because I believe it the duty of every American citizen to take part in such administration of the government as comes to him.

This was an explicit enough declaration. Wanamaker undoubtedly meant what he said. He was disgusted with politics. Attractive as his life in Washington had been for two years, the game did not seem to be worth the candle. In administration circles at Washington his associates were all that a high-minded Christian gentleman could wish for. But he knew that it would be difficult to play a rôle in Pennsylvania politics without either turning against his party or accepting the strange bedfellows that politics imposes.

After the Democratic administration returned to power, Wanamaker's one thought was getting back to business. Before he did so, however, he decided to take his family and some friends on a transcontinental tour. Four delightful weeks were spent in Mexico, and then from El Paso to San Francisco the route of the former presidential tour was followed. From California the party went north to Tacoma. Salt Lake City was revisited, then Kansas City. The last objective was the Chicago World's Fair, where the merchant reasserted himself. Friends say that while Wanamaker was interested in the Fair, he spent a good part of his time at Marshall Field's and other stores. There had come into his mind the thought of New York or Chicago, or both, for the test that he had to make. The next chapter in his career would be the demonstration that the Wanamaker principles of business and genius for merchandising, advertising, and organization could compete successfully with other great stores in a field where there was not the advantage of an early start and a location acquired at comparatively little cost.

Judging from a letter of his old friend, Rev. Dr. James R. Miller, who joined the party at El Paso, the American part of the journey was largely spent in visiting Presbyterian educational institutions and addressing religious gatherings. At the end of the sixth week Dr. Miller wrote to his wife:

The tour has not been a mere vacation from work for Mr. Wanamaker and myself. We have held services at every point. I am sure that Mr. Wanamaker has left encouragement and new strength in hundreds of Christian hearts, especially by his words to college and Y. M. C. A. gatherings and to Sunday-school teachers. Certain it is that we would hardly have done as much preaching and speaking if we had been at home. It has been almost like some of St. Paul's journeying through the country to confirm the souls of the brethren. This fact reconciles me to the sightseeing which seems to me almost a waste of time.

Dr. Miller was a good preacher and one of the best writers of his day on religious topics. But that was his whole life. He had little interest in anything else. If they reach the rank of master, most men are masters of only one trade. Wanamaker was the man in a million who could use his mind simultaneously in doing thoroughly well widely divergent things. The trip may have seemed only an evangelistic tour to Dr. Miller; but while his host did his full part in what Dr. Miller was interested in, he made notes on department stores everywhere, and wrote about the people, the growth of cities and their post-office facilities, the scenery, and the climate. All the while he was planning to return to active business, studying the financial panic, and making drafts of arguments to use against the Cleveland administration in the 1894 congressional campaign.

The latter half of 1893 was a bad time for business, and the panic left disturbed conditions that greatly affected retailing through the winter and into the spring of 1894. Wanamaker found that he was needed in the business, and devoted himself to the skillful steering that was necessary in the storm. Much commercial paper was out, and in 1895 he told a life-insurance convention that he had been thankful to have large reserves for borrowing on his policies, and that he had used them to the limit.

In the summer of 1894 he went to Carlsbad for a cure,

after a lapse of seven years. Except for a flying official trip to study the experiment of sea post offices, he had not been abroad since he had taken Mrs. Wanamaker and the girls over the year before he became Postmaster-General. But he was back in the autumn, and entered the congressional campaign. In view of the way the party had honored him, he felt the obligation, of course; and the path had been made easy to speak without reserve in Pennsylvania, for Quay had heeded the lesson of 1891 and consented to the belated nomination of Hastings for Governor.

Wanamaker's excoriation of the Cleveland administration proved that he had learned a lot about political speaking. He made the most of the lukewarmness of many Democrats to the sound-money issue, which was just coming to the fore, and of the panic of 1893. He charged disturbed business conditions to the Democratic tariff policy. He called the assumption of the Democrats to be reformers ridiculous, in view of Tammany's control of the party. In several speeches he accused Tammany of having bought Cleveland's second election by the use of a huge campaign fund. "The Democratic party," he said, "has not for forty years had within it sufficient material with which to carry on the public business. It was a conspicuous failure in Mr. Cleveland's first four years, and the present experiment is little or no better."

At Columbia, Pennsylvania, he amazed everybody, delighted many, and worried not a few, by a resounding speech, the tenor of which can be judged by the peroration:

"Notwithstanding the oratorical riot going on from the hills of New York to the crisp breezy mountains of Georgia, the people are not going to be deluded again. Soon there shall rise another Abraham Lincoln—not to free three millions of slaves, but to emancipate the land from the blighting curse of inadequate protection. Undying courage and herculean strength shall be equal to the emergency. In spite of all that threatens, the country is not to be swamped after the strikes and lock-ups. After the lower wage scales and patient suffering will come again the sunshine of prosperity, but it will not be until the Republicans return again to their proper place in governing the land. The fight is now on and we are sure to win."

The Republican victory throughout the country was overwhelming. For Congress and state offices the North and West registered Republican gains everywhere. Wilson, author of the tariff bill, was unseated by a Republican opponent in West Virginia. The Democrats lost Tennessee. Aside from the reversal of the congressional majority, the notable feature of the election was the loss of the governorship to the Democrats in the largest three states. Altgeld was defeated in Illinois, and Senator Hill lost to former Vice-President Morton by 150,000 in New York. The blow to the Tammany bosses in New York City, already shaken by the revelations of the Lexow Investigation Committee, was especially severe. The 1894 election influenced profoundly for nearly two decades the history of American political parties. The disaster to the Democratic party was nation-wide. It was split up into factions, and did not present a solid front in a national election again until 1912.

The magnitude of the victory, the revelation that Pennsylvania was still overwhelmingly Republican, and the fate of the Hill machine in New York, combined to make Wanamaker believe that Pennsylvania could be freed from boss rule by a movement of revolt within the Republican party. Having this belief, the temptation to get after Quay was irresistible.

CHAPTER XXX

PENNSYLVANIA POLITICS: THE FIGHT AGAINST QUAY

QUAY realized that he had to reckon with Wanamaker when a successor to Senator Cameron was to be chosen by the legislature elected in the autumn of 1896. There was no question about Cameron's intention to retire. That he would not succeed himself had long been known. That Wanamaker wanted to go to the Senate was also known.

Wanamaker made no move to arrive at an understanding with Quay. He gave his usual contribution of $10,000 to the national campaign fund, and announced his intention of taking the stump for McKinley. With Bryan as the Democratic candidate and free silver as the issue, his wholehearted eagerness to go into the campaign was patent. In the private files we find in his own hand the following note for a speech:

Going straight to the point, it is a case of natural selection. I have great confidence in the ability, experience, and patriotism of Governor McKinley. I have faith to believe that the people of the United States after the cyclones of panic and disaster in the past three years will unite now to advance national prosperity rather than party successes. A financial system for the public good of the whole country is far above considerations affecting the interests of any one section of states or any single industry.

That this was how everybody felt in the East was shown by the split over free silver in the Democratic party. Cleve-

347

land himself could not indorse Bryan on the Chicago platform. McKinley's election seemed a foregone conclusion.

Wanamaker had every reason to believe that he could run for Senator without putting the success of the Republican ticket in Pennsylvania in jeopardy, whatever attitude Quay might take. This being the situation, Quay decided that it would be wise to come to an understanding with Wanamaker. As in 1888, he asked for an interview, and went to talk things over with the man whom he could not afford to ignore. But again, as in 1888, he found Wanamaker unwilling to finance a campaign where he had no control of expenditures. Wanamaker was nervous about Quay's methods. Quay feared that if Wanamaker were elected Senator, without being under obligations to him, the state organization might pass out of his hands and he would fail of re-election when his term expired in 1898. The two men tried sincerely to come together, and it was reported that they had actually arrived at an agreement. But at the last moment, when Quay insisted on naming the financial agent for the campaign, Wanamaker's suspicions were aroused. It brought forcibly home to him the risk he was running of getting tarred with the organization brush. He asked of himself whether he could stand as the organization candidate without tacitly accepting responsibility for the organization's methods. There was only one answer. He let Quay know that he was going to seek the senatorship openly—without the aid of bosses.

This decision lost him the certainty of election. Had there been direct election for Senator, or preferential pri-

---

[1] But Wanamaker was afraid of lack of vigilant effort. On September 26, 1912, in the midst of the Taft-Roosevelt-Wilson campaign, he wrote to National Chairman Charles D. Hilles, urging missionary work among employers, to get them in turn to educate their employees on the tariff question, and added: "I gave such advice to the managers of our campaign in 1896, and Mr. Hanna thought enough of it to create a special bureau in Chicago, with Hon. John M. Farquhar of Buffalo in charge, the results of which were magnificent."

maries, in Pennsylvania, Quay would have stood little chance of thwarting Wanamaker's ambition. It was presidential year, and the Senatorship was a national, not state or local, issue. Wanamaker tried, of course, as it was the only way, to get candidates for legislature pledged to him before the voters in every county of the state; and to this end his friends formed a campaign organization. In his own speeches he dealt with national issues and clean and efficient politics without specific attack upon Quay or any other boss.

The McKinley landslide in November returned to Harrisburg a virtually solid Republican legislature, but how these men would vote was problematical. The Wanamaker forces claimed the majority, and seemed to be able to count on above a hundred definite pledges. This number was more than Quay's candidate could muster. Quay had given the organization indorsement to Boies Penrose, member of an old Philadelphia family, with a Harvard education, who was by background and training of excellent senatorial caliber. But Penrose had the instincts of a gang politician. No scruples held him back from putting himself unconditionally in the hands of Quay, and his subsequent career proved that his goal in public life was to follow in the footsteps of Quay. Penrose did not hesitate to advance his candidacy by defaming Wanamaker, and at the same time charging that Wanamaker had hired a band of ministerial agents, whom he called "filth throwers in politics," to carry on a "campaign of scandal."

Wanamaker thought he had learned all there was to know about political abuse when he was Postmaster-General. In December, 1896, he woke up to the fact that his experiences in Washington had been those of an amateur! The guns of the organization were trained upon him through the press and by flooding the mails with circulars. In his private life Wanamaker proved invulnerable. Nothing could be found against him save the vague accusation that he must be a hypocrite because of his excessive religious activities.   But the old stories about cheating the customs in import declarations were revived, and much was made in rural districts of the charge that the Wanamaker store put the country merchants out of business, and that Wanamaker was a millionaire who wanted to go to the Senate to represent big business.

Wanamaker's categorical statements and his warm advocacy of the McKinley tariff did not prevent his loyalty to this great Republican issue from being questioned.   Pennsylvanians were told that it was against Wanamaker's business interests to believe in a high tariff, and that as an importer he would work against the party if elected to the Senate.

An attempt was made to inject the religious issue in the campaign by the secret circulation of a special Christmas issue of *The Republic*, the national organ of the American Protective Association and the Junior Order of United American Mechanics.   Mailed to their members from Washington and distributed in lodges, this paper came out strongly for Penrose, who, it was asserted belonged to their orders. Wanamaker's name is not mentioned; but there was the specific statement that the opponent of Penrose did not belong to anti-Catholic organizations and could not therefore be relied upon.[1]

At the last moment before the legislature assembled the big broadside of the Quay forces was released.   A professional detective, who had been dismissed by several em-

---

[1] The venom of the politicians against Wanamaker was extended even to intrigues in the Masonic fraternity.   These failed, of course, but it is interesting to note that on July 28, 1902, Wanamaker received a letter from a prominent Mason, in which we find the following statement: "Several years ago, when you were proposed for membership in the Commandery, a suggestion was made to keep you out, to one working on an afternoon paper. The inducement was made that the newspaper man would stand in great favor with the owner if you were not admitted.   I understand that the object was to use the news for political purposes at the time of the election."

ployers and who was out of a job, was found to sign an affidavit to the effect that the Wanamaker forces were trying to buy members of the legislature.

When the joint caucus of the Senate and House met on January 5, Penrose received 133 votes and Wanamaker 76. It was a surprising revelation of changes that had occurred in seven weeks. At least 20 votes had shifted, if not more. And the dozen or less uncertain votes had all gone to Penrose. When the result of the caucus was announced, Wanamaker withdrew his name. The Republican candidate before the legislature was Boies Penrose.

An eminent citizen wrote that evening, urging Wanamaker to stay in the fight, and volunteering to drop everything to come to his aid. On the side of the letter in the private files Wanamaker jotted down in pencil the reply, as was a custom of his. He wrote:

It was very kind of you to offer to come to the front in the Senatorial contest, but there was nothing left to be done to win the battle but outbid the buyers of the votes. I could not reverse my life to become a Senator and come back home with any other honor than clean hands. It was too much to expect to break down a thirty-year-old machine by one bold dash.

In this last sentence we see what was in Wanamaker's mind. He had a keen sense of realities. The "one bold dash" had not been sufficient to overthrow a system that had been intrenching itself in every part of the state during a generation. In his campaigning, as we have seen, Wanamaker had not gone out of his way to attack the machine. He had confined himself to national issues. After the election there was not the means, nor was the utility apparent, of meeting calumny and abuse throughout the state. The members of the legislature had been chosen. The decision and the responsibility were theirs.

Business and personal considerations combined to urge upon Wanamaker the advisability of giving up the fight.

The great adventure of the New York store had just been
entered upon, and while everything had started auspiciously
over there under the leadership of Robert C. Ogden, it was
certain that the magnitude of the undertaking called for
the attention and talents of the head of the business. New
York was not going to prove an easy nut to crack. And
competition in his own field was becoming more acute in
Philadelphia.

Wanamaker was rich, and he had come to the age when
it seemed natural that a man of his position should yearn
for leisure. He had acquired the taste for travel. He enjoyed crossing the ocean, and vacations in Europe offered
attractions the power of which he had come to know. Then,
too, taking the cure at Carlsbad did him a lot of good. His
one great physical handicap was a weak throat. Family and
friends believed that the Sundays at Bethany were already
too great a tax upon his voice. When he got tired he was
peculiarly susceptible to colds, and physicians warned
against traveling and speaking. They said it was the worst
thing he could do, and that it would be folly for him to keep
up the fight against the Pennsylvania machine—a fight that
he could hope to win only by speech-making. Pneumonia
was a real danger that might develop at any time from a
severe cold.

But reform sentiment had now been thoroughly awakened
in Pennsylvania, and Wanamaker was only too ready to
listen to the men who told him that he had become the
standard-bearer of the movement against the bosses. The
purport of thousands of messages pouring in from every
part of the state was that Wanamaker's leadership had become the hope of the decent citizens of Pennsylvania. If
he was going to allow the blocking of his senatorial ambitions to discourage him to the point of abandoning the fight,
how could he reconcile this surrender with his impassioned

preaching of the responsibility of all the voters to strive with every nerve and make every sacrifice for better citizenship?

As a tangible demonstration that the fight was not over, the 76 members of the state legislature who had resisted every form of pressure and had remained Wanamaker men to the end formed a bloc at Harrisburg, and stood up valiantly on the floor of the House and the Senate for honest government. Their loyalty to him and to the principles of which he had made himself the embodiment stirred Wanamaker deeply. He might have found argument against the urgings of zealous friends in business and church circles in Philadelphia. But when he thought of the "seventy-six" he knew that he would have to go on. To his oldest son, who had remonstrated with him, more from filial anxiety than business interest, he cited the "seventy-six" struggling at Harrisburg, and said, simply, "You know, Tom, that our Wanamaker loyalty never fails to match that of those who serve us. 'Am I a dog to do this thing?' "

From that day until the son's death there existed between him and his father perfect understanding and sympathy in the matter of the father's political activities. More than that, the son's brilliant mind was directed to the problem of how he could help. The answer was *The North American*, with which he carried on after the elder Wanamaker's forced retirement from leadership of the reform forces.

Immediately following the senatorial contest in January, 1897, the "seventy-six" began their defiance of Quay. They declared that they were banded together to correct legislative abuses; to oppose legislative corruption; to protect Pennsylvania's educational and business interests; and to compel the wise and honest expenditure of the state's money.

Quay and his advisers were of the opinion that the best method of putting an end to the revolt was to show dissatisfied Republicans who was the master of Pennsylvania.

Quay astounded his opponents by announcing, nearly two years before it was time for a new Governor to be elected, that William A. Stone was to be the party's candidate in November, 1899, and that it was important for all "good Republicans" to work for party harmony in view of the crucial presidential election ahead. It was a contemptuous challenge to all who thought that boss rule in Pennsylvania could and should be ended.

The move was skillful and logical. Republican voters would want to return a large administration majority to Washington in the congressional election of 1898. The machine would have an advantage in a year when national and state issues could be confused. However anxious Pennsylvanians might be to rid the state of the machine, they would hesitate to put in jeopardy Republican success in congressional contests by a revolt within the party. Political machines always try to hide behind national issues.

Wanamaker's candidacy for the senatorship, however, had so thoroughly aroused decent Republicans throughout the state that there was an open revolt against the slating of William A. Stone for the Governorship. On February 2, 1898, more than four hundred leading Republicans, representing fifty-five counties, held a meeting of protest at the Philadelphia Bourse. Wanamaker was in the South. Without his knowledge or consent he was unanimously named as candidate for the Governorship in opposition to Quay's man. A committee of influential citizens was appointed to notify Wanamaker, and to assure him that all who were present at the Bourse meeting were eager to contest, under his leadership, Quay's ownership of the Republican party in Pennsylvania.

Many personal friends, viewing the situation objectively, advised strongly against acceptance. They pointed out that a third of the delegates had already been chosen, all Quay men, and that his chances of securing the nomination were *nil*. There was less hope, they said, of breaking the machine in 1898 than there had been when he was running for Senator fifteen months before. War with Spain was on the horizon, and the gang were certainly going to make the most of the plea to "stand by the President." But when he realized that his refusal would mean the end of the revolt, Wanamaker could not bring himself to remain deaf to the call. On March 9 he wrote to the Committee of Notification of the Bourse Meeting:

> I consent to be a candidate for Governor in pursuance of your request presented to me on February 7th.
>
> Somebody must begin. I am ready to do my part. The fight must be fought—and fought to the finish—if it takes all summer, with the autumn and the winter thrown in.

In every way Wanamaker was as good as his word. His conduct throughout the gubernatorial campaign revealed him as a man inspired wholly by a sense of duty. He did not hesitate to sacrifice personal ambition, and to devote time, strength, and talents in a losing fight. The record speaks for itself.

The war with Spain, which came in April, complicated the pre-convention campaign. But Wanamaker traveled over the state, speaking with telling effect, and succeeding in winning delegates not only in friendly districts, but also in places where the machine was strongly intrenched. He handled State issues without gloves. But before the convention assembled, at the beginning of June, it was realized that the Wanamaker delegates would not be in a majority. There was another anti-Quay candidate, Charles W. Stone, who had secured instructed delegates in districts where the feeling was against the machine, but where personal enmities, distrust, and misrepresentation had militated against Wanamaker.

Wanamaker proved that he had not gone into the fight for self-advancement by volunteering to withdraw in favor of Charles W. Stone when he found that the delegates instructed for him were willing to vote for the other anti-Quay candidate. It looked like a sure victory, for the Stone and Wanamaker delegates seemed to number 199. But on June 3 the convention named William A. Stone, giving him 198 votes against 164 for Charles W. Stone. It is impossible, of course, to state beyond the shadow of doubt when a pledge is a pledge. But just as in the senatorial contest eighteen months earlier, it seemed that bribery and intimidation had again been resorted to.

The result was so close that the anti-Quay leaders felt encouraged and justified to carry the issue before the people. Charles W. Stone was named for Governor on an independent ticket. The insurgent movement thus developed into the most formidable rebellion Quay had ever faced. His re-election later as United States Senator was at stake. Looking ahead, people facetiously remarked that while the issue, from the personal angle, seemed to be Stone *vs.* Stone, it was really Wanamaker *vs.* Quay. The defeat of William A. Stone would mean more than placing an anti-Quay man in the Governor's chair and more than putting an end to corruption at Harrisburg. Eventually it would mean Wanamaker in the Senate and in control of the party organization in Pennsylvania.

Quay made the fight of his life. So did Wanamaker. To Quay it meant everything,—power, prestige, livelihood; and every resource of the gang at bay was mustered in the battle. To Wanamaker, if he viewed the situation personally, victory would bring obligations and responsibilities that could hardly be welcomed. He was far from being as keen about the Senatorship as he had been during the years when the glamour of Washington official life still had him in its spell. But his conception of the duty of citizenship was broader and at the same time more specific. Added to the unusually keen sense of loyalty of which we have already spoken, this conception, prevailing over all other considerations, made an inspired man of him for months. It lifted him to the highest level of his career, if we except the panic days of 1907. It gave him the power to become the herald of a new day in American political life.

Wanamaker had a curious habit, as valuable to his biographer as it has proved hard on his eyes, of picking up old date books and pocket diaries years after he had carried them, and using the blank pages for jotting down notes and even for writing letters. In a worn-out diary for 1898, which he had used only for some of the days of his speaking tours, we find under date of January 24, 1908:

My little book wants me to apologize for its shabby dress. It was worn out by living in my pocket ten years ago while I was being knocked about all over the state in a political campaign. It was present at some speeches that were terribly exciting and long. But Mr. Quay was defeated for the Senate, though he managed to get back afterward by buying the two Democratic votes that re-elected him.

This is the only mention that we have found of the 1898 campaign. Were it not for the fact that he always was too busy with his multiplying interests and too enjoyably engrossed in what was going on at the moment to give time to the might-have-beens, there would be reason to imagine that his silence about the closed doors indicated painful memories. There is abundant proof that open wounds in Wanamaker's life did not go beyond family bereavements. He was too buoyant ever to brood. And while others tried, generally with little success, to impress upon him the lasting influence of what he accomplished in politics, he himself, while feeling intensely at the time, let it go at that. He never appreciated the full significance of the gallant fight, first to secure his own nomination, and, when that could not be done, to elect the man who had been nominated by the insurgents in his stead.

Fortunately, the Business Men's League collected in book form sixty-seven of his speeches during the gubernatorial campaign. The foreword says:

During the autumn campaign lasting seventy-two days Mr. Wanamaker made the most remarkable series of political speeches ever delivered by one man in so short a time. They are of such wonderful versatility that no two speeches are alike and no two sentences in all the speeches are identical. The national attention they have attracted attests to their great merit. The Business Men's League is in receipt of thousands of requests from all parts of the country for these speeches, and having exhausted the files of the city papers which published them, we have deemed it expedient to have the speeches printed.

From the beginning of the campaign to the end there were one hundred and forty speeches; and those not included in the collection could have been put in without modifying the statement that "no two speeches are alike and no two sentences in all the speeches are identical." Wanamaker wrote his speeches while he was traveling, and he delivered them in local halls and theaters and often in the open air. As the tour was made before the automobile era and many places in Pennsylvania, in adjacent counties, are difficult to reach by train, the inconveniences and hardships of intensive campaigning would have broken down most men of sixty. Wanamaker had, too, his weak throat to contend with. But he never gave up for a single day, and did not hesitate at any uncomfortable stunt to meet an engagement. Once he had to ride for a long distance, crowded into the cupola of the trainman's caboose, blinded and begrimed with soot, half deafened with the noise of the engine to which it was directly attached, to reach Erie in time to speak to an audience of two thousand. And it was like him to insist upon including in the itinerary towns where his managers had assured him that few would listen with a friendly ear and to keep on campaigning when the situation had become hopeless.

The effort was possible only to a man who believed that what he had to say was necessary for the salvation of the people. The Spanish-American War had aroused the nation to a patriotic expression of feeling such as it had not experienced since the Civil War. Wanamaker kept sounding the note of love of country in his appeals to the voters of Pennsylvania, and he used to remark, when told that he was killing himself, that it was a poor time for any man to hold anything back of himself or of his talents in the service of the nation.

The crescendo at the end, in the first week of November, had something of the superhuman in it. There were thirty speeches in eight days.

Of course his opponents claimed that he did not write the speeches himself. A man with Wanamaker's background, they asserted, could never have written such speeches. How was it possible for a man who had spent more than forty years in business to get up day after day and tell graphically, with a wealth of detail, the story of political corruption at Harrisburg, finding new stories to illustrate every speech, and varying his scathing denunciations in new and felicitous phrases each day? But the larger part of the originals of the speeches, which he wrote in longhand, are in the private files.

The tenor and vigor of his campaign speeches can be judged by this appeal to apathetic voters:

You fought for liberty at Valley Forge, and you surrender it without a struggle in the same county within sound of the spot once foot-marked with the blood of the soldiers of the Revolution. You fought for liberty for the Union. Why not fight for liberty for Pennsylvania? You voted down black slavery, why not vote down slavery to one white man, even though for a quarter of a century he has been your master? There are people who do not care what comes; but are they the true friends of the Republic? I believe the storm is coming, that it is near and that it is time to prepare for the change close at hand. The old Republican ship was built to carry an honest cargo to be shared by all the people, and it was not intended to be captured by pirates, and scuttled rather than give it up to its owners. Let us throw overboard the dangerous freight and save the passengers.

Voters of Pennsylvania, are you dumb and are you blind? Is not this one chapter of shame enough to make you strike for freedom? You will risk your life to defend your home and your property from thieves at night, yet you applaud the robbers who by day take millions that belong to you.

He emphasized the fact that the centering of the fight around his personality was accidental:

Is it not possible to put Wanamaker entirely out of the case, while we resolve together for the undoing of the captivity of Pennsylvania?

He was not stirring up trouble merely to annoy:

I am not a wasp in speech or action. I am a surgeon, ready to make heroic operations to save the patient's life. The patient is the Republican party, born of Lincoln and Grant, mangled, run over and overrun by the Quay-Andrews sacrificers.

His own high purpose and determination are beautifully expressed:

There are two freedoms—the first where a man is free to do what he likes; the other where a man is free to do what he ought.

Neither wars without nor treasons within deter me. There must be sturdy plowing in the chilly winds of early winter if there is to be spring wheat.

In one sentence he summed up the reason of the revolt:

The steady demoralization of the Republican party in its political management has made the Harrisburg legislature a toll-gate on the people's turnpike that no honest man can pass without a sneer, and where all men must halt and give the countersign of a dividend to the sentinels, however worthy his cause, before he can pass on.

He gave the example of plain speaking on the trusts which Roosevelt and other advanced Republicans followed only years later:

The time is far passed when the interests of the people and those of the corporations were identical. Human selfishness, the origin of inequalities and the source of dangerous power, has gradually divorced and made the interests of the masses diametrically different from those of the corporations.

The great combinations of capital, realizing the power of organization, discipline and concerted energy, have mustered in and equipped great armies of talent and genius, such as money can always command. On the principle that might makes right, and that they are entitled to all privileges that can be obtained through legislation, by fair means or foul, they have waged an unceasing war against the people. A long-continued series of victories has made them thirsty for more. Continued success in their schemes has intoxicated them, and they are arrogant and defiant. Conscious of their strength they proclaim by word and deed their mastery over the people.

On the evening before election he summed up the burden and the spirit of the campaign:

Wanamaker was denounced by the machine speakers as an anarchist and socialist. Because he has told the farmers that they were unjustly taxed, because he has shown that the taxes of the people are thirty-five percent. too high as the result of the machine's plundering and wastefulness, and because he has said that the corporations should relieve them of a part of their burden of taxation, he was called an anarchist. Because he has given to the taxpayers of the state the records of their public servants; because he has sounded a note of warning against the increasing and dangerous power of pools and trusts, and because he has pleaded for the working-men of Pennsylvania, speaking against unrestricted privileges, and advancing their right to equitable conditions of labor that can be regulated by state laws, he was called a socialist. If these things make a man an anarchist or a socialist, Wanamaker must plead guilty.

Thus it has been throughout the entire campaign. Rocks of slander and vilification have been heaped in our paths, reservoirs of wrath and abuse have been poured upon our heads in the machine's vain attempt to divert us from the one straight path. A constant stream of threats have come to our ears, and friends have begged us to desist for fear of our personal safety. But to-night as we go into camp for a few days between battles, we leave a sadder if not a wiser gang of character-wrecking tools of a perishing machine.

William A. Stone, picked by Quay nearly two years earlier, was elected. His plurality was nearly 118,000. Only six anti-Quay Fusionists, or Independents, won seats in the legislature. But eighty-four Democrats—an unprecedented number for Pennsylvania, were returned. The Republicans numbered 164, but by no means all of them, as was soon proven, could be counted as machine men.

Wanamaker expressed himsef as being "more than well satisfied with the results." In an interview he said:

"I was mustered in to stand against Quayism, and if the battle is not won this time, I shall stay on the field until the war is ended. I want to see the State start anew out of the wilderness of political corruption into a land of economy and justice, of hope and prosperity."

And on the day after election, he summed up his record in Pennsylvania politics with a hearty laugh. "No other man in Pennsylvania," he declared, "has been defeated for Governor, United States Senator, and Mayor of Philadelphia."

CHAPTER XXXI

PENNSYLVANIA POLITICS: THE AFTERMATH

THE blow dealt to Quay's personal fortunes by Wanamaker's speechmaking activities was not long in making itself felt. Indicted in Philadelphia on charges of corrupt practices, this fact did not prevent him from presenting himself at Harrisburg for re-election. The first ballot for United States Senator was taken on January 17, 1899, a little over two months after the gubernatorial election. Public opinion had been so thoroughly aroused by the Wanamaker revelations of corruption at Harrisburg that Quay could not whip into line enough votes. It was a long-drawn-out contest; and all the newspapers except those owned by the machine expressed themselves frankly on the impudence and indecency of an indicted man seeking re-election before his trial.

Quay was acquitted. But still he could not swing the election. Congress was in session. His term had expired. Then Governor Stone promptly did what he had been chosen for; the contingency had been foreseen by the machine. The Governor of Pennsylvania appointed Matthew Stanley Quay to fill a senatorial vacancy caused by his inability to get himself elected!

This travesty of popular government caused an outcry throughout the country; for the Wanamaker-Quay fight had attracted nation-wide attention. Leading Republican newspapers warned the Senate against giving the Democrats ammunition for 1900 by accepting into its membership on a party vote a man who had been rejected in his own state.

The establishment of a precedent of this character would be a shameful betrayal of the principle of representative government. In the future all one who belonged to the majority party would have to do to become Senator would be to own the Governor of his state. Election to the office would not be necessary. If the aspirant blocked the other candidates, that would be as much of a victory as he needed. Quay received the surprise of his life when he discovered that some Republican Senators placed the interest of the party and the question of principle above the personal interest of a colleague. Among these was one of Quay's own good friends and fellow-bosses, Senator Hanna of Ohio, who deplored Quay's ill luck, but who did not intend to jeopardize McKinley's chances of re-election by voting to seat Quay. Quay was rejected by 33 to 31.

In November, 1900, McKinley was sweepingly returned to the Presidency. Never had the party received so overwhelming a majority in Pennsylvania. But the scandals unearthed and pilloried by Wanamaker in 1898 still tarred Quay and crippled his machine. When the legislature met in January, 1901, Quay again found himself without a majority. He had marshaled every Republican that could be induced to support him, and was short two votes. Then the machine went to work on the Democrats, and managed to discover two of easy virtue. By their change of vote Quay got back to the Senate with a majority of one. His prestige, however, was irretrievably lost. The mantle of Republican boss soon passed to the shoulders of Penrose.

The discomfiture of Quay was viewed philosophically by many Republicans who did not approve of Wanamaker's efforts to smash the machine. Some saw in it the inevitable result of too large majorities over a long period of years. In their minds the lesson of the fight was that political power should not be abused by a party organization. Unlimited power caused politicians to "go too far" in graft and mulcting taxpayers. Overconfidence and belief in their immunity led bosses to risk exposure of their methods. As one political writer put it:

We hear much about opposition to Quay as a sort of treason and about Wanamakerites as "insurgents" deserving of being led to the party's scaffold and dispatched without benefit of clergy. But the fact is, it is essential to the public welfare for the public crib not to become top-heavy with a long-continued dynasty of office-holders. Whatever may be the ambition of millionaire Wanamaker and whatever the inconsistencies and selfishness that may be charged against his allies, they are useful brakes on the machine. It may be all true enough that they are "soreheads" and "ingrates" and "traitors," but when a dominant party has a chronic majority of two or three hundred thousand, it is not a bad idea to keep its professional leaders lying awake o'nights with a row in the party household.

Another newspaper of independent, but not Wanamaker, tendencies, said:

The beneficial effects of the Quay-Wanamaker row may be seen in many directions all over the State. The opponents of Quay have circumvented or crushed scores of jobs and extravagances which would have passed the last two legislatures had all hands borne aloft the M. S. Q. standard when that trademark was as all powerful in its significance at Harrisburg as S. P. Q. R. once was in the seven-hilled city on the Tiber.

This was in keeping with what Wanamaker himself had frequently declared was the real purpose of his leadership in the Republican revolt. In 1898, when he was exposing the reign of graft in Harrisburg, he used to declare that he was not out for personal advertisement or aggrandizement and that his daily recital of the abuses of the machine was simply to arouse good citizens to the necessity and determination to clean house in Pennsylvania politics. On the stump in the second McKinley campaign in 1900 he was in the unassailable position of a man no longer seeking public office, but performing a sacred duty of citizenship. He said at Pottstown:

"A Legislature must be elected overwhelmingly hostile to the machine in all its works, and to its whole corrupt and sinister spirit, in order that the present protection to fraud at the polls shall be swept away by an act of enforcing true ballot reform."

To this end he had secured at the Johnstown convention of the Pennsylvania State Sabbath School Association the passage of a resolution, personally presented by himself, calling upon clergymen to preach Sabbath sermons on good government at least four times a year and requesting the International Lesson Committee "to include in the future course of lessons two lessons each year upon good citizenship and the duties of Christians in relation thereto."

His vision of the importance of the crusade he was carrying on, irrespective of the outcome of the fight upon his personal fortunes, was tersely expressed at one of the greatest meetings he ever addressed, the "Town Meeting" at the Philadelphia Academy of Music, on October 14, 1898. Few of his audience forgot what he said that night, long before Roosevelt or Wilson, about the new era that was dawning in American political life:

"To me the greatest element of victory in this war is already won in the restoration of the old town meeting system for the discussion of public affairs. And if it be necessary in order to wipe out the last vestige of Quayism, they shall not cease until every church, school house and country store has become a class room for the study and teaching of good government."

The fight that he was in and the company that he kept during these stirring years led him—temporarily at least—to approve and counsel party irregularity. Despite his ardent Republicanism, which was almost a religion with him, he found it impossible in Pennsylvania to keep a clear distinction between municipal and state politics, on the one hand, and national politics on the other. He tried his best to do so, but logic made him admit that if the Republican party could not be reformed from within, the good citizen had to act independently of party. Nothing was harder for him to do. And yet in 1900 he saw that fusion with Democrats in very many districts was demanded by common sense. He made a statement that was twelve years later—much to his annoyance—used by the Bull-Moosers in the 1912 Presidential campaign. It was this:

"Young men of Pennsylvania, Republicans, Democrats, or Prohibitionists, ought not to be willing to begin life by falling in with a ready-made political creed. It is their plain duty to think and act and unite to exterminate the existing political machine, and build up a new system beginning with the old-fashioned New England town meeting where the people have a say.

"All believers in good government, willing to do something besides talk, must get together for action with batteries of their time, personal effort, and money to spread the truth. Mere intrepidity or sentiment will amount to nothing without self-denying endeavor.

"It is a great work to make and maintain good government. It requires the type of men not given to hesitation or fearful of failure—men who are fearless of criticism, contempt, and murderous hatred—roughriders taking their lives in their hands.

"The young man who has concluded that to purify politics is a hopeless task, must re-enter the ranks and do his best."

This heresy, which he could not avoid getting into, and the general results of his long fight in Pennsylvania, put Wanamaker in wrong at Washington, where, at the beginning of the McKinley administration, his word had carried weight. When Roosevelt became President through the assassination of McKinley, the new President and his Cabinet were nervous about the congressional election of 1902. They wanted things "made up" in Pennsylvania. The word went out that the internal strife must end, irrespective of the questions and principles involved. As President, Roosevelt had no patience with party irregularity in Pennsylvania, and he was greatly displeased with an interview Wanamaker gave to the New York *World*, deploring and denouncing "the political conditions in Pennsylvania," in the height of the congressional campaign. The Republicans in New York were using for ammunition the Democratic party's control by corrupt Tammany, and it hurt to have the *World* come out with a former Republican Cabinet member's statement of corrupt gang control of the Republican party in Pennsylvania. It made the New York campaign arguments, which the President himself was using, appear like the pot calling the kettle black. It was not until years later that Roosevelt came publicly to Wanamaker's views. And by that time Wanamaker had gone back to party regularity, and felt badly about Roosevelt following in his footsteps!

To the biographer of John Wanamaker, who has been told by numerous people as facts malicious gossip about his subject's business and private life (gossip of the kind that gathers around the name of every man long in the public eye), the most remarkable feature of the Quay fight and its aftermath is the clean bill of health given to the Philadelphia merchant by the people among whom he lived and worked after a scrutiny as minute and exhaustive as was ever made of the actions of a man who had lived in one place for sixty years. In his famous column, "Men and Things," in the *Philadelphia Bulletin*, January 23, 1900, William Perrine ("Penn") wrote:

Wanamaker, as the responsible leader of the insurgents, has for a long time been under almost as much surveillance by the Quay men as if he were a suspect shadowed by detectives. Claudius in his closet, offering up his prayer, with Hamlet ready to run him through and trip him that his heels might kick to Heaven, was not more closely watched by the avenging young prince than Wanamaker is by Penrose. The business, the habits, the comings and goings, of the ambitious merchant are under the espionage of all the sharpers and snappers up of unconsidered trifles who are eager to carry "important information" to the Quay headquarters. To discredit Wanamaker, to bring him into personal disrepute, or to pick out the weak points in his trade establishment, have been the chief features of this retaliatory policy.

"Penn" went on to say that few men could stand such a pitiless searchlight on their private life and business methods. No more than during the lottery and telegraph fights at Washington a decade earlier could any scandal be dug up and proved about Wanamaker personally. The Keystone Bank charges had been refuted for all time by the return of the fugitive bank president and the evidence brought out at his trial. Wanamaker had suffered defeat of the most decisive kind in politics. If he had really set his heart on being Senator and a national leader in the Republican party, that ambition was definitely thwarted. But he had gone through the fire of personal attack unscathed. His great business, too, had stood the test of publicity.

Pennsylvania returned to gang control, but only temporarily. There was the State Capitol graft, but the punishment of the grafters was swift and complete. Wanamaker's pioneering bore fruit. Raw deals and unblushing corruption, such as he had exposed, public opinion no longer tolerated.

In writing the history of the Progressive movement in the Republican party and Wilson's successful resistance to the state bosses when he became Governor of New Jersey, students of the regeneration of American political life and the awakening of public conscience must go back of the ten-cent magazines and the "muckrakers" to Wanamaker's leadership of the Pennsylvania insurgents in 1898.

John Wanamaker, Philadelphia.

Private Office.

April 14/98

Notice

In order that our men may have easy minds in considering and arranging their plans in the event of being called upon for military service, this notice is posted to say

First That all positions thus vacated will be re-opened for return when the military duty is over.

Second That all salaries continue in such absence while on actual duty, to be paid to the authorized representative of the respective families.

Third An insurance of to the amount of One thousand dollars will be paid by the firm in case of death while actually engaged in military service

Signed Jno Wanamaker

Note. All details of absence will be arranged by the Manager Mr Drewes

NOTICE OF CONTINUANCE OF SALARIES AND INSURANCE OF EMPLOYEES VOLUNTEERING
FOR WAR IN 1898

CHAPTER XXXII

THE SPANISH-AMERICAN WAR

IN THE second round of the fight against Quay we have seen how aptly Wanamaker used in his political speeches the coincidence of the war against Spain with the campaign for the gubernatorial nomination in Pennsylvania. The sinking of the *Maine* occurred within a fortnight after the protest meeting at the Philadelphia Bourse. When war was declared Wanamaker was in the thick of the campaign. But he acted instantly in the national emergency.

On April 14, 1898, he telegraphed Secretary Alger that although he was opposed to war, "unless honorably unavoidable," if it came he would raise a regiment and serve with it. On the same day he wrote to Governor Hastings:

Anticipating the call likely to be made today I desire to tender and urge acceptance of 1,000 men to be ready to report to you for service in 48 hours. If the fact that I have not had military experience stands in the way I waive all preferment of place and will be willing to take a subordinate position or go in the ranks. I earnestly beg your early authority to form this regiment.

Without waiting for a reply he wrote a notice to his employees, which was printed in facsimile and circulated in both stores before evening, offering to keep open the places of men who volunteered, continue full salary during absence under the flag, and pay to families $1,000 in case of death while actually engaged in military service.

While opposed to war, if any peaceable means could be found to settle the Cuban question and deploring efforts of the "yellow press" to force President McKinley's hand,

Wanamaker let it be understood that he was ready to stand whole-heartedly behind the decision of Congress. He never made a secret of his hatred of war, and he abhored jingoism. He was sympathetic with the Quaker spirit of many of his friends, and spoke and prayed at Bethany that the impending war be averted. On the other hand, he could not go the full way with those who believed in non-resistance as a Christian virtue, and he thought that military training was a splendid thing for young people. He had already introduced it in his stores, having organized his boys and girls on a military footing, with uniforms and flags and bands. Drills and marching played an important part in their activities, and they were called cadets.[1] It was because he had a large body of young men already prepared that he was confident of his ability to make good in the offer to have a regiment enrolled in forty-eight hours.

Wanamaker had always been interested in the movement for the emancipation of Cuba and had shown his sympathy with Cuban revolutionaries whenever the opportunity offered. To this one of them bears eloquent witness:

Years ago Hilarion Cisneros, General Jesus del Sol, and he who writes these lines, arrived one afternoon at the store of Wanamaker & Brown. We were looking for a suit for the General, who had just come from the Cuban jungle. We found it and the clerk took us to the cashier. Cisneros asked for the bill and indicated that the package was to be sent to General del Sol at the Continental Hotel. A genial man who was there left the books he was examining and came to us. He wanted to shake hands with one of the illustrious commanders in the redemption of Cuba. Later there arrived with the suit a magnificent overcoat and a beautiful military cape with a card, "From John Wanamaker to General Jesus del Sol."

This was one of many acts of kindness we received from this grand and generous man. He lived through the great hours of his own country; and he exercised through his spirit, a great and profound interest over our people. At no time has he failed to concentrate his labor to their

[1] See vol. ii, chap. xx.

uplift. Cuba and the Cubans have always known him as an excellent friend.[1]

Acceptance of Wanamaker's offer hung fire, because the rôle of the National Guard had not yet been decided upon. Anticipating the calling out of the Guard and believing that Pennsylvania would need more troops than were available from the peace-time enrollment, Wanamaker continued his work. On May 23 he telegraphed the Governor that he could raise eight full companies for service in the First Brigade, National Guard of Pennsylvania, and when the offer was published in the newspapers, letters poured in from men who wanted commissions. To one who wrote from New York on May 31, asking for the lieutenant-colonelcy of the regiment, Wanamaker answered: "I have concluded to take the lieutenant-colonelcy myself." The private files show that he kept a daily report from June 4 to June 28, of those who volunteered, with enlistments, examinations, and rejections. On the latter date 900 had been accepted. The next day he wrote to the Governor:

Up to last night I have had 1,033 men in the city and as many more outside of the city apply for enrollment. I declined to accept any enlistments outside of the city and up to last night there were 907 accepted men. These drilled in companies at the First Regiment Armory.

Answering requests for commissions of majors and captains, he penciled the letters with the statement: "The places in the regiment I am raising will be chosen by vote, and I, therefore, cannot comply with your request."

The acceptance of Wanamaker's offer came on June 24, 1898, when General Edward Morrell, who commanded the First Brigade, N. G. P., wrote:

In accordance with your letter of May 23rd, I have the honor to state that I am prepared to accept the offer made in that communication, namely, eight full companies, fully equipped and armed with Springfield

[1] *La Discusion*, Havana, May 4, 1921.

rifles, for service in the First Brigade, N. G. P.   A skeleton battalion of four companies, the major and captains of which will be commissioned, will also be part of the regiment.   The number of the regiment will be No. 11.   Upon hearing from you I shall immediately appoint a time for the examining and mustering in of the companies referred to.   I would like to have a personal interview with you on the subject.

Following the official acceptance, a board of officers was organized on June 27.   John Wanamaker was elected "major and president."   Wanamaker's war activities excited a great deal of comment throughout the country, and his example was followed by other wealthy and prominent citizens.   A Cincinnati newspaper said that "in his proposition to raise a regiment and to pay each member out of his own pocket John Wanamaker has followed Revolutionary example, and has evidently been reading history to a purpose."   And the New York *World* commented editorially:

Mr. Wanamaker has illustrated his versatility.   He is making spicy speeches all over Pennsylvania in behalf of his candidacy for the Governorship, and at the same time conducting a business whose trade per year is larger than the cost of running the whole Pennsylvania state government, and recruiting a regiment for the war.   Mr. Wanamaker expects to lead the regiment in person.   He will arm and equip the men at his own expense, and will march with them as their colonel.

But this great dream of national service was not realized. Only one volunteer marched with the regiment he raised—and he only as lieutenant-colonel.   Aside from the Rough Riders, none of the privately raised regiments saw active duty.   The United States army could not organize quickly enough the facilities for a national army, and took only a few National Guard regiments from the different states. The war was over before the machinery for a large army could be put in motion.   John Wanamaker's regiment was not needed.

But as he had volunteered his services to the government, with no string attached to the offer, it was felt in many quarters that he could be used to great advantage as purchasing officer for the War Department. The rank incompetence in this vital branch of the service was soon discovered. There were newspapers wise enough and courageous enough to declare that Wanamaker should have been put in charge of the Quartermaster Department. Had the war lasted longer, this step would probably have been taken. It would have needed a Wanamaker as Quartermaster-General to prevent a scandal embarrassing to the administration. In this field, too, the swift ending of the war deprived Wanamaker of the opportunity of service.

If he was disappointed, he never showed it, any more than he showed his disappointment in the failure to become Senator or Governor. He proved by what he did and said that personal ambition did not enter into his eagerness to serve his country. He rejoiced in the victory, and was generous in his praise of those who were priviliged to do what was denied him. At the convention of the Pennsylvania State Sunday School Association at Johnstown, on October 18, 1898, he said:

"The world at large wonders at, and America is justly proud of, the volunteer army that turned its face towards the southern waters as if the shattered and sunken *Maine* were a shrine at which to worship. The splendid fellows in the colleges filled the ranks so quickly that there was no room for city clerks. These sons of rich fathers who had carried little else than canes, who were thought to have but little of the practical in their plans of life, threw their culture, wealth, and enthusiasm into the military service on land and sea. No labor was too humble, no duty too irksome. They cleaned horses, raised and struck tents, cooked meals and served tables, swabbed guns. Nothing was too heavy or too menial for them in their desire to strike a blow to free Cuba.

"All honor to the Roosevelts and the Hobsons and the thousands of heroes whom we embrace with admiration and affection, and crown with unstinted honors. For them we are thankful this night when no hand the wide world over is lifted against the old flag. We commend them to God and a grateful people, who will not weigh out rewards to them in an apothecary's scales."

CHAPTER XXXIII

ADVENTURES IN MUNICIPAL POLITICS

THE statue of Philadelphia's greatest merchant on City Hall Square bears the inscription:

JOHN WANAMAKER

CITIZEN

1838   1922

This is as he would have had it; and it justifies the emphasis that must be put upon public service in telling the story of this man. The achievements of Wanamaker as Postmaster-General and his sally into Pennsylvania politics were, as we have seen, episodes. Their influence was far-reaching and permanent. But he never went back to Washington to live and work; and six or seven years bounded his active participation in the political life of the state. Because they were episodes it has been possible to narrate them connectedly, and to place them at the point chronologically when Wanamaker was a Cabinet member and a state leader above all else.

His rôle as a citizen of Philadelphia, however, covered the entire period of his sixty-four voting years. "Beginning at Jerusalem" was a modifying clause by which he set great store. A man's mission in life may carry him far, he used to say, but only if he is faithful at all times in his home duties. "Tie up the loose ends as you go along," he told his Bible Union, "but don't forget that there will always be loose ends to tie. The dishes must be washed before another

377

meal is prepared.   And then there will be dishes to wash
again!   That is life."   Daily he had to drive home the
same truth to his business family.   Nor did he forget himself.   A friend reports his having remarked: "I love to
repeat that proverb, 'The fool's eyes are at the ends of the
earth'—but more often to myself than to any one else.   I
am so full of ideas!"

He was fanatically fond of Philadelphia.   The city of
his birth had his full devotion.[1]   As a boy he began to think
of Philadelphia and business together, and he never got
over mixing up the two.   Oak Hall, the Grand Depot,
Wanamaker's—the business was an integral part of the
history of Philadelphia.   Built on Philadelphia traditions,
it had to keep pace with Philadelphia's growth.   Its success
and its future depended upon the well-being of the city
he loved.   The store belonged to the people and served
them.   So did its owner.

Affection for Philadelphia and the identification of the
city with his business were often spoken of by the unfriendly
and the unknowing as a pose, just as his Bethany activity
was called hypocrisy.   Were they not both advertising
stunts?   But Bethany was older than the business.   The
Sunday-school superintendent antedated the merchant.
Similarly, John Wanamaker was an active worker for the
Centennial Exhibition before he knew there was to be a
great store bearing his name at the heart of the city; and
in the last days of his life his whole heart and soul were
wrapped up in a Sesquicentennial for 1926.   With these
facts before us, and the souvenirs of old Philadelphia, gathered with painstaking care, on the walls of his private office

[1] In a letter to a Town Meeting at the Academy of Music, on September 27,
1917, convened to protest against lawlessness on election day in the fifth ward,
Wanamaker wrote: "Born in Philadelphia, I love its history and have spent
my life in striving to build up its institutions and the glory and power of its
name."

as we write, we understand why Wanamaker advertising has so much of Philadelphia in it and why the Golden Book of his business and his speeches during more than half a century are shot through with allusions to the history of Philadelphia and to the lives of Philadelphians. He could not tell the story of the Wanamaker business without talking about William Penn, Benjamin Franklin, Robert Morris, and Stephen Girard.

Given the deep sense of the obligations of citizenship so eloquently proved by his services to the nation and the state, it is not difficult to see why Wanamaker always felt the deepest interest in the political life of his city. In the middle years this interest translated itself into active participation in municipal politics, wholly aside from the bearing they had upon his fortunes in business and in the wider range of national and state politics. It is with the picturesque adventures of this period that we deal here.

As early as 1882, six years before Quay induced him to help elect Harrison, Wanamaker had a chance to go into national politics through being a Philadelphian. He was offered a nomination to Congress, which in the Philadelphia district meant certain victory for a Republican. His new store was still in the experimental stage and was just beginning to reap a rich harvest. The time had not yet come when he could leave his work and spend long months in Washington. This would have been a legitimate reason for declining. But he did not hesitate to let it be known that he did not care to be slated for any post by "Cameron and his ring." There was a reform movement in municipal politics that year, led by a "Committee of 100." Wanamaker's name was not included in the list of prominent Philadelphians, many of them fellow-merchants; but there is a copy of the committee's booklet in the private files, with pencil marks to indicate that he had given its platform careful study. Both he and Ogden contributed to the reformers' municipal campaign fund.

Wanamaker first appears prominently in Philadelphia politics in the defense of municipal ownership of public utilities against the assaults of private interests. There had long been an agitation against the germ-laden Schuylkill River water, by reason of which typhoid fever was endemic in Philadelphia, when a private corporation, with ring connivance, proposed to take over the water works and sell the city and the people pure water. Wanamaker joined the movement to frustrate this scheme, and to insist that the city itself provide for pure water by a filtering plant and by securing legislation at Harrisburg against pollution of the river by upstream cities.

The politicians and grafters were afraid of the uncertain expenses that might have to be incurred in filtering the water—that science was still in an experimental stage—and desisted when they saw that prominent citizens were determined to impose conditions that would really mean pure water. Here they were dealing with human life. So they turned their attention to getting control of the gas-works. Electricity had not yet begun to compete with gas for lighting, and the prospects of rich returns were alluring. In 1886 a syndicate of politicians, headed by Thomas Dolan, proposed to lease the gas-works for twenty-five years, offering to spend three million dollars in improvements, pay the city half the profits on gas at $1.50 a thousand feet, and guarantee that the city's share would net at least a million dollars a year. The guaranty itself betrayed the tremendous profit that would accrue to the operators. The newspapers began to denounce the steal, and its magnitude was demonstrated by an offer of a New York syndicate, which met the Dolan proposal, and added five hundred thousand dollars as a bonus.

The corruption of local politics was revealed when the Finance Committee of Councils ignored the more favorable New York terms and reported an ordinance accepting the Dolan offer. There was no valid reason why the gas-works should be leased at all, and, if leased, why the more advantageous proposal should not be taken. Despite newspaper outcry and public meetings of protest, the Common Council took up the ordinance, and there was no doubt that it would be passed.

On the morning of the meeting Wanamaker dramatically intervened. He sent a letter to the Select and Common Councils offering to lease the gas-works himself. He agreed to spend three million dollars of his own money for improvements, and to pay half the profits of the lease for five years without deducting cost of extensions and new improvements. For the remaining twenty years he was willing to "pay a sum each year equal to three-quarters of the net profits, which will enable the city to reduce the price of gas to consumers if it desires." As an alternative, "in order to enable the people to become a party to this lease and hold the control thereof," he expressed his willingness to form a $5,000,000 stock company to operate the gas-works, paying himself for three-eights of the stock in cash, and offering five-eighths in small lots to the people of Philadelphia. He pointed out that the lease was more valuable than either the Dolan or New York proposals would indicate, and that if there were any lease at all it was the business of Councils to keep in mind the most advantageous terms for the city and the problem of selling gas at as low cost as possible to the people. In conclusion, he stated:

I am clearly and strongly of the opinion that the city should not at the present time lease its public works to any person or persons, for the reason that the profits that individuals or corporations can produce from said works can be equally well produced by the city, and the entire profit should belong to the city for public improvements or be distributed in cheaper gas or lower taxes.[1]

Common Council, responding to the ring whip, made a slight amendment to the Dolan lease, and passed it. But the outcry was now so strong that the lease was withdrawn and the steal temporarily dropped. Philadelphia grew rapidly, and the saving both to the city treasury and to the people year after year was enormous. This was proved by the fact that in 1897, eleven years later, the United Gas Improvement Company, headed by the same Thomas Dolan, offered to lease the works again for thirty years, spending $15,000,000 on improvements, and selling gas at $1 a thousand feet, with a fixed return to the city of fifteen cents a thousand for the first twenty years, and twenty-five cents for the final ten years. The lease that Wanamaker blocked would have been in force during fourteen years of the second Dolan offer, during which time the people would have paid fifty cents more a thousand feet for their gas, and the city would have received much less revenue.[2]

In 1905 private interests, in collusion with local politicians in their pay, brought up the proposition of getting an extended gas lease for seventy-five years, mortgaging an unborn generation to terms and conditions that would make them for their whole lives tributaries to a corporation. A mayor had been elected two years before who was supposedly the creature of the ring. John Weaver emigrated to the United States from England as a boy of seventeen, and had worked in Wanamaker's before becoming a lawyer

[1] There were two letters. They are published on pages 279-281 of the *Journal* of the Common Council of Philadelphia for 1886, forming appendix 174.

[2] In an editorial, January 1, 1923, after Wanamaker's death, the *Philadelphia Record* said: "By a conservative estimate it is safe to say that Mr. Wanamaker, by blocking the 1886 lease, saved the gas consumers about $4,000,000 a year for the twenty-five years of the proposed lease, or a total of $100,000,000."

and politician. He was in Canada on vacation when the extended lease was being rammed through Councils. It was too big a steal for him to tolerate. He hurried back, threw off the yoke of his masters, and stood valiantly for the rights of the people who had elected him. Because of the early association as a Wanamaker employee, the merchant's hand was seen in the Mayor's bold stand. But Wanamaker was far off in Europe. On May 31, 1905, we find him writing in his diary at Biarritz:

> I have some regrets that I could not be in the new gas-works battle. The Gang are worse than I ever painted them.

The blocking of the gas-works steal gave new heart to Philadelphia reformers, whose Committee of 100 had been disbanded, and the thought occurred to them that Wanamaker would be the ideal leader in a new movement to wrest the control of the city from the politicians whose unworthiness and shameless corruption he had so strikingly exposed. Rudolph Blankenburg, Henry C. Lea, William H. Jenks, Morris Perot, E. W. Clark, and other independent Republicans called on Wanamaker and urged him to head a fusion ticket against Edwin H. Fitler, the Republican mayoralty candidate. They pointed out to him that the moment was ideal, not only because of the gas-works incident, but also because there was widespread dissatisfaction in the city over the failure to name Edwin S. Stuart, who was the popular candidate with the rank and file of Republicans. In Christmas week, 1886, Wanamaker attended several conferences of the Independents, and freely expressed his opinion that Fitler's election would put back the prospect of reform for a generation. But he told them that if he ran people would say that it was "only one of Wanamaker's advertising dodges." To prove his interest in the reform movement he offered to pay a large part or all of the expenses of another Independent candidate, suggesting John Field. After several conferences he made clear that his refusal was definite.

It may be true that Wanamaker was sensitive to the criticism of advertising his business if he ran for public office in his own city. It may be true, too, as some of the disappointed Independents charged, that he refused the nomination because he was afraid that the Democrats would not unite to support him and that the Independents could not muster strength enough to make good the deficiency.

But correspondence in the private files seems to indicate that Wanamaker's eagerness to help crush the gang was counterbalanced by his suspicion that the Democrats would make capital in the next presidential election out of the Philadelphia situation. He was troubled by the presence of William F. Harrity, Cleveland's Postmaster-General and an astute Democratic strategist, in the fusion movement. Much as he wanted to help, he was unwilling at that time to commit himself to an electoral campaign that would lay him open to the charge of working against the interests of his party. It was one thing to fight for a nomination inside the party, and quite another thing to make an alliance with Democrats against a Republican ticket on the eve of a critical presidential year. Viewing the situation purely from the local point of view, some of the Independent Republicans believed that Wanamaker's stand was inconsistent, and there were several who never got over the feeling that after attending their conferences he had let them down. On the other hand, had he decided to run against Fitler, whether the campaign ended in success or failure, he would have been barred from the high place he attained so soon after in national affairs, and he could not have later fought the battle of clean politics effectively in Pennsylvania.

After the election of Fitler there was a persistent rumor

that the gang had experienced a change of heart about Philadelphia public utilities, to give proof of which the new mayor would name Wanamaker to the important post of Superintendent of Public Works. The newspapers took up the rumor with rejoicing, and heralded a revolution in the water and highway departments that would "go far toward redeeming the fair name of Philadelphia from the national disgrace into which it has fallen."

The invitation did not come. Since the gang lived by graft, and public contracts were the bread and butter of municipal politicians, it would have been suicide to place an honest and energetic business man where he had authority over the expenditure of the people's money.

In describing the early years of the Grand Depot, we spoke of the amazingly difficult time shoppers had to reach the center of Philadelphia in the late 'seventies and early 'eighties. Only as the city grew did public opinion awaken to the connection between comfort and prosperity on the one hand and cheap and rapid transit on the other. John Wanamaker started his business when means of transportation in American cities were what we would call now astonishingly primitive. Horse cars, with straw-covered floors for warming the feet in winter, were the only means of communication. There were many railroad stations, and none of them came into the heart of the city. The biographer is still some years on the sunny side of fifty, and yet his childhood recollections of Philadelphia transit accommodations carry him back before cable cars and trolleys. He remembers his father speaking at mass meetings of good citizens held to protest against the introduction of electric trams. He remembers the newspapers with their daily display on the first page of the "toll of victims" of the trolleys. He remembers the sudden jerk one had to be on guard against twice at every intersecting street on the Market Street line—the stopping jerk and the starting jerk. Such was rapid transit.

As a business man, with a great establishment at the heart of Philadelphia, it was natural that Wanamaker should be interested in every improvement in the city's transportation system. It meant more customers when shopping in the center of town was made easier. As his employees mounted rapidly into the thousands, and, with the growth of the city, had to move farther away from the store, it meant less time in transit for them, less hardship, less fatigue. It is easy for materialists to point out that his great interest in Philadelphia transportation facilities was not altruistic. But as he showed himself throughout his long career consistently interested in everything that pertained to the welfare of his city, may we not also be allowed to put to the credit of his citizenship record the adventures in municipal politics that had to do with improving transportation?

In 1887 his pioneering spirit comes to the fore once more in his advocacy of an elevated railroad system for Philadelphia like that which New York was beginning to construct. He formed the Consolidated Traction Company for the purpose of erecting elevated railways, and proposed a line on Market Street and a line to Frankford. The money could have been found. But Common Council was not in the mood to grant any favors to the man who blocked the gas-lease steal. It was an unpropitious moment. The project fell through, and was not revived for another generation.

Wanamaker was in favor of the consolidation of the little traction companies, formed in the early days when the construction of single lines by individuals was the limit of capital enterprise. At first, in common with other business men, he co-operated in the formation of a transit system under one management. This was in line with the evolution of American business, of which his own success was an example. But he was opposed to the conspiracy of capitalists and promoters to put watered stock into the consolidation, on the strength of a value dependent upon monopoly of franchises and high fares. He felt, too, that the privilege of exploiting a public utility entailed the obligation of good and full service.

In December, 1895, when Christmas shopping was at its height, a strike of employees paralyzed Philadelphia's trolley system. The strike was ordered by the Amalgamated Association of Railroad Workers, whose delegates had been unable to secure from the president of the Union Traction Company what they thought was satisfactory consideration of the demands of the employees. We remember that this was the period when organized labor in all trades was endeavoring to secure recognition. The merits of the question did not greatly interest the people of Philadelphia, who understood imperfectly the issues. Public sentiment was not strongly on either side. But the employment of scab labor brought the usual results. Mob violence met the effort to run the cars, and the new question of keeping scabs permanently on the pay roll arose to complicate the settlement. All over the country the same thing had happened in conflicts between labor and capital. Capital was willing to make concessions and take back most of the strikers. But labor was to be intimidated by the punishment of strike-leaders. If the principle were established of not taking back the men who had been instrumental in organizing the empoyees, unions would receive a death blow; for organizers and leaders would always have the fear of losing their jobs.

In his business John Wanamaker had never had a strike; and, although artisans of organized trades were working for him in the store factories, their number was negligible, and they had no grievances. The problem of unions was, therefore, outside his ken. He had had to formulate no policy for himself on this question. All the same, for a man with his background and associations, it was a delicate matter to intervene in this strike. And yet, at the request of Railroad Workers' Union, he accepted the task of arbitrating between the employees of the Union Traction Company and the president and directors. The union representatives, on December 19, 1895, agreed to call the strike off in return for Wanamaker's promise that "if the men shall resume work at once, he will guarantee their positions to them during the term of sixty days from date hereof, and will have all the men who were discharged from the company immediately restored to the positions they formerly occupied, excepting in such cases where the men so discharged were guilty either of the offense of drunkenness or of malfeasance while on duty."

Wanamaker soon found that he had stirred up a hornets' nest. The general manager of the Union Traction Company declared that while the company did not propose to forbid membership in unions, "unions cannot be recognized in the business conducted between us"; and that while "all men unjustly discharged since December 10 would be reinstated," they were "not to have the runs made by the present employees, meaning those who have entered our service since the evening of December 17." Refusal to recognize the union, with whom Wanamaker had made the. agreement, was not essential to settlement, but the statement about keeping on scabs made impossible what Wanamaker promised. Christmas was coming and the city was in confusion. The employees in mass meeting passed a resolution "earnestly and respectfully requesting that Mr. John Wanamaker use again his best efforts to settle the impending difficulty to the best of his ability."

We reproduce a photograph of the characteristic letter prompted by this move. Wanamaker wrote to Mayor Warwick, stating that he would deposit with him or any trust company a sufficient sum to pay any just or future obligations incurred for the new men "that they may be immediately retired to leave all the places open forthwith to all the old employees that are deserving." He added:

I do this in the interest of public safety, believing it to be dangerous to bring to this city at the present time the unemployed of other cities.

Wanamaker's notes on this crisis, and the letters and stenographic record of his conferences with the union delegates and the strikers' committee, bear eloquent testimony to their confidence in him. Some Wanamaker employees and Bethany folk belonged to the families of motormen, conductors, and switchmen, and some of the strikers themselves had been in the Wanamaker store. In their hour of perplexity and dire need it was remarkable how they felt that this fellow-citizen, who had been one of the largest employers of labor in the state for over thirty years, was the friend to whom they could turn. The stories they told of how men identified with the union movement in the period of formation had been persecuted by the Union Traction Company stirred Wanamaker's indignation. He was opposed to unions, and did not hesitate to say so. But in this investigation it began to dawn upon him that in great corporations, where personal contact and personal interest were lacking, employees did have grievances that could be righted only by concerted action.

The adventure of arbitrating the trolley strike had an unhappy aftermath. Wanamaker found himself unable to do what he had promised the men he would do for them if they gave up the strike. He had counted upon a different spirit on the part of the company officials, and it worried him

Philadelphia 23 Dec 95

Hon Charles F. Warwick
    Mayor of the City of Philadelphia
My dear Mr Warwick
    If the newspaper statements are correct
that the failure to adjust the strike
arises from the employment of one
thousand men by the Traction Company
since their men went out, who now have
a claim prior to the older workmen
— this is to say that I will deposit
with you or any Trust Company you
designate a sufficient sum to pay
any past or future obligations incurred
for the new men that they may be
immediately retired to leave all
the places open forthwith to all of
the old employees that are deserving
        I do this in the interest of public
Safety believing it to be dangerous

to bring to this city at the present time
the unemployed of other cities.

It is proper also to add that
while I make myself responsible to
you I count upon my fellow citizens
suffering from the strike to join me
in contributing the sum needed to pay
off these men—but however that may be
as I cannot at this moment consult
with any one I hereby obligate myself
to pay on call whatever amount you
notify me is needed for the
purpose above indicated.

Thanking you for your indefatigable
labors and success in preserving the
peace I beg you to remember that a
very considerable part of the public
outside of the Corporation involved
have a large interest in maintaining
facilities for uninterrupted street travel

to think that the grievances of the men, far from being remedied, had in many cases been aggravated. Pay was less after the strike, and the number of trips the same. There were abuses, such as cutting out lay-overs, speeding up on time of trips, and counting the crew's day not from the car barn or depot, but from the stand from which trips began. The crew had to call at the depots in the morning for their car, take it to the stand, and return it to the depot from the stand. This morning and evening time was not counted in the working day, and to it had to be added the time it took for the crews to go all the way to the depots for their cars and return from the depots to their homes after taking back the car. It is indicative of how Wanamaker felt that we find a number of letters from trolley employees which, from his notes on the margin, we know that he had read carefully. This was like him. He was not the man to dismiss from his mind a thing in which he had been mixed up. A marked passage from one of these letters reads:

I arise at 4:20 a. m., work six hours, go back at night and work six and a half hours, get into bed about half past twelve the next morning. My health is completely ruined; No time for reading; for home; for anything. I suffer all the tortures of the lost. Were you to know our sufferings; were you to hear the cursing and swearing of motormen and conductors, brought about by utter despair, I believe you would keep your promise to help us.

There was nothing that Wanamaker could do, and he must have said to himself that he would never get again into a position where the responsibility or odium of a situation beyond his control should be put upon him. It often happens that way with arbitrators. The one who proposes an award or solution is expected to see that it is accepted and carried out. Wanamaker was employing more people than the Union Traction Company, and he probably comforted himself with the thought that if he could not make others treat their employees humanely, he at least was setting an example of what the relations between capital and labor should and could be.

It was when he was receiving these letters that a serious complaint of incivility was referred to him. An official of the Pennsylvania Railroad wrote that a salesman at the necktie counter had threatened to punch him in the face. Was this, he asked, the way the store practiced its policy of courtesy? The man complained of had an excellent record and was regarded as being particularly obliging. Wanamaker sent for him and showed him the letter.

"If you did what Mr. X says, there must be some explanation," said Wanamaker.

"Yes, I did tell him that, and I'm sorry. I ought to have kept my temper. But it was a morning when a sale was on, and he took up my time showing him ties. He picked out half a dozen, and then said he guessed he wouldn't take any, after all. I had missed several other sales."

Wanamaker said nothing.

The man went on: "You know, Mr. Wanamaker, that it gets on your nerves just to be selling ties year in and year out. I just blew up—the last straw, I suppose. I'm not excusing myself."

"How long have you been selling ties at that counter?"

"Nine years, sir."

"Well, I guess the medicine you need is a change of scene. Do you think you could sell men's clothing without volunteering to punch people in the face?"

This incredible question, to the man who expected to be discharged, was too much for overwrought nerves. The salesman broke down.

"There, there," said Wanamaker, "it's not so bad as all

that. I guess we'll survive this." He wrote on a piece of
paper as he talked. "Take this to Mr. Brewer."

As the man reached the door, Wanamaker called, "Just
a moment, Blank."

"Yes, sir."

In a stern voice, but with a twinkle in his eye, the merchant repeated the sentence his advertising has made classic.
"Remember, Blank, the customer is always right."

After Quay's re-election to the Senate by the 1901 legislature, the Philadelphia bosses had a bill introduced called
the "Transit Ripper," which provided that the state grant
charters for overhead and underground railway systems to
the Union Traction Company. There was an outcry about
thus mortgaging the future by giving to the Philadelphia
traction monopoly a blanket charter for every kind of railway that might ever be constructed in Philadelphia. But
Governor Stone signed the bill. That was what he was
there for! This "job" was completed by the prompt passage through the Philadelphia Councils of ordinances giving
the Union Traction Company franchises covering all the
streets named in their charter without compensation. There
was no debate on the reasons for or merit of the proposal,
and no consideration of the unanimous protest of press and
people.

Wanamaker intervened in the same dramatic way as at
the time of the gas-lease steal fifteen years earlier. He
wrote a letter to Mayor Ashbridge, who had not yet had
time to sign the ordinances, stating:

> The fourteen ordinances were rushed through the Councils with un-
> precedented and reckless speed. Every effort to postpone action until
> investigation could be made, as well as all amendments offered looking
> to the conservation of the interests of this city and the people and intended
> to secure the benefits of cheap transportation to citizens, were summarily
> voted down.

Wanamaker went on to say that he was sure that the mayor did not intend to see the city cheated, and that he wanted to help him get something for the city in return for these franchises. Therefore he offered $2,500,000 for them, and included in the letter a certified check. He added that he was making this offer wholly for the city's benefit, and that he would fall in with any plans that might be made to give the city adequate and cheap transportation and a good income from its investment.

Two copies of this letter were made. One was sent to the mayor's office in City Hall. The other, in which the certified check was inclosed, was taken by Wanamaker's secretary and a newspaper editor to the mayor, who was attending the dedication of the new Mint. It was handed to him in the presence of guests assembled for the ceremony. When Ashbridge saw who the letter was from, he threw it away without opening it. A reporter picked it up and tried to give it back to him; he refused to take it. He knew well enough what was in it, for Wanamaker had said that he was going to make a large offer for the franchises, and that if the bill was not a steal that fact would soon be proved. The afternoon newspapers published Wanamaker's letter—and also the news that Mayor Ashbridge had signed the ordinances. The deal netted the organizers nearly twenty million dollars in watered stock, which was promptly passed on to the public. The Republican and Democratic city bosses, the mayor, and most of the members of Select and Common Councils were paid for their part in the affair either in cash or Union Traction stock. After Wanamaker's death the *Philadelphia Record*, commenting on his attempt to block the notorious steals, wrote:

As a result of his failure the blackmailing franchise-holders of that day perpetrated the steal through which for 999 years the people of Philadelphia are obligated to pay the Union Traction Company $1,170,000 a year on $19,500,000 of stock upon which not a cent has ever been paid into the Union Traction treasury. For twenty years now the 6 per cent dividend paid on the watered stock of the Union Traction Company has amounted to $23,400,000.

Wanamaker was a consistent opponent of proposals to increase Philadelphia's bonded indebtedness to finance grandiose building, highway, and improvement schemes. He contended that city management was like any other business, and that because the city had borrowing capacity was no reason why the people should go ahead with no thought of to-morrow. Interest would have to be paid on every loan by raising the tax rate. He more than hinted that the concern of the politicians in getting loan authorizations voted was the hope of having contracts to farm out, thus enriching themselves. He referred to the building of the Philadelphia City Hall as an historic example of municipal corruption carried on through many years. What was to have cost $5,000,000, and could have been erected for approximately that sum, was so maneuvered as to mulct the city out of $20,000,000, with an unfinished, unsuitable, and hideous building to show for it! On occasions he did not hesitate to use large advertising space in the newspapers to campaign against loan propositions.

It will readily be seen that these adventures in municipal politics, which interfered with the gang's exploitation of Philadelphia, did not make John Wanamaker popular with the local politicians. At Harrisburg his interference with graft schemes was only for a few years. In Philadelphia it never ceased. Consequently, in Philadelphia the persecution of Wanamaker by the politicians was a continuous performance. They tried to get him on his taxes. Instead of aiding in the development of the great business that was one of the city's glories, public officials delighted in creating as much trouble as possible for the store. City Hall inspectors made themselves obnoxious. This was particularly true whenever there was building going on, and especially when the great new building was in process of erection. And always the hint would be dropped that if Wanamaker kept his mouth shut about city affairs he would have no trouble with city taxes and ordinances.

These annoyances were generally met with the contemptuous silence they deserved. But once an official went too far. Abraham L. English, Director of Public Safety (head of the police department) in a notorious administration, tried to browbeat Wanamaker. On May 11, 1900, accompanied by the Commissioner of City Property, English came to the private office and asked to see Wanamaker. He was received, but Wanamaker, having already had unpleasant experiences with these representatives of the gang, called in his secretary to take down the interview. English objected, saying that what he had was for Wanamaker's ear alone.

"Oh no," answered Wanamaker, "you have your witness," pointing to Pierie. "I shall have mine. Now go ahead."

English declared that the mayor and he were not going to stand any longer the criticisms of the *North American* on the way the city was being run. Wanamaker denied owning the paper, or having anything to do with shaping its policy. It belonged to Thomas B. Wanamaker, who was the man for English to see, or, better still, the editor. English broke in: "Why nobody will believe that; not one in ten will believe that you do not own and run the paper."

"That implies that you do not believe it, either, though I have reiterated the fact to you; that is as much as to say that you think I am a liar."

"I do not say that you are a liar, but I want your answer, yes or no, whether you are going to stop this *North Ameri-*

can matter. You can if you want to, and if you don't we have been looking up your personal record and have followed you even to Europe. We have fortified ourselves with affidavits against you, and since you have been attacking other people, we will now take our turn on you."

Wanamaker jumped up and ordered the men out of his office. Then he gave the press a transcript of the conversation, adding:

No more insidious and terrorizing form of blackmail could be devised. To be silent under such circumstances would be an encouragement to lawless officials and would embolden the perpetrators of such practices to put weak men at their mercy.

Wanamaker requested the newspapers to get from English the discreditable things his police agents and detectives had found out at home and abroad. "Let him go ahead and do his worst," Wanamaker told the reporters. "He is a scoundrel—he and all his kind—and it is a sad and tragic day for Philadelphia when blackmailers like English hold the highest posts in the City Administration." The next day he asked again why English did not make good his threat, and referred to the Director of Public Safety as a "contemptible weakling."

The city enjoyed hugely the discomfiture of English, but there were many who believed that the incident should not be allowed to pass without an expression of public opinion. On May 25, 1900, a mass meeting was held at the Academy of Music to discuss the charges against Director English. But nothing ever came of it on one side or the other. Philadelphia had the kind of government she deserved at that time. Wanamaker was a prophet crying in the wilderness. His adventures in municipal politics were exciting and furnished excellent newspaper copy. But they could have had an aftermath only if thousands of others had proved themselves as fearless and tireless in the practical expression of civic pride and affection as he did.